My Dear Sister

My Dear Sister

NATHANIEL HAWTHORNE AND HIS SISTERS

Kris A. Hansen

MOUNTAIN ASH PRESS

My Dear Sister
Nathaniel Hawthorne And His Sisters
Copyright © 2024 by Kris A. Hansen

All rights reserved. No portion of this book may be reproduced in any form without written permission from the publisher or author, except as permitted by U.S. copyright law.

Cover permissions: Charles Osgood (1809-1890), *Portrait of Nathaniel Hawthorne*, 1840. Oil on canvas. Frame (Outer) 36 x 31 x 3 ¼ in. (91.44 x 78.74 x 8.26 cm) H x W x D. Gift of Professor Richard C. Manning, 1933. 121459. Courtesy of the Peabody Essex Museum. | Cover script: Hawthorne, Nathaniel, Letter from Nathaniel Hawthorne to Maria Louisa Hawthorne, June 18, 1852, Nathaniel Hawthorne Papers, MSS 68, Box 1 Folder 4. Phillips Library, Peabody Essex Museum.

Back cover and in-text photographs and graphical scanning by Kornel A. Krechoweckyj

Permissions to Publish, with sincere gratitude: The Phillips Library at the Peabody Essex Museum, Salem, Massachusetts; Saratoga Springs History Museum, Saratoga Springs, New York

Library of Congress Control Number: 2024924945
ISBN: 9781952430992 (print), 9781965889008 (ebook)

Dedication

To my husband Kornel,
for his continuous love, assistance,
support, and encouragement,
with all my love.

Charles Osgood (1809-1890), *Portrait of Nathaniel Hawthorne*, 1840. Oil on canvas. Frame (Outer) 36 x 31 x 3 ¼ in. (91.44 x 78.74 x 8.26 cm) H x W x D. Gift of Professor Richard C. Manning, 1933. 121459. Courtesy of the Peabody Essex Museum.

Contents

Preface   ix

Part I: A Life Incomplete
1. The Curse of the Hathornes   3
2. A New Life (1808-1818)   23
3. Wild and Free (1818-1819)   45
4. Salem Is Home (1819-1821)   71
5. Separation (1821-1825)   95
6. Solitude (1825-1837)   123

Part II: A Life to Fruition
7. Cupid's Arrow (1837-1842)   155
8. Louisa Visits! (1842-1845)   189
9. Transition (1845-1852)   213
10. Nathaniel's Tears (1852)   245
11. The Spirits of the Hawthornes   273

Acknowledgements   307
Photography and Illustrations   309
Bibliography   313
Notes   317

Preface

It was simple then. Two hundred years ago, people took the time to compose handwritten letters. It was the best method for communication and keeping in touch. Envelopes traveling through the mail could be addressed with only a name, and a town written in ink on its front. Securely closed with a wax seal and an official post office stamp, the envelope and an enclosed letter arrived at its destination. Glancing quickly at the letter reveals a notation of the location where the letter was written followed by the day, month, and year. In most instances on a space below the location and date, the letter was addressed with "Dear" followed by the name of the recipient. This salutation could be formal such as Mr. or Mrs. or simply a last name. More informal correspondence may include a first name, a nickname, a familial relation such as "Sister," or "Brother," or "Mother," or "Father." In informal correspondence, sometimes a single letter, instead of a fully spelled name, would suffice.

My Dear Sister

Letters were mailed between Massachusetts and what is now Maine, from Salem and to Salem, from Salem to Raymond and back, letters from Concord, to Concord, from Lenox and back. So, it continued, decades of letters between one brother and his two sisters. The simple events of life were recorded in pen and ink upon paper in sealed letters sent through the mail. These letters provide a remarkable yet incomplete narrative of the life of Nathaniel Hawthorne.

Hawthorne loved both his sisters, but his younger sister, Maria Louisa, "little Loiza,"[1] was possibly his favorite. Maria Louisa was the cheerful and supportive sister, always eager to read his infrequent and long-awaited letters. He often addressed them to "Dear L" or "Dear Louisa" and signed them "Nath'l" or "Nath" or N.H. His elder sister was Elizabeth, a different character than the continually happy Maria Louisa. Elizabeth's remarks could be cutting and blunt. She accepted the world only from her exacting and critical viewpoint. Although sometimes in contrast to her reclusive nature, she did reveal a particular sense of humor.

Both sisters brought different elements into Hawthorne's life. Maria Louisa was the sweet, light-hearted younger sister. She was at times Hawthorne's only playmate, a little pixie ready to sprinkle some magical dust onto his oft somber mood. She possessed an innate skill to temporarily alter her brother's disposition from a persistent emotionally cluttered sadness to one of momentary joy that passed all too quickly. Elizabeth, on the other hand, challenged Hawthorne's mind. She was intelligent and longed to learn. She believed the Hawthorne family had been endowed with "the best brains in the world,"[2] and she may have spent her life trying to prove

PREFACE

it. However, in educational interactions with her brother and in his personal life, she often exhibited an attempt to control.

Hawthorne, unfortunately, burned volumes of old letters to erase and protect private thoughts from future inquisitive minds. His personal journals, family correspondence and recollections from friends and family provide clues to Hawthorne's life with his sisters. After Hawthorne's death his wife, Sophia, and their three children wrote about him or edited his writings. Hawthorne's sister, Elizabeth, was also instrumental in making her brother's life more known to the world through the letters she had written. However, the substance depended on her memory and interpretation. At the outset, she had not purposely planned to record a biography, but her writings survive to tell parts of the story. Although these remembrances of her brother have been published in many biographies written about him, Elizabeth had deliberately instructed Boston publisher James T. Fields, "I depend upon your assurance that no one shall know that I write this ..."[3]

I was introduced to one of Hawthorne's sisters while researching for my first book *Death Passage on the Hudson: The Wreck of the Henry Clay* (Purple Mountain Press, 2004). There were several people, both survivors as well as victims of the disaster, who interested me. However, it was Hawthorne's sister, Maria Louisa, who gently tugged at my heart drawing me to research what had been her story.

Since many in Hawthorne's family have either edited his writings or written their own articles and books about him, this consequently allowed for some subjectivity. There could be the deletion of unflattering or painful entries leaving many blanks and missing pieces of information. Creative additions may have altered some original text. However, allowing for editorial changes, these writings still serve as a framework to learn about Hawthorne and members of his family. In addition, there are also surviving unedited letters which allow for further study.

In writing this book, I have relied largely upon these original sources such as family letters, Hawthorne's own writings, and those of his children and descendant Manning Hawthorne who wrote extensively about his family. These resources represent the writings of those closest to Hawthorne during his lifetime, offering his own words as well as the recollections of his family and friends. There have been many biographies written about Hawthorne, his wife, and his family. None, however, has devoted its subject specifically to Hawthorne's life with his two sisters. Therefore, in this book on the pages that follow is their story, often depicted through the letters they wrote to each other, often-times addressed:

"*My Dear Sister ...*"

Part 1

A Life Incomplete

Birthplace of Nathaniel Hawthorne, Union Street, Salem, Massachusetts

Chapter 1

The Curse of the Hathornes

"God will give him blood to drink."

—Nathaniel Hawthorne,
The House of the Seven Gables

It was Independence Day!! Twenty-eight years had passed since this country's rebellious forefathers had signed the Declaration of Independence initiating a journey to self-determination for the peoples of an upstart country. Thomas Jefferson, a famed writer of that document, was running for reelection as the third President of the United States. The new nation by this time had grown. There were seventeen states in the Union plus Indiana Territory, Mississippi Territory, and the recently acquired Louisiana Purchase. The land mass of the United States had increased across almost two-thirds of what would eventually become the continental United States. Lewis and Clark had, two months earlier, commenced an

My Dear Sister

historic expedition westward into uncharted territory. This was 1804.

There was much to celebrate in this new and growing, freedom-loving country with festivities reaching every corner of its boundaries, north, south, east and west. In New England, a few miles up the coast from the bustling city of Boston, Massachusetts, sat the village of Salem. Here too, its citizens were celebrating Independence Day. Salem enjoyed an economy powered by international trade as huge ships with billowing sails traveled in and out of the harbor for destinations across the Atlantic Ocean and beyond. Many residents relied upon those ships for their livelihood and, for some citizens, their wealth. Although modern commerce ruled life in Salem, promoting a lengthy prosperity, there was something sinister buried far within the annals of history. It was here more than a hundred years earlier that the taint of witchcraft left a legacy that still lingered in the port's salty ocean air.

A short distance up the street from the docks stood a simple colonial house at 27 Union Street. On that day, there came a small celebration of a different kind. A new baby boy was safely born in his family's home. His life would be affected by the ships sailing from Salem port as well as by the tales of witchery and cruelty from generations past. The child was born destined to endure the burdens of a family history that shared both ill-repute and long-lost prosperity and prominence. Nonetheless, he would celebrate each of his future birthdays on the Fourth of July.

The child's father, Nathaniel Hathorne, was not present to welcome his offspring into the world. He was a captain in the merchant marine[1], not owning his own ships but hired out to command them. Although at sea for months at a time, he had always returned home safely to entertain his family with tales of exotic adventures in equally exotic lands. With such success, there was the optimistic prospect for supporting his wife and growing family through the future years of his life.

During inevitable long absences his young wife, Elizabeth Clarke Manning Hathorne, waited at home. She became in her marriage a lonely spouse spending but a few tender moments with her husband. Those moments were stolen away quickly with his next voyage, thus forcing her to await again his safe return home after several months at sea. Although lonely, this seafarer's wife was not alone. She lived with her mother-in-law, Rachel Phelps, the widow of Daniel Hathorne who had died in 1796. While her husband sailed the vast ocean waters, Elizabeth dutifully brought his children into the world.

The first child, a daughter, was Elizabeth Manning Hathorne who had been born on March 7, 1802. This child was possibly the reason the roving sea captain settled down to wed Elizabeth Clarke Manning on August 2, 1801. The townspeople of proper Salem may have been counting the passing months in discreet whispers among themselves. Baby Elizabeth Hathorne was born a scant seven months after her parents' marriage vows were exchanged. Two years later, their son, Nathaniel, was born on the fourth of July in 1804 while his father was again out to sea. Another four years passed when Elizabeth Hathorne brought another daughter, Maria Louisa, into the family on January 9, 1808.

About the time of Maria Louisa's birth, Hathorne stood as the captain of the ship, *Nabby*.[2] The winds took Hathorne out of Salem port. He sailed away from Essex County and the bitter damp and frigid cold winter of Massachusetts. The

My Dear Sister

Nabby traveled over the horizon toward distant South America. In Hathorne's imagination were the call to foreign ports and the smell of spices in the warm winds that tugged at his senses to reach deep into his soul.

Unlike sea captains who brought their families on voyages, Hathorne instead stocked his cabin with plenty of books that served as his companions.[3] In contrast to many men in that era, Hathorne could read and write. He filled the innumerable hours of tedium at sea, thousands of miles away from his family, reading. In later years, his three children would become devoted admirers of classic literature to minimize the episodes of loneliness or boredom in their respective existences.

These three children were the latest in a line of Hathornes who almost two centuries earlier had first arrived as immigrants in New England. The family's patriarch, William Hathorne, was a committed Puritan emigrating in 1630 from England, arriving in colonial Boston on the ship *Arbella*. He understood the advantage that politics offered for advancement in life and pursued that opportunity. He was soon elected a Representative after moving to Dorchester. He married his wife, Ann Smith, and later moved northeast of Boston to a village named Salem.[4]

Hathorne wasted no time in making a name for himself in this seaside community on the New England coast. He became so entrenched that succeeding generations of Hathornes continued to call this village home. Salem had thrived by the mid-seventeenth century from its fishing industry, and this solid economic foundation served the elder Hathorne well. Prospering from his commercial ventures, he did not wish to simply make money. He wanted prestige and found it by serving in various governmental positions including Speaker and Deputy. Hathorne eventually was appointed Magistrate for Essex County.[5] He had successfully achieved a dignitary position for himself, enjoying both success and prestige.

Hathorne's good fortune, however, did not result in a worthy or reverential personal disposition. He relished targeting the religious sect of Quakers who had arrived in Massachusetts in the 1650s. Hathorne and other like-minded Puritans passed laws against the Quakers who had previously met persecution elsewhere as "... every nation of the earth rejected the wandering enthusiasts who practised [sic] peace towards all men ..."[6] For these gentle souls, there was little peace, only harassment which commenced at the hands of zealots like Hathorne. Local officials punished the Quakers with whippings or locked them in wooden stocks for several hours in the center of town.[7]

During these punishments, the accused were forced to suffer extreme heat in the midday summer sun, pelting rain or cold and darkness during the harsher seasons of the year. This mistreatment served as a warning to others to not interfere with established Puritan ideals. Hathorne became notorious for his cruelty toward the Quakers and in the words of his descendent, Julian Hawthorne, "Justice, with him, does not seem to have been tempered with mercy."[8] Little did the innocence of these persecuted people affect the self-righteousness of those who caused the suffering. More so this perverse "justice" fed upon itself. It demanded more persecution and finally a call for death to blameless people:

> The fines, imprisonment, and stripes, liberally distributed by our pious forefathers, … the persecution which was at once their cause and consequence, continued to increase, till, in the year 1659, the government of Massachusetts Bay indulged two members of the Quaker sect with the crown of martyrdom.[9]

The unjust treatment of the Quakers had progressed from targeted intimidation to severe punishment and ultimately to a sentence of death. All occurring in the village named for peace.

Hathorne died in 1681 a successful man, although a repugnant one. "There was scarcely any field of activity open to him, in which he had not exerted himself. Even religion received the benefit of his zeal and eloquence."[10] Infamy passed down to the next generation of Hathornes from the elder William to his son John, "who lived to enjoy the sinister renown of having, in his capacity of Judge, examined and condemned to death certain persons accused of witchcraft,—one of whom, according to tradition, invoked a heavy curse upon him and upon his children's children."[11]

Three decades after his own father's involvement in persecuting Quakers, John became a judge at the witch trials in Salem in 1692. Records from the trial indicated that Hathorne and Jonathan Corwin served as magistrates and "entered the village in imposing array, escorted by the marshal, constables and their aids, with all the trappings of their offices and a great crowd gathered to hear the testimony taken."[12] The trappings of the office may have been what interested

Hathorne and not the prospect of fairness to any of the accused in a Massachusetts court of law.

John Hathorne indeed had followed closely in his father's footsteps. He quickly learned well in the dealings of cruelty and acted with malice during what became known as the "witch delusion." He was most brutal in his demeanor toward the defendants as Thomas Putnam had instructed him to be particularly stern to the accused.[13] Hathorne took heed of those instructions and performed his duties exactly as ordered. History recorded how Hathorne and his fellow magistrate, Corwin, diligently issued arrest warrants for those accused of witchcraft. One of the first was Sarah Good, dated February 29, 1692:

> Sarah Good, wife of William Good of Salem Village for suspicion of "Witchcraft by her Committed."[14]

Transcripts of the trial detailed the proceedings where John Hathorne coldly questioned the defendants. "Have you made no contracte [sic] with the devil?"[15] he sternly interrogated Sarah Good. For six months in a similar manner, other defendants and witnesses were questioned. Indictments followed. All the while Hathorne sat at the center of the proceedings. His participation ensured his long-lasting political esteem.

The entire town was drawn into the frenzy. Neighbors became fearful of neighbors, trusting no one, as more and more accused were arrested. Some residents offered names of their neighbors to simply protect themselves from suspicion. Others may have been settling personal scores by pointing fingers for revenge or retribution. Many victims were thrown into the Salem jailhouse, which was located on a passageway appropriately named "Prison Lane," to rot or worse to die. In Judge Corwin's house, where the grand jury met, the prosecutors forced confessions from the fearful accused. Nearby was the Meeting House where the examinations took place while the actual trials occurred at the Courthouse on "Townhouse Lane."[16]

All was done at the word of a few children acting out such unexplainable behaviors that town leaders concluded witchcraft was responsible. The authorities of the day were quite disposed to believe in the authenticity of such claims made by children. It was a time when witches held as much authority over human nature as gods and demons. However, unlike gods and demons, supposed witches could be rounded up, prosecuted, and ordered to their deaths.

Hathorne acted toward the accused witches in as ruthless a manner as his father had treated the Quakers. He was possessed and ruled by his own personal demons, failing any sense of justness or fairness. The defendants, both young and old, were sent to their deaths, mostly by hanging at Gallows Hill. One of the first to be condemned was Sarah Good, and in the following months, others shared the same fate.

Elderly, eighty-one-year-old Giles Corey, whose wife Martha had been sentenced to hang for witchcraft, was also executed. He was not hanged but sentenced to death by the judges in a manner both depraved and cruel. At a location between the Howard Street Cemetery and Brown Street in Salem, Corey suffered a prolonged and grisly death because he refused to enter a plea.[17] Over a period of several days heavy stone upon heavy stones were placed upon his prostrate body with the intent of forcing him to plea. He declined and was crushed to death taking a last labored breath in silence under a pile of heavy rocks. He was the only accused to die in this manner. The other victims of this outrage were sent to the gallows to hang until their last breaths were snatched from them by a tight rope around their necks.

Hysteria was the unseen witness and judge during those first months of the witch trials. Hathorne acted as a willing instrument in those proceedings. He was cruel, unfair and self-righteous. Yet, he slept well at night in his bed, feeling no remorse in performing his civic duties while the accused languished in a cold and dark jail … waiting. Meanwhile during those vicious months, nineteen victims were hanged, Corey was crushed to death, and several others died in jail.

Slowly over time, some Salem residents began to question secretly among themselves the validity of the children's claims of witches. Were these children telling the truth or making up outlandish lies? The witch delusion had caused Salem to become not only a bewitched town but a cursed one. It wrote a history for itself that it may possibly never live down.

As the grim infamous months passed, an altered mood slowly crept into the environs. This change did not come like the swift wind of a storm but rolled in quietly like a heavy fog permeating through the tainted air of equally tainted Salem. A new disposition worked its way across the fields and down the deserted streets of this distressed village spreading doubt, possibly remorse, among the residents hiding behind closed and locked doors. In time, judicial officials had a change of heart.

My Dear Sister

A new "Superior Court of Judicature" was appointed to take over the proceedings of the witch trials, without Hathorne and Corwin's participation. Additional trials continued into the following year, 1693, resulting in the accused being either pardoned or acquitted and released. Unfortunately, this reckoning was far too late for those who had already been executed or died in the Salem jailhouse awaiting their fates. Mercifully, during all the turmoil of the past year, some Salem residents had escaped to safety,[18] starting new lives elsewhere in more hospitable environments.

Since the injustice of the witch trials had poisoned the courts, its flaws needed to be addressed. It was a long time in coming. On October 17, 1711, after almost two decades since the delusion, a new generation of provincials was called upon to oversee the legal system. Finally, something was achieved, if not to make things right, at the least to make things more palatable for history's sake. The court publicly reversed ill-thought decisions made during the initial witch trials under Hathorne and his participating magistrates. Many of those accused who had been executed were officially exonerated with some monies awarded to their families.[19] The final exhibition of contrition on the part of the authorities was noted in official transcripts:

> Be it Declared and Enacted by his Excellency the Governor Council and Representatives in General Court assembled, and by the authority of the same that the several convictions Judgments and Attainders against the said George Burroughs, John Proctor, George Jacob, John Willard, Giles

Core and his wife, Martha Core, Rebecca Nurse, Sarah Good, Elizabeth How, Mary Easty, Sarah Wild, Abigail Hobbs, Samuel Wardell, Mary Parker, Martha Carrier, Abigail Faulkner, Anne Foster, Rebecca Eames, Mary Post, Mary Lacey, Mary Bradbury, and Dorcas Hoar, and every of them Be and hereby are reversed made and declared to be null and void to all Intents, Constructions and purposes whatsoever, as if no such convictions Judgments, or Attainders had ever been had or given.[20]

Such legal verbiage could not bring the innocents mentioned back to life. Their mortal lives were gone forever and thus irrevocably altered the lives of their families and futures. Salem's history was forever transformed with witchcraft, not peace, becoming synonymous with the name for the now infamous village. However, with this legal pronouncement recorded into history, Massachusetts, once again, was able to live with itself.

Hathorne suffered no consequences for his disreputable actions. He lived long enough to know of the reversal of judgment and exoneration of all those he had brutally sent to death. It made no difference. A decade after presiding as a magistrate in those infamous trials, Hathorne was offered the honorable position as Judge of the Supreme Court.[21] He thus distinguished himself in the footsteps of his own father by receiving an undeserved reward for his despicable acts.

However, Hathorne's descendants may not have been destined to share in his good fortune. Legend passed down in the Hathorne family history points to words spoken by one of the accused women at the witch trials conjuring a curse upon Judge John Hathorne, his family, and his descendants. Thereafter, any early death of a Hathorne family member or some unexplained misfortune gave rise to suspicion about the existence of a curse on the family. Elizabeth Hathorne, the older sister of Nathaniel and Maria Louisa, had written to her niece years later mentioning "the witch's curse."[22]

Was there truly a witch's curse, or was it simply a supposition made at a time of hysteria? One of the accused, Sarah Good, had been convicted of witchcraft and sentenced to death. Prior to her hanging she glared at the judges and glanced particularly at Reverend Nicholas Noyes, who was present at the trials. Without hesitation, she proclaimed:

> You are a liar! I am no more a witch than you are a wizard! And if you take my life, God will give you blood to drink![23]

Her threats were ignored by the magistrates, and Sarah Good was executed at the Salem gallows. Regarding the perceived curse she pressed upon the judges, there is no such evidence concerning the fate of the judges involved in the witch trials. Legend has it, however, that Reverend Noyes died of a brain hemorrhage in 1718 as blood streamed from his mouth. Coincidence or curse?

Clearly, succeeding generations of Hathornes believed in a curse that had been pressed upon John Hathorne. Yet, he suffered no ill effects during his lifetime. Enjoying both prosperity and prestige, Hathorne lived to the age of seventy-six.

THE CURSE OF THE HATHORNES

After his death he was buried in the Charter Street Burial Ground, a cemetery also known as the Old Burying Point Cemetery, where many of Salem's early residents were interred.

However, it can be questioned whether John Hathorne, or his father William, rested in peace after all. According to the writings of Nathaniel Hawthorne, their descendent, in his story, "The Custom House," there is mention of a stain on his ancestor. It may have been the stain of sin, murder, disgrace:

> So deep a stain, indeed, that his old dry bones, in the Charter-Street burial-ground, must still retain it, if they have not crumbled utterly to dust! I know not whether these ancestors of mine bethought themselves to repent, and ask pardon of Heaven for their cruel ties ...[24]

This "stain" preoccupied Nathaniel Hawthorne. In his story "Fancy's Show Box" from *Twice Told Tales*, Hawthorne asks: "What is Guilt? A stain upon the soul."[25] And in "The Gentle Boy," he references the persecution of the Quakers and writes that:

> An indelible stain of blood is upon the hands of all who consented to this act ... his uncompromising bigotry was made hot and mischievous by violent and hasty passions; ... his whole conduct, in respect to them, was marked by brutal cruelty.[26]

My Dear Sister

Hawthorne took very personally the detested exploits of his ancestors upon the innocent. He included in his piece, "The Custom House," that some forgiveness may be held upon his descendants. Hawthorne wrote:

> At all events, I, the present writer, as their representative, hereby take shame upon myself for their sakes, and pray that any curse incurred by them—as I have heard ... would argue to exist—may be now and henceforth removed.[27]

Only the passage of time would determine if such repentance for the sins of his forefathers would protect later generations of the family. Yet possibly not.

Nonetheless, John Hathorne's remains, with or without an indelible stain, rest forever flanked by the graves of family members in Salem's Old Burying Point Cemetery. Upon his stone, which still exists today, states a simple epitaph. There were no words inscribed to note his involvement in the witch trials or any terrible curse passed down to his heirs. Nor were there words of his former prestige or his infamy, simply:

HERE LYES INTERD YE BODY OF COLO
IOHN HATHORN ESQR AGED 76 YEARS
WHO DIED MAY 10 1717.[28]

Hathorne entered eternity not knowing what future tragedies may befall his familial lineage. He was the father of several children including a son, Joseph, born near the time of the witch delusion, who would carry descendance down to Nathaniel Hathorne and his sisters. Joseph Hathorne did not follow in his father's footsteps to a political career sending victims to their deaths during a witch frenzy. He also rejected a long and lonely life at sea, finally settling down to follow the plow. Known as "Farmer Joseph" he lived an extraordinarily quiet existence supporting his wife and seven children by the humble and land-bound profession of farming Salem soil.[29]

Joseph, who had inherited the Hathorne family homestead, "was a quiet, home-keeping personage."[30] His son, Daniel, however, was endowed with the spirit of adventure. In between his exploits and after an unsuccessful romance with a woman named Mary Rondel of Boston, this rogue married Rachel Phelps. Among their seven children were daughters who would marry into prestigious Salem families. A daughter, Rachel, married wealthy Simon Forrester, and another daughter named Sarah, married into the influential Crowninshield family.[31]

During the American Revolution, Daniel made a name for himself commanding the *Fair America*, a privateer ship. He was a pirate of sorts, who was endeavoring to capture, pillage, or sink enemy ships. Known as "Bold Daniel" he was the subject of a ballad noting his daring exploits and sung during that era. The words of the ballad were recorded in "Griswold's Curiosities of American Literature."[32]

While he was often at sea, Daniel's family resided in Salem. They no longer lived on the modest Joseph Hathorne farm. Daniel had sold the family home and bought another property in town, a more convenient location near Salem Harbor. Nathaniel Hawthorne, the author, wrote decades later of this transaction made by his grandfather:

This old man of the sea exchanged it for a lot of land situated near the wharves, and convenient to his business, where he built the house (which is still standing), and laid out a garden ...[33]

Daniel's son, Nathaniel, "a silent, reserved, severe man, of an athletic and rather slender build, and habitually of a rather melancholy cast of thought"[34] married his bride in 1801. She was the gray eyed Elizabeth Clarke Manning, known as Betsey to her family, who was both "beautiful and highly gifted."[35] They moved into 27 Union Street.

Betsey had, prior to her marriage, resided in a large and adequate house in Salem filled with many family members. She was raised in a financially secure home life with comfortable means provided by her father. Richard Manning was a successful businessman owning several operations including a profitable stagecoach company, stables, and substantial real estate.

Lurking in the Manning family may be found shadows of scandal. The widow of Richard Manning of Dartmouth, England, had brought her children to the New World on the *Hannah and Elizabeth* in 1679.[36] Shortly thereafter, a salacious court case was recorded in Essex County records alleging incest with a punishment carried out against two Manning sisters:

> Antis Maning and Margret Maning, now Polfery, for incest, their brother Nicolas Maning being implicated, were committed to prison until morning, and then at Ipswich to be whipped

... and stand or sit upon a high stool ... in the open middle alley of the meeting house, with a paper upon each of their heads, with their crime written in capital letters, the constable of Salem to see it performed.[37]

According to the record, the brother who was allegedly involved, Captain Nicholas Maning, meanwhile had disappeared. The written record indicated that Nicholas' wife, Elizabeth, may have made the accusation for having to live in "terror of her husband and his sisters."[38] It is unclear if any of the allegations were true or ever proven. A fine was paid in lieu of the punishment and the official written court entries remain to attest to the incident.[39] Nathaniel Hawthorne may have heard this sordid tale directly from the Manning relatives. If the story was so secret and unspoken by them, he may possibly have come across it while browsing through old Essex County records. In an 1837 entry to his personal journal, Hawthorne indicated that he had seen certain family related papers that had been stashed in a desk at the Salem Custom House.

Thus, the three Hathorne children drew their first breaths preceded by the secret scourge of scandal in the Manning family and the cursed misdeeds of their infamous Hathorne forebears. Would a dark shadow be cast over these children's lives? Would they be forced to suffer the consequences ordained for the family to which they were born?

The answer, in part, came quickly. Maria Louisa was only a few weeks old when Betsey and her family awaited her husband's return from his latest voyage. Day after lonely winter

My Dear Sister

day in early 1808 slowly passed. As the daylight hours grew longer and early spring flowers popped their petals through the vestiges of the lingering New England winter snow, ships arrived at Salem port. Betsey's anticipation grew.

However, it was not Nathaniel Hathorne at the ship's bow of a returning vessel as he neared his arrival home. Nor was he walking up Union Street for a happy reunion with his family. There were no tales to tell of exotic ports or packages of small gifts. This was the time before the invention of telegraph, or telephone, so letters and messages arrived through the mail carried overland or from overseas on sailing ships. Therefore, in Hathorne's place came a message, one that every seaman's wife feared. Word came that her husband, the father of her children, had died a continent away in South America by the scourge of yellow fever.[40]

It had not been the sea that took her husband's life in a shipwreck or in an unforeseen fierce storm or brutal pirate attack in the Caribbean. He was taken by a much feared and mysterious disease. Betsey had lost her husband far from home, where she was unable to care for him in his illness, hold his hand, offer expressions of love or say goodbye as he slipped away into eternity. Her three children lost their father before they had the opportunity to know him.

Still, it was not unusual for seamen to never return home. Cemeteries along the New England coast include empty graves with engraved stones or monuments attesting to those lost at sea. However, the occurrence becomes real when news arrives at a family's door. Hathorne had been taken by an early death. No one spoke of it, but possibly the family may have thought to themselves about the witch's curse.

Spring would not arrive for Betsey Hathorne. The cold and dark winter of Maria Louisa's birth may have never ended for her suddenly widowed mother. At only thirty-three years of age, Nathaniel Hathorne left his wife a widow at age twenty-eight with three small children no older than six.

Chapter 2
A New Life (1808-1818)

"There were aunts and uncles…"

—Elizabeth Manning Hawthorne

aptain Nathaniel Hathorne had died almost three thousand miles from home. The cold reality for Betsey's family was reinforced as an announcement appeared in the Salem newspapers:

> At Surinam, of yellow fever Captain Nathaniel Hathorne of this town, aged 33, Master of the Brig Nabby[1]

In the grief following his death and the perpetual loneliness she experienced, Betsey had to think about caring for her now fatherless children. Therefore, on an early spring New England morning in April of 1808, Elizabeth Clarke Manning Hathorne, gripped with a crushed heart, delivered the news to her only son, Nathaniel, that his father had died in a distant land. Four years of age was terribly young for a child to learn such a devastating truth and fully understand the implications. However, he was informed. His sister Elizabeth was only six years old at the time, yet throughout her life she never forgot the scene. Years later, she recollected, "I remember that one morning my mother called my brother into her room, next to the one where we slept, and told him that his father was dead."[2]

Unbeknownst to Nathaniel and Elizabeth that day, life would be different for them, their mother and their little sister. Lost were the tender moments of family life together with father. Also vanished were their father's voice, the touch of his hand, and the emotional security of his presence. The family would never again anticipate or rejoice in his return from the sea or revel in listening to wild tales of adventure in foreign lands. Although it was difficult to understand the depth of all the implications, they knew their father was never returning home again.

Besides the emotional loss, another harsh reality for his widow, Betsey, was that she no longer had her husband to support her children. During her marriage, she had lived in the home of her in-laws, the Hathorne house on Union Street. Betsey and her husband held very few assets. They did not have their own home nor did her late husband own any ships that could have provided a source of income. With her husband's death, there was no longer any income. The questions swirled. What would become of Betsey? Her children? Would she be welcome to live in the Hathorne house without her husband? If not, where would she go? Would the

A NEW LIFE (1808-1818)

curse, set upon John Hathorne more than a century earlier, offer Betsey and her Hathorne children, not death but a life of destitution? Was this the blood for them to drink from the witch's curse?

Shortly after her husband's death, Betsey received the answer she so desperately needed. Oftentimes a widow with children married quickly to obtain a means of support for her own family. On the other hand, a widower may require a new mother for his own motherless children. This kind of marriage was not a romantic solution to a difficult situation, but it was a practical one. Men and women often agreed to such arrangements for the sake of family survival. If they were fortunate, the new couple might eventually develop a mutual fondness for each other or possibly a newfound romance. Conversely, no emotionally comfortable feeling might develop at all. However, for practicality and survival, these types of marital unions continued sometimes, adding even more children to the names already written on the fragile pages of the family Bible. The Hathornes were certainly well-known in Salem. Surely there were men with an eye for this new widow and knowledge of her sudden plight. Was there a prospective husband ready to step up and enter her life?

For Betsey, the answer was simpler. There would be no marriage proposal from a near stranger to rescue her. The solution came closer to home and without any demands or unwanted propositions attached. Her devoted parents had kindly invited her to live with them. No longer a child but a struggling widow with three children, Betsey received the help she desperately needed.

Betsey packed her modest belongings and departed from

the Hathorne house for a final time. Returning to the home she had left seven years earlier on her wedding day, Betsey was welcomed by her parents, Richard and Miriam Lord Manning, along with a houseful of relatives. Her three sisters, Mary, Maria, and Priscilla Miriam were the children's aunts while her brothers, Robert, William, John, Samuel, and Richard were their uncles. Although most of the aunts and uncles remained in Salem, Richard eventually moved to Raymond, Maine, where the Mannings owned substantial tracts of land. Maine at the time was a part of Massachusetts, until 1820 when it became the 23rd state.

Betsey's return home, although emotionally fraught from sudden, tragic change, was not a long or difficult journey. She remained in Salem, relocating to her father's home at 12 Herbert Street, which ran parallel to Union Street, where the Hathornes lived. The Hathorne and Manning back yards were situated close to each other. This proximity of the houses may have been the reason Elizabeth Clarke Manning came to meet for the first time her husband Nathaniel Hathorne. Their families were neighbors.

Richard Manning house, Herbert Street, Salem, Massachusetts

Carrying her baby in

her arms, Betsey, along with her two other young children, crossed the short distance to a new home and life provided by the abundant Manning relatives. The little family approached the front door of the large, austere, and somewhat square box of a house. For many future years, Betsey and her children would walk in and out of that very threshold into the respective chapters of their lives. Sometimes, they would depart through that door for an hour or a day or two while other times for long periods. Then, after an absence, they would return as their lives journeyed through the circumstances of their existence. On this day of reunion, Betsey's parents willingly brought into this unassuming yet adequate home their young and suddenly destitute daughter. For the remainder of her life, Betsey would depend on family members to provide her with a home.

The Manning house, which had been settled to the quiet order of the residing adults, was made ready for three small children. Although the house was large, there were many adult family members living there already, and thus rooms were filled almost to capacity. The new Hathorne arrivals were squeezed in with their baggage among the numerous other relatives. Betsey was offered a single room on the second floor that she would share with her daughters, Elizabeth and baby Maria Louisa. At four years old, Nathaniel was ordered up to the third floor to share a room and possibly a bed, common in that time, with his Uncle Robert,[3] who was twenty years older. The age difference alone left no opportunity for commonality between them and, thus, was an adjustment for both. Robert was accustomed to adults; Nathaniel was accustomed to his sisters.

My Dear Sister

Betsey and her children were afforded a roof over their heads and nourishment for their bodies. Their earthly needs were modestly satisfied in equally modest surroundings. "The rooms had but little furniture of the plainest kind. No carpets or curtains."[4] Abundance in the Manning home consisted of the people living in the house not of extravagant possessions. With the move to their new home, Betsey's three children were immediately surrounded by attentive grandparents, aunts and uncles, all with diverse personalities yet all sharing the name of Manning.

Herbert Street was located a short distance from Washington Square and the Salem Common, a veritable New England town green. In the other direction from Herbert Street was Derby Street along the busy wharves of Salem Harbor. Large fashionable homes of the wealthy on Derby Street dotted the coastal environs offering a life of luxury unknown to most of Salem's citizenry. Noisy shipyards and docks stood where the Hathorne children's father had taken his final fateful ascent aboard a sailing ship bound for South America.

Shipping had made many men quite well-to-do in Salem. From about 1760 through the American Revolutions and until the War of 1812, Salem was known for its shipping strength. Large sailing vessels departed for months at a time then returned to Salem port laden with fabulous cargoes brought back from far-off lands.[5] Salem bustled from global commerce. This was the era into which the Hathorne children had been born.

Betsey's father had become quite affluent through his successful land-based business enterprises. Therefore, the Mannings were in a far better financial position than the

Hathornes, who may have enjoyed esteem from generations past but no longer enjoyed wealth.[6] Betsey's husband left little money for his family as a result. While Hathornes lived in the shadows of glory days long gone, the Manning family thrived.

Thus, fate had dictated Betsey's future. Her married life in the Hathorne house, previously with her husband and children, would never be known. That life was gone along with the hopes and dreams that Betsey and her husband had once cherished for themselves and for their future. Tragic circumstances had forced her into a new life, not of her making, as she and her children adjusted to living with her numerous relatives. Their lives from that point forward were influenced and primarily structured by the Manning family. Yet, Hathorne blood left its own legacy for the three children, a legacy which strangely influenced them in different ways for the rest of their lives.

Living in the home of her parents, Betsey should have flourished with the support and love of her family. However, history and legend recorded otherwise. Stories had circulated that she languished in a self-imposed prison at home, rarely speaking to anyone, remaining reclusive and distant. Considering her situation, it was the respectable thing to do for a young widow. Social norms may have required that she remain at her family home and focus on her children's upbringing. Betsey could have simply been avoiding any unwelcome marriage proposals. Or possibly, she may have already become reclusive in the Hathorne house. Her husband was often months absent, and she may have spent her time in her room with her children around her. If this was true, she carried this behavior to her new home locking herself away from the reality of her life in Salem without her husband.

Decades later, a descendant, Manning Hawthorne, attempted to tackle this very complicated question about Betsey's seclusion. Hawthorne supposed that Betsey was not reclusive in earlier years but may have become more so in her later years due to illness.[7] There is a possibility that his explanation is correct, or at least partially. Stories of Betsey's dark and mysterious widowhood provided a curious folklore that painted a picture of a withdrawn and suffering woman. However, Betsey was a committed mother to her children, who were quite attached to her.[8] Contrary to the myths surrounding her, when her health permitted, there was a period when she succeeded in living a productive community life almost entirely on her own.

Thus, Betsey initially had not set an example for her children that would have encouraged them to live in their own self-imposed prisons. That characteristic was to emerge later resulting from life circumstances, possible family tendencies, and her example. For the present, the children studied in school, played with friends, and enjoyed their relatives. The three Hathorne children flourished while living with their extended Manning family. They were very fortunate. Betsey's oldest daughter, Elizabeth, later wrote to one of her nieces about their life growing up in the Manning house explaining that:

> All through our childhood we were indulged in all convenient ways, and were under very little control except that of circumstances ... We always had plenty of books ...[9]

A NEW LIFE (1808-1818)

The extent of Manning prosperity could not be judged by their furnishings, but if wealth were measured in books, they were rich. The Hathorne children were permitted to read whatever volumes they wished from the Manning collection of books at their disposal. They read often from classic literature including Shakespeare. Nearby was the Athenaeum, "a dreary old library," where young Elizabeth, called Ebe, would pick up books for herself and her brother because he didn't want to go inside.[10] Books and reading were mainstays in the Manning house and offered the children hours of entertainment. As the children grew, at least one, two, or all three of them could be found reading books at any one time, sometimes reading the same book.

Nathaniel, called Nath or Natty, became a voracious reader and practiced his skills by reading aloud from the classics and entertaining his mother with his readings from books as she sat in the parlor.[11] The stories he read helped to develop creativity and imagination in his young mind. At times, he fashioned his own fanciful tales of faraway adventure which ended with an ominous warning, "And I'm never coming back again."[12] His boyish threats were something for his mother and sisters to truly ponder. His sisters were amused by the thoughts he fancied, but the mischievous words pierced his mother's heart.

Her family often called Maria Louisa by her middle name, Louisa. She had an aunt named Maria Manning, so the name Louisa may have been used to differentiate between the two. Louisa had been the luckiest of the three Hathorne children. She started her life with a blank slate, never having experienced what life was like when her father was present at home and her mother content. As a newborn she had not experienced the long months of waiting for her father's return. Nor did she witness her mother desperately longing to see her husband's face once again and to be held in his embrace. As Louisa awoke from sleep each morning, she did not suffer the realization that her father was never to return. He was an unknown entity to her, a name, a person who had once existed but without a tangible emotional connection to her that brought sorrow.

In contrast, her mother suffered this sorrow each day as she quietly grieved for the husband she lost. Nath and Ebe witnessed for themselves how their mother endured. They had experienced the loss of their father and understood he was never coming home. They missed his presence although it had been fleeting. There may have been a level of grieving shared by Betsey, Nath and Ebe that developed into a life-long disposition set in loss. It was only Louisa who did not suffer bereavement. Without such hurt or memories, she cheerfully grew to toddlerhood among her many Manning relatives. This was the only home and family she knew, and she loved them all. As a playful infant, it would have been impossible to avoid at least some attention by the numerous Manning relatives and from her older siblings as well.

Nath and Ebe, respectively four and six years older than Louisa, were available to watch their little sister as she learned to crawl on the floor. Often, they heard her voice, a laugh with joy or a scream with discontent. They watched as she learned to take her first toddler steps. They picked her up as she tripped over her newfound feet. As she improved in her footsteps, Louisa could follow them around the house. Even if Nath and Ebe preferred other pastimes, there was little opportunity for them to hide from her.

A NEW LIFE (1808-1818)

Then, suddenly Louisa was old enough and adept enough to run after them with glee, especially after her beloved brother. She'd catch a few moments with him before he was off to do the things he needed to do. It was a rarity for her to catch him, possibly for a moment or two, before more years passed. However, sometimes he would slow or stop and turn around to see her and wait for her. Louisa was his little sister, and he loved her.

Ebe had interests more mature than the playful antics of her baby sister. Often, oldest daughters in families are called upon to become caregivers for the family taking on various household duties. They become substitute parents themselves to their siblings. Many oldest daughters struggle with such responsibilities pressed upon them at a young age. Others have an instinct or pick up such domestic duties almost naturally. This was not Ebe.

Household occupations were uninteresting to her, and there is no record that she willingly pursued those domestic endeavors that were usually expected of young girls at the time. She preferred cerebral pursuits and was an avid reader. Ebe proved to be quite self-disciplined and took advantage of every opportunity to educate herself. Her preferences were a book in her hand or a challenge for her intellectual mind. As a youngster in the Manning house, she was allowed the freedom to explore her exceptional intellectual interests.

Ebe was sociable enough in her young years, but she preferred doing so at her own design rather than being required to visit or entertain. She liked to make her own rules as much as she could get away with in the family. This trait may be the result of her being the oldest of the three children or simply her own personality. She visited with family and friends and travelled to nearby environs. However, her degree of desired sociability would change as she grew older. She desired to be emotionally independent although she would never become monetarily independent from her relatives.

There appears to have been a wide intellectual variance between the two sisters. This may be partly due to their age difference since the two sisters would never share the same chronological or developmental stage in their lives. They also had divergent personalities with Louisa being quite sociable and amiable while Ebe was more intellectual and strong-willed. Louisa could have looked up to her older sister, but Elizabeth could have dismissed her. There is the possibility that the sisters were not particularly close.

However, the sisters could always enjoy certain of the same activities either together or apart as young children. They both enjoyed reading, loved their mother, and played with the household pets, which invariably ran around the house. There was at least one cat or kitten to lavish affection upon throughout their young lives.

Nath, in his youth, was intent on creating indoor pastimes to entertain himself, his sisters, or the cats for that matter. In one instance, the Manning book collection came in handy for his mischievous pursuits. He collected a pile of books from around the house and used them to construct a system of tunnels into which a cat could run.[13] The three children watched as their frisky pet entered one end of this construction marvel and disappeared from their sight. The children then waited and listened for any hints of cat scratching or meowing from inside the wobbly maze. The intensity of the moment lingered with silence until the furry little creature peaked out at the

A NEW LIFE (1808-1818)

other end of the tunnel to see daylight. The quick thumping of soft paws could be heard as the cat quickly scurried off out of sight followed by excited glee from the children.

In time, Nath happily shared another peculiar creature with his sisters that mysteriously had come into his possession. Possibly it had stowed away on one of those huge sailing ships returning to the Salem docks from a land far away. The creature was a monkey who provided hours of entertainment climbing or jumping while causing the children to laugh at its clownish antics. The adults in the house may not have shared in the excitement of having such a wild thing living under their roof. In any event, the commotion was short-lived. Considering the climate of New England, the food sources available, and lack of other monkey playmates, alas, the unusual pet eventually succumbed to nature and died.

Nath, with his sisters at his side, could have easily walked to Salem Harbor to conduct a burial at sea for their pet. However, they decided upon a more practical intention and prepared for a proper burial in the Manning backyard. The threesome escorted the deceased monkey to its final resting place. Nath and Ebe were aware of death; they understand their own father's death and the monkey's death. Louisa, however, was too young to understand death. Ebe recollected years later in a letter mentioning the pet funeral:

> We buried it in the garden; Louisa, who was very little, said it was planted. We also carried a Cat to the grave with a long procession, and he [Nathaniel] wrote its epitaph upon a piece of slate. It was this:

> "Then, oh Thomas, rest in glory!
> Hallowed be thy silent grave,—
> Long thy name in Salem's story
> Shall live, and honour o'er it wave."[14]

Nath had to start somewhere, and the spark igniting his own literary genius was aroused by writing a rhyme to memorialize the passing of a deceased pet. The period of mourning for any lost pet for Ebe, with her matter-of-fact personality, and little Louisa, too young to understand, was most likely minimal. For Ebe, a good book served to bring her world back to normal. For Louisa, a playful kitten could quickly replace the lost monkey in her heart, and a new kitten could easily have been acquired.

Unfortunately, the pet funeral reflected the true situation for the children's extended family. There had been much adult sadness during the children's younger years. Five years after they lost their own father, the children's Hathorne grandmother, Rachel Phelps, died as well as their grandfather and benefactor, Richard Manning in 1813. His son, the children's Uncle John, had already disappeared at sea during the War of 1812, and the children's aunt, Maria Manning, died in 1814.[15] On the national front that same year, the British succeeded in burning the Capitol Building and the White House in Washington D.C. with President James Madison and his wife, Dolley, safely evacuated to Virginia and then Maryland. Although the War of 1812 with Britain covered a two and a half-year period, the lives of the Hathorne children for the most part were not materially nor physically affected.

The management of the Manning businesses enterprises

A NEW LIFE (1808-1818)

were rearranged following their grandfather's death. The children's Uncle William managed the office, their Uncle Samuel oversaw the stables and carriages, and Uncle Robert served as company agent.[16] Thus, the Manning business enterprises continued under new supervision. The Hathorne children's lives continued under the care of renewed benefactors, not one with the name of "Grandfather" Manning but several with the names of "Uncle."

Sometime near his grandfather's death, Nath, who had always been an athletic young boy, running and playing outdoors, experienced his first and possibly only physical hardship of his young years. He seriously hurt his foot while playing ball with his neighborhood friends. The injury turned Nath into a housebound invalid. He lost his independence since he was prohibited from playing outside to protect his injury. He witnessed Ebe enjoying her liberty as she ventured out of the house. His little sister, Louisa, ran about the house with ease, having no limitations placed upon her. There must have been some envious feeling toward his friends and sisters as he watched them outside through the window or scurrying in and out as they pleased.

In addition, Nath was unable to attend school, and therefore, his convalescence required him to continue his education at home. A local schoolteacher named Joseph E. Worcester, who had written a dictionary, stopped by each evening to tutor the injured lad with his lessons.[17]

The large austere Manning house was no longer a home to Nath. It was his prison. The restless boy was forced to learn other occupations to pass the long hours of time during his incarceration. His studies, of course, consumed a part of each

37

day. Also, this period in his life cemented his lifelong habit of reading books as he spent many hours each day reclining on the floor with a book to occupy his time. He enjoyed classic literature such as *Pilgrim's Progress, The Fairie Queene,* and the works of Shakespeare, which became some of his many favorites.[18] These were adult level books, quite advanced, yet valuable classic reading for such a young boy.

Nath's convalescence gave his five-year old sister, Louisa, an opportunity to come hopping around visiting as her brother lay stretched out on the floor. One can envision her climbing over him to fall on the other side laughing all the while and causing him to lose his page. Annoyed, Nath may have teased her or shooed her away so he could read in peace. Or possibly she fell asleep dreaming securely with big brother by her side. All the while Nath read page after page of books, which offered a temporary escape from his present immobile situation.

Louisa, following the example of her older siblings, also developed a deep satisfaction from reading books. One of the earlier noted incidents of the interaction between Louisa and her brother was Nath's plan to address Louisa's education. Appointing himself as her personal tutor, he had learned the ins and outs of such activity from his own tutor. However, his tutor was an educated man; Nath was a boy. Nonetheless, he had this plan for Louisa. There were plenty of books in the Manning house for him to choose from for her lessons. Therefore, the sessions progressed with Nath as the sage, although somewhat lame professor, and Louisa as his dubiously agreeable pupil.

Their older sister, Ebe, the objective bystander, made her

own pragmatic observation and held serious doubts about the endeavor. She skeptically wrote in a letter, "Nathaniel keeps school for Louisa, who is his only scholar. I expect she will soon leave him."[19] The tender scene between older brother and younger sister lasted until perchance a first spat between them threatened to end it all. Apparently, this educational endeavor was quite brief since there are no records to indicate any length to this venture.

Ebe helped fill some of the interminable hours her brother suffered during his recovery by discussing the books they both had read. They shared common interests in reading the classics, and she appeared to be the equal to her brother in intellect. A neighbor, Elizabeth Peabody, later recalled that Ebe "used to do her lessons with me. I vividly remember her; she was a brilliant little girl, and I thought her a great genius."[20] Nonetheless, there was a distinct difference between the brother and sister. Nath avoided serious study while Ebe seriously pursued it.

Louisa, on the other hand, was a more average student when compared to the aptitude of her older brother and sister. While Ebe was more involved in intellectual pursuits, Louisa became the playful target for her brother's pestering and sporadic annoyances. Regardless, Louisa looked up to her older brother. They shared a close relationship even with their differences in personality, age, and intellect. They seemed to nicely complement each other. Over the years, Louisa developed social skills and niceties, which fostered many friendships for her in Salem. Nath, intellectually gifted yet quiet, felt more comfortable with his family or by himself rather than in the social situations that Louisa so enjoyed.

My Dear Sister

By early January 1815 after months of being confined, Nath's injury had healed, and his life returned to normalcy. He was free to run out the door and resume strenuous activities playing with his friends. However, this caused the months of sibling bonding between Nath and his sisters to abruptly end. He was no longer the continually available brother stuck in the house ready to read with his sisters or interact endlessly with them and their pets. He now had other plans. However, the time spent indoors during his long convalescence had established a strong pattern for the two sisters. They expected, almost demanded, that their brother would always be with them and available to them. When they matured to adulthood, this expectation would prove to cause troublesome tension.

Inside the Manning house, the dynamics of the house had changed once again. Since Nath was no longer the permanent fixture on the Manning floor, Ebe and Louisa had their mother along with Aunt Mary and their aging grandmother Manning for companionship. A favorite aunt, Priscilla Miriam, would soon leave the house to marry John Dike, a local and widowed merchant. However, the ties to the children would stay strong after her marriage. She and her future husband would treat the Hathorne children as if they were their own.

Although all the Manning uncles and aunts shared some time and support for the children's well-being, their Uncle Robert had the most profound influence on them. He willingly took on most of the responsibility for looking after his widowed sister and her three children. Ebe and Louisa were offered education until their early to mid-teens. They were encouraged to have friends and pursue social interests, at which Louisa was the most adept. Nath was offered a comprehensive education to nurture, perhaps force, him into eventually becoming a productive adult.

Well occupied as an agent for the Manning businesses, Uncle Robert successfully juggled his professional and family obligations. However, that success came with a steep price since he delayed his own personal pursuits and marriage. Uncle Robert was especially interested in Nath's future and endeavored with intensity to secure the education of his nephew.[21] It was an effort that the young boy stubbornly resisted. Nath had neither appreciation nor patience for his uncle's determined devotion.

Louisa viewed her uncle differently. She loved her Uncle Robert and exhibited a quiet respect and recognition for all he did for her. She grew to be a happy and affectionate little girl. Her light spirit and playfulness were evident in the letters she wrote to her uncle while he was away on business. In an 1816 letter, she wrote with a candor that surpassed her age: "As so good an opportunity offers of putting a letter into the trunk I thought I would write to you and to inform you that you have no longer power to dispose of your own clothes …"[22] Louisa then proceeded to tell her Uncle Robert how his coat had been sent off to be woven into the makings of a carpet.

Always the genial child, Louisa added that, "… I want to see you very much."[23] In the letter, Louisa also anticipated the return of a young distant relation who had been brought to help in the Manning household, "we expect Hannah Lord back again today or tomorrow."[24] Closing her letter to her uncle, Louisa added, "I have written all that I can think of so good bye."[25]

Julian Hawthorne, Louisa's nephew, remembered her from

his early childhood. The memories of her remained with him through his adult life. He wrote of her:

> As for Louisa, the youngest of the three, she was more commonplace than any of them; a pleasant refined, sensible feminine personage, with considerable innate sociability of temperament.[26]

Louisa always seemed to be very content with family and friends around her and life the way it was.

Ebe grew to be a very different character. She did not possess an easy-going nature like her younger sister. Her nephew, Julian Hawthorne, described Ebe's personality as "a cold, clear, dispassionate common-sense, softened by a touch of humor such as few women possess."[27] Her relatives would come to understand her strong personality although they did not wholeheartedly accept it. Nath was aware of his sister's temperament. She may have somewhat frightened him as he once remarked, "The only thing I fear is the ridicule of Elizabeth."[28]

Ebe, although not one to be sentimental, years later spent much time reminiscing and writing in letters about her brother and his life. These letters often offer her viewpoint about her family as well as her relationship with her brother. In one of her letters to her niece, Ebe wrote, "Your Papa used to call me the severest critic he knew, and sometimes he told me I was not amiable in my tastes ..."[29] Bluntly, Nath revealed his thoughts about the shortcomings of Ebe, to Ebe!

If Ebe intimidated her brother, the same could not be said about Louisa. Nath found her so agreeable to spend time with. Louisa did not have the edgy personality that caused their older sister to be aloof and overly critical. Louisa was drawn to her brother. She was very happy to be with him without any competition between them. Louisa's congenial personality, warmth, and loyal friendship that she offered endeared her to all she knew including her brother.

Thus, the three Hathorne children, Nathaniel, the athletic yet quiet boy, Ebe, the strong-willed older sister, and Louisa the youngest, a happy, pleasant child developed their own distinct personalities while living with their widowed mother among the diverse Manning relatives. They lived as guests, for the present, in their grandparents' house in Salem.

Betsey Hathorne house in Raymond, Maine

Chapter 3
Wild and Free (1818-1819)

> "At fifteen I became a resident in a country village, more than a hundred miles from home."
>
> —Nathaniel Hawthorne, "The Vision of the Fountain"

As the first two decades of the nineteenth century progressed, Salem's economic luster had begun to dim. The two years of Thomas Jefferson's 1807 Embargo, which ceased American foreign trade, had decimated the entire country's port commerce. This was followed later by the War of 1812 against Great Britain, which added to the economic misery. The once thriving shipping port of Salem struggled to recover and return to its former days of prosperity. However, although the economic climate was challenging for transatlantic shipping, inland transportation proved important. Thus, the well-connected Mannings remained prosperous due to the strength of their carriage business. As a result, the Manning enterprises continued to adequately maintain financial support for Betsey and her three children.

This support included a family trip to undeveloped Maine, where the Mannings held substantial real estate. "Raymond, Maine, in the year 1816, was a tiny hamlet consisting of three or four houses, and a mill by Dingley Brook."[1] At that time, Maine, was a place of vast wilderness with scented pine forest and untouched natural beauty. It was bounded by mountains and dotted with lakes. Its eastern shore, bordering the Atlantic Ocean, provided miles of craggy, rocky seashore. The Hathorne family, on holiday removed from Salem, spent a pleasant summer in Raymond. Their Uncle Richard was already living there, so the Hathornes sometimes stayed with him or at another family-owned farmhouse.

It was an enchanted time for the mother and her three children as they experienced a newfound autonomy far from Salem's dark and ghostly heritage. In her mid-thirties by this time, Betsey summoned a dream after this pleasant summer excursion to reside in a house of her own. She simply may have wanted to escape her current life. Achieving this fantasy would be impossible without the assistance of her brothers, Manning money, and the family real estate holdings. A relocation to the village of Raymond would offer Betsey a certain amount of independence and a permanent reprieve from living in old Salem. It would allow Betsey to remove herself from the constant reminders of her life without her husband and from the oblique stares of its gossipy residents. Living on her own in Maine may have offered Betsey an opportunity for self-determination to pursue long-ignored interests.

Written correspondence among the scattered relatives

became a necessity. The families were split between Salem and Raymond, resulting in the three Hathorne children commencing a lifelong career of writing letters to keep in touch with their various family members. Surviving letters serve as a record of the years when the Mannings and the Hathornes lived apart in multiple locations. Letters usually contained family news and activities, updates on health, weather, and visitors. Often the writer's personal feelings were imparted to the reader of the letter where happiness, anger, or frustration may be gleaned from the written words inked on paper. Although Maine was still under the jurisdiction of Massachusetts, envelopes for mailing purposes were addressed to Raymond, Maine.

Though the village was a rustic outpost compared to the civilized world of Salem, it did offer a small semblance to the niceties of society. Local citizens attended religious services, gathered for weddings or funerals, and perhaps enjoyed a summertime picnic. These occasions offered an opportunity for social interaction beyond the difficult work necessary to survive in a challenging environment. People living in more remote regions depended on resources that they provided by themselves alone. They raised their own livestock for meat and milk. They grew their own vegetables, hunted for game, and made what they needed.

However, neighbors tended to look after neighbors because they knew a time could arrive when they also may need help. Hazardous circumstances could arise such as severe or contagious illness, accident or weather-related catastrophe, flood or fire. In these times, the locals would be called upon to assist one another. There was no fire department down the street for emergency medical help or for extinguishing flames. Doctors could be miles or days travel away.

Betsey's neighbors may have been somewhat sociable in a New England sort of way. New Englanders could seem distant and aloof, but they came when they were needed. "It was a wild spot, but a lovely one."[2] Ebe, enjoying her surroundings well enough during her summertime visit, also enjoyed that no one bothered her. She resisted social visits intensely during her stay. In Salem, she may have been required to be friendly, but there was not the presence of aunts and uncles and grandmother to insist she visit the neighbors or relatives now. Ebe wrote in a defiant letter to her Aunt Mary in Salem, "I shall not make one visit while in Raymond: I always dislike them,...The society here almost equals that of Salem, & it is much pleasanter living here."[3] She, Nath, and Louisa equally enjoyed their visit to Raymond.

Betsey was accustomed to Salem society although since her husband's death she hadn't been a very active participant. In Raymond, she seemed attracted to the culture of the quiet, remote village and enjoyed the life it offered. Following the summer sojourn, Betsey returned to Salem, making plans for a renewed and productive life for herself.

During the next two years, Betsey patiently waited while her dedicated brothers prepared and planned to fulfill her wishes. They arranged for the construction of a new house on Manning land in Raymond. Although Betsey by this time had reached her thirty-eighth year, maturing from a young widow to middle-age, her desire to move to Maine with the freedom it offered had remained steadfast. As the heat of the summer of 1818 began to wane, Betsey wrote to her brother, Robert, who had been overseeing the house construction in

Maine. She indicated she was anticipating the move, "... we are very glad to hear the house is to be finished this fall, if we can move in Oct. I think it will be very well."[4] Betsey contained her excitement but felt the realization of her dream approaching.

Ebe relished the thought of Raymond and its remoteness. She desired an escape from living with too many relatives and entirely too much Salem. She anticipated living without anyone else's rules, familial constraint, comments, or requirements. She'd had a taste of such independence two years earlier, and she dreamed of uninterrupted hours that she could fill with what was most important to her: reading, study, and long walks.

Nath, impatiently waiting, dreamed of his new life of boundless independence far away from Salem and his relatives, especially his Uncle Robert. He may have nurtured the notion of abandoning his schooling in that far off and primitive place. Nath preferred the outdoors and looked forward to having unencumbered hours to walk or hunt in the forest and fish or skip stones into the waters of Sebago Lake. This would be the best life for him.

Louisa hadn't the thought of independence in a way her brother, sister, and mother dreamed. She had her family around her, and that was all she needed wherever they lived. She understood that she would soon be leaving to live in a new house. Her prior visit prepared the little girl for the relocation, and she looked forward to her new home. Although she was just about ten years old, Louisa was not timid. She wrote a few words to her Uncle Robert exuding her excitement for Maine although too late to enjoy its summer harvests:

My Dear Sister

> We miss you here very much and am glad to hear that you intend to return by the first of September next. I want to see Uncle Richard and Aunt Susan very much and I hope that I shall in October, but I suppose that the berries will all be gone then and that I shall be sorry for I love berries very much ... I wish I was down there to eat some with you.[5]

Her Uncle Richard had married a local girl, Susan Dingley. His marriage guaranteed he would be staying in Raymond for a long time. As it happened, Richard remained there for the remainder of his life. Up the road from Uncle Richard's house was the nearly completed construction project which would become Betsey's future home. Louisa would be trading Salem relatives for the Maine relatives living nearby. This was totally suitable to her expectations.

Louisa and Nath excitedly waited in Salem with their mother for their house to be completed. Ebe, who was sixteen years old by this time, was enjoying an extended visit to Newberryport, close to the New Hampshire border. Ebe apparently enjoyed her visit writing to Uncle Robert when she returned, "I had a very pleasant visit to Newberryport, I like it much better than Salem ... I go to see my relatives and acquaintances quite as much as is desireable."[6] Several of the Hathornes preferred to be out of Salem rather than in it. Over the course of time Betsey, Nath, and Ebe had all expressed their desires to leave Salem. However, Salem refused to let them go entirely. The ties never seemed to be totally severed, and for many years, Salem kept pulling them back ... back ... back.

WILD AND FREE (1818-1819)

As the Hathornes were busily preparing for their long journey to their own future home, news arrived that completion of the house was delayed. Betsey took the news well. However, Ebe, exhibiting her usual straightforward manner, wrote of her disappointment to Uncle Robert:

> We were sorry to hear that the house will not be finished till November, because so long a journey in cold weather will be disagreeable ... you must not complain of our not writing, for two letters have been sent you, and we can tell you nothing but what you know already.[7]

Although Ebe was totally dependent on the Mannings for her support, she often overlooked that inevitability in her life. She appeared, even at a youthful age, whether tactfully or not, to disregard the generous efforts of others made on her behalf. She did not mince her words.

Eventually word arrived that it was time for the family to move. On an autumn day, the Hathorne children were packed up along with their belongings for the long journey to their new home. Nath and Ebe were very pleased to leave Salem with their mother while Louisa was prepared to make the trip with them. The New England landscape, losing the yellow and gold hues of the apex of autumn, transformed to bronze, signaling the coming of winter. The crispness in the air easily turned to a cold dampness as the day waned toward sunset. The excited travelers were carried away from civilized and familiar Salem. As each mile passed over primitive unpaved roads, the journey took several bumpy days.

The Hathorne children entered a new life, which was far

removed from the familiarity of the Manning household in Salem where they had lived humbly yet comfortably for ten years. The journey to Maine had taken them away from their Hathorne relations, the last connection to their long-deceased father. It had been a lengthy decade since Betsey's life had been turned upside down at the death of her husband. After all the interceding years of heartbreak and loss, there were new dreams for Betsey. She would have her home and a life of her own in Raymond with her children.

Life suddenly was no longer set with familiar countless days residing as guests in the Herbert Street house. Now there was the prospect for a great adventure. The Hathornes had the opportunity to create a different way of living in their newly built colonial house. So new that the wood in the house still smelled freshly cut and not yet affected by mustiness or mold as old houses tended to suffer. It offered an abode where the four Hathornes could happily live on their own terms in a spaciousness unfamiliar to them.

Each season at the new Hathorne homestead offered a dream of something different for Betsey and her children. They already witnessed the change in season and the crisp air scented with a hint of pine from the thick native forests. The cold winter would soon arrive to bring mounds of fluffy snow that afforded sleighing and playfulness in the frozen white crystals layered several feet deep. Looking ahead to the next Spring, warmth would melt away the snow and nourish fragrant, colorful flowers and welcome new young wildlife. Summer would open endless space for the children to run and hide and get their feet wet in the cool waters of nearby Dingley Brook. There would be tiny fish to tickle at the children's ankles as the trickling waters flowed downward and mingled with the calm and pristine water of the massive Sebago Lake. A fishing rod in hand offered a fresh catch for dinner every day and endless memories of summer adventure.

Nath, Ebe, and Louisa would have the chance to follow the water's path, leading them to view the huge lake from solid ground. The lake appeared as if its water spread for miles to the horizon. The shadows of the evening sun rested on the nearby islands, huge lumps emerging from the sparkly waters. One of these protrusions like a giant sleeping turtle was close enough to the mainland to be reached by a small boat. It was a perfect target for exploration for the restless young boy and his devoted sisters.

The children would learn, during their tenure in the expansive wilds, that danger lurked, if not for them, then for the animal life they so enjoyed. The islands out in the lake were needed at times to safely keep the domestic goats away from one such danger—packs of ravenous wolves. To Louisa's relief, the goats were brought out to the island for safe keeping from such a threat. Another lesson for the children—nature itself may cause harm or at least allow certain natural events to occur. Louisa wrote to her Uncle Robert on one occasion that, "Mr Hamlins went of [sic] to the island where the goats are and found the old one dead on the point of a rock and he thought he was killed by lightning, the other two were well."[8] Such was the harsh reality of rural life in Maine.

Nath, at fourteen years of age was ecstatic and he possibly was the happiest he ever had been in his life. Of course, his healed foot injury added to his enthusiasm. If he had been an invalid at the time of the move, his situation would not have changed much, simply the address of his affliction. Physically capable, then relocated, Nath had the opportunity to experience an undemanding independence that he had not experienced in Salem. He wrote years later of this splendid time in Maine:

> Here I ran quite wild, and would, I doubt not, have willingly run wild till this time, fishing all day long, or shooting with an old fowling-piece … Those were delightful days; for that part of the country was wild then, with only scattered clearings, and nine tenths of it primeval woods …[9]

Nath felt no loss away from the upstairs chamber where he had slept in Uncle Robert's room. The old graveyards filled with the bones of Hathorne ancestors were now distant. Nath suddenly found himself living in an expansive land where there was scarcely a building to cast a shadow upon him. He could look out his chamber window to see the sunny sky, bright daylight, and great expanses of trees. At night, the stars with a glowing moon cast light upon the earth. For the most part, Nath lived quite contently in Raymond.

He spent some spare time, "reading a good deal, too, on the rainy days, especially in Shakespeare and 'The Pilgrims Progress,' and any poetry or light books within my reach…"[10] Reading provided a haven for him, an escape from the ordinary life he led in Salem. Although Nath loved the outdoors and spent the boundless hours of his days outside to enjoy his natural surroundings, he found solace and comfort in printed words.

Regarding Louisa, "so sunny and cheerful was her disposition, she could be happy anywhere."[11] In Salem there was much to make this sparkling personality happy in her surroundings; she seemed to be always delighted. Could she be happily content in a new home so different from Salem? There were no narrow streets like in Salem or small back yards, no harbor with tall sailing ships or pretty town green, no grandmother or loving Aunt Mary to run to for hugs. However, Louisa's immediate family at her side and some Manning family residing down the road buoyed her contentment.

Preferring the isolation it offered, Ebe was supremely satisfied with her new situation in Maine. She had the opportunity to read to her heart's desire. A walk in the Maine forest provided total solitude with only the ancient trees for companionship. In her mind and heart, she hoped to never leave Raymond and wrote to her Aunt Priscilla that:

> I do not feel at all surprised that people think it strange we should remove from Salem, but I assure you we are extremely well contented here, and that nothing could induce us to return ... we shall expect a visit from you all next summer, and then perhaps you will not pity us quite as you seem to do now.[12]

The relocation miles away from their former home in Salem could have caused some apprehension for the children, but the three siblings were quite happy in their new environment. The entire earth became their backyard. Sebago Lake replaced the familiar Salem Harbor. The landscape offered an expanse infinitely larger than the familiar Salem town green. There were wild acres to run and hide or sit in the shade of a tall tree and breathe the cool fresh air.

Raymond offered a quiet so quiet that perhaps the children could hear the gurgle of Dingley Brook or the crunch of pine needles beneath their feet. Cheerfully skipping and running, Nath, Elizabeth, and Louisa could easily visit their Uncle Richard and Aunt Susan if they wished. They were Manning family, too. As the Mannings of Salem had done, these Maine Mannings enveloped the fatherless Hathorne children and showered them with the kind of familial love and closeness that nurtures in children a sense of security and acceptance.

Thus, as the remainder of their first autumn in their new home swiftly turned cold, winter soon blanketed the small

A View of Sebago Lake, Maine

WILD AND FREE (1818-1819)

village of Raymond. 1818 had closed, heralding in a new year with renewed hope for the future. New Year's was the day for celebration in that time. Tradition had not yet established the coming of Saint Nicholas or Santa Claus on Christmas Day. Therefore, it was New Year's Day and not Christmas that brought holiday spirit into the home. The small family shared in its own quiet festivities for that day. It was a different holiday for the Mannings in Salem who may have felt quite lonely without the commotion of three children who were no longer in residence. Betsey, though, celebrated the coming of the new year in her new house with her children but without her mother or sisters nearby.

Nath, Ebe, and Louisa spent the winter days outdoors running and playing in the snow. They were free to scramble outside as the first snowflakes began to fall, catching some on their tongue before the tiny white crystals made their descent to reach the frozen earth. As the snow accumulated to sufficient depths, piling onto the pine trees and across the landscape, the sleighing commenced. The children whole-heartedly participated in wintertime frolicking until their woolen clothing, becoming heavy and wet, produced shivers from the cold.

Nath made every effort to take advantage of the fun that the cold winter months offered. Occasionally he hiked into the woods with the hunting gun to shoot small animals or track a bear. Opportunities for skating and climbing over deep mounds of newly fallen snow in the forest were a daily treat. Sometimes he took such long walks with Ebe that it seemed they would walk till springtime arrived. Years later, Ebe fondly reminisced about her excursions with her brother:

My Dear Sister

> When we lived in Raymond, I generally went with him, and one cold winter evening when the moon was full, we walked out on the frozen Sebago to a point which we were afterwards told was quite three miles from our starting place, and that we were in danger from wild animals ... The walks by the Sebago were delightful, especially in a dry season, when the pond was low and we could follow, as we once did, the soundings of the shore, climbing over the rocks until we reached a projecting point, from which there was no resisting the temptation to go on to another, and then still further, until we were stopped by a deep brook impossible to be crossed, though he could swim, but I could not, and he would not desert me.[13]

Although Nath was almost entirely irresponsible toward his studies, at an early age he had a sense deep down inside him to look after his sisters. This was not a responsibility that he particularly sought; it was simply there. Occasionally circumstances arose where he was called upon to mind the wellbeing of Louisa and Ebe. Often during his life, his own personal circumstances, his finances, his location physically elsewhere proved an inability to always live up to this responsibility. There would come a day some decades into the future where Nath would suffer crushing heartbreak caused by a calamitous situation involving one of his sisters that he was powerless to prevent or resolve.

Once the winter's white blanket of snow melted away at

the arrival of spring, Louisa busied herself with her new vegetable garden and flowers. She scouted about the property in search of flowers, making a bouquet in her small hand. She searched for wild berries to pick enjoying the blooming abundance of vegetation. Such memories of Louisa as a child may have been noted by her brother years later describing the child, Pearl, in his book *The Scarlet Letter*, writing when she "grew big enough to run about, she amused herself with gathering handfuls of wild-flowers ..."[14]

Louisa immersed herself in rural farm life, unlike her sister. She fed the chickens, played with the baby kittens, kept watch over the sheep and baby calf, tended to the apple trees and vegetables. Sometimes when she was able to sit in one place long enough, there was butter to churn.

Louisa spent precious time with Nath as they walked in the endless acres of forest or crossing along Dingley Brook to fish at Sebago Lake. Big brother Nath escorted little Louisa to the water's edge and helped her to bait the line and then throw it into the water. The two spent hours patiently waiting for an unsuspecting fish to bite and become their prize catch for the day. The times were memorable, and more than twenty years later, when Louisa was an adult, she reminisced to her brother asking:

> Do not you remember how you and I used to go a-fishing in Raymond? Your mention of wild-flowers and pickerel has given me a longing for the woods and waters again; and I want to wander about as I used to in old times ...[15]

My Dear Sister

Those "old times" that she would recall far into the future were her present now. Louisa found enjoyment in the little things in her surroundings like the flowers, the pets, and the garden in the summer. She wrote to her uncle, "there is a little squirrel runs about in our yard in the day time and sleeps in the shed at night. Mother says she hopes he will stay here all winter …"[16] Like the mischievous pet cats or the strange little pet monkey in Salem, this small furry creature had unknowingly provided amusement for all the Hathornes. However, Nath may have preferred to hunt the small wildlife rather than watch any scurry around the yard.

Interestingly, the exposure that Nath had to Louisa's domestic endeavors became very useful years later in his life. The skills of gardening, gathering food, and the preparation of simple meals eventually offered him a pleasant pastime in his adult life. For the present, however, knowledge of these domestic purposes and skills were somehow seeping into his consciousness to be stored in the far reaches of his memory until a situation arose where he would make use of them.

Their mother delighted in her newfound life, which she had dreamed about, planned, and accomplished. These circumstances offered a diversion away from her former life where she was labeled as the Widow Hathorne, dependent upon the kindness of her relatives for support. That chapter in Betsey's life was temporarily closed. The neighbors didn't necessarily know her life history or business nor reliance on family money. She was intent on becoming an active participant in their small community, where she pursued personal interests, most particularly, in teaching a religious Sunday school for the church-going residents.

Her sister, Mary, was most supportive and helpful to

Betsey's effort. Mary offered her assistance by collecting religious books from ministers or churches in Salem. She sent packages of books to Betsey as often as she could gather them. Mary wrote to Betsey that, "I am very much pleased with your account of the Sabbath School, I was allmost [sic] affraid [sic] to hear thinking the news might not be good..."[17] Mary continued in her letter that the deacon in Salem "was much pleased with the manner in such I disposed of the books and offers me more, wich [sic] I shall endeavor to send as soon as possible."[18]

This endeavor may have been a matter of charity for the Salem church members to contribute toward this project, but Mary truly believed in this undertaking that Betsey had embraced in Raymond. Mary was also equally devoted to helping her sister as she wrote:

> I have been [ ] favored in finding Friends in the Trustees of the Bible Society here they have commited [sic] to my care another box of Bibles & Testaments wich [sic], I shall transmit to you as soon as I have a convenient opportunity. I hope you will do the best in your power with them...[19]

Betsey had found a new purpose for her life outside of raising her children. The Bible school provided a challenge and the joy of making a true contribution to the small society of people who lived in rural Raymond. Betsey made a place for herself and her children. She successfully created a new life for her family, coincidentally largely removed from most of her own relatives.

For little Louisa, busy with all her interests and playful

pastimes, there were hints that she at some point soon would grow from a little girl into a young woman. Just as Nath would eventually grow into a man, beyond the childhood games, the fishing, and playing with pets, his sister would grow up too. One indication of this was Louisa's concern for clothing as she wrote to her uncle: "I hope you will not forget my gown I shall be obliged to Aunt Mary or Aunt Dike if they will get Miss Blackney to fix it ..."[20] Louisa then added in the letter some special instructions on the subject. A few months later, Louisa wrote again about clothing: "I should like to have a dark gown fit to wear everyday Elizabeth wishes to have hers light."[21] Apparently, the sisters did share a common interest. Like many young girls, they both appeared to be interested in the fashions of the day.

The Hathornes were not simply dropped off and left to fend for themselves. Their relatives, especially Robert, were careful to provide whatever they needed to survive including supplies and laborers to help with chores. Betsey took it upon herself to actively engage in its operation. Nonetheless, with life, things sometimes may get out of hand as did one of the workers that Uncle Robert had hired. In a letter she wrote in early spring, Betsey defined the problem to her brother Robert that this hired man simply didn't care to work:

> Dear Brother I have forebore saying any thing about Joe concluding you has cares enough, but ... he has been a great deal of trouble to me ... Richard took him away more than a fortnight ago ... he wishes to go back to the poorhouse and says he shall not be oblige to work there ...[22]

Instructions in the same letter to Robert regarded his nephew: "Nathaniel wants a pair of pantaloons 2 pair of short cotton stockings and a thin waistcoat."[23] Robert carefully attended to his responsibility for his sister and her family and provided for their needs as consistently and as best he could. He often travelled back and forth between Salem and Raymond in part to check on his sister and her children and provide for their well-being.

For their first few months Ebe, Louisa, and Nath enthusiastically enjoyed their new life. However, the Manning uncles, especially Robert, did not forget about education, most importantly their nephew's. Louisa could be schooled at home, if necessary, and Ebe, by this time, was not offered an education any longer. Nath along with Jacob Dingley, "had gone to school to a clergyman, a Mr. Bradley, near Portland …"[24] at Stroudwater for a more formal education. This may have been the first time that Nath was separated from his mother and sisters for any significant length of time. His family learned to do without him for the immediate future. However, this future was not so long as Uncle Robert had planned.

As it turned out, Nath was totally miserable at school and begged to be brought back home. The experiment with boarding school had failed, and shortly thereafter, Nath was joyfully reunited with his family. Still, Nath's lack of formal schooling did not sit well with his frustrated Uncle Robert. As the tenaciously devout guardian of his nephew's education, the uncle devised another plan which would be equally as distasteful to Nath.

By June of 1819, it had not been a full year since Nath had been relocated to Raymond with his family. The early summer provided opportunities for delight with Nath looking forward to a season equal to or better than the summertime visit he enjoyed in 1816. Unfortunately, he was going to be very disappointed. Uncle Robert ordered his nephew to return to Herbert Street. Two things were waiting for the boy upon his arrival. Nath was enrolled in Mr. Archer's School for preparation for entrance to college, and he was given work in his Uncle William's office.[25] Uncle Robert had meticulously worked out all the details to his own satisfaction regarding the education and training of his errant nephew. Summer fun had not been scheduled into the plan.

Not long after his arrival back in Salem, Nath's true feelings surfaced. Nath was separated from his mother and sisters. Any previous friends of his could have moved on after he had left town. He felt abandoned, especially by his mother. He had lost any control of the situation and was helpless. He decided his only option was to complain and complain often. Louisa and Ebe remained with their mother through the summer and autumn of 1819 and into the winter of 1820. They fared quite well without Nath at home because they thoroughly enjoyed living in Maine. Nath, on the other hand, was unhappy and struggling. As autumn chilled the air, Nath unburdened himself, complaining to Louisa in a sorrowful letter:

> DEAR SISTER, We are all well, and hope you are the same. I do not know what to do with myself here. I shall never be contented here, I am sure. I now go to a five-dollar school,—I, that have been to a ten-dollar one. ... I wish I

was but in Raymond, and I should be happy But 'twas light that ne'er shall shine again on life's dull stream ...[26]

Despondent Nath, the unruly student nephew, was stuck in a school he didn't wish to attend, stuck in the Manning house in which he didn't want to live, and stuck with Uncle Robert watching his every move, all in Salem where he didn't want to be. However, no one except Louisa and his mother knew of his true feelings. Confiding to Louisa in the letter he wrote:

> The knowledge I have of your honor and good sense, Louisa, gives me full confidence that you will not show this letter to anybody. You may to mother, though ... I remain Your humble servant and affectionate brother, N.H.[27]

Although Ebe would have relished tutors and schoolteachers for herself, she did not have to deal with the intensities of a forced education. For her, any educational opportunity provided distinct pleasure. Nath, however, did not realize how fortunate he was in being given an education during a time when many boys were simply sent off to work at manual labor. Nath would have preferred to be sent off to the Maine woods to hunt or fish. However, his uncle persevered.

Ebe spent her time reading or taking long walks in the countryside. This may have been when she discovered that she enjoyed isolation and solitude. Meanwhile, Louisa was occupied with the workings of the household. Through her

My Dear Sister

detailed letters, she kept Uncle Robert up to date on the status of the property. She delighted in the progress of the season, "the corn and potatoes turned out very well."[28] As though she was the foreman of the family operation, Louisa wrote in her letter of some of the season's accomplishments, "The nuts and seeds are planted according to your Directions … I hope they will come up well."[29]

Meticulous with the specifics, Louisa offered her uncle an inventory of all the vegetables and animals on the property while adding, "We have excellent butter of our own making."[30] Eleven-year-old Louisa concluded that the harvesting at the Hathorne place went very well. The outlook for the coming months looked favorable as the Hathorne women held their own in the wilds waiting for the winter snows to blanket the landscape in frozen white.

Although Ebe sometimes enjoyed social encounters when it suited her, this is where Raymond failed miserably in her opinion. A rural outpost, the population was small, and most likely those living in the small community were not well-travelled nor well-read. Their lives were engaged in a constant struggle toward survival. Ebe understood the realities of living there but wrote to her Uncle Robert, "… it is certainly much to be lamented that so pleasant a place should be inhabited by people so rude and uncultured."[31] She accepted the bad with the good, and for the most part, Ebe preferred to stay.

The utopia that Raymond provided for the Hathornes also included certain realities. The distance to Salem made it very difficult to visit relatives or help when sickness or tragedy struck. The weather also presented challenges, sometimes bringing forth dangerous perils. Snow and freezing temperatures could make living in their home harsh, lonely, and deadly. Then add one, two, or three illnesses during the winter of 1819 to 1820. However, Betsey would endure to the severest of challenges to stay in her own home with her daughters. She did not want to abandon her new life.

In some ways the winter season could be delighting for the Hathorne women. It was a time to hunker down and enjoy each other's company or read favorite books. The winter offered a solitude to live among one's thoughts, memories, or dreams while enjoying the magic of a newly falling snow. Years later, Hawthorne remembered his precious days there and would write about the magic of the season in his story "Snow-Flakes":

> I love to watch the gradual beginning of the storm. A few feathery flakes are scattered widely through the air, and hover downward with uncertain flight, now almost alighting on the earth, now whirled again aloft into remote regions of the atmosphere ... By nightfall, or at least before the sun shed another glimmering smile upon us, the street and our little garden will be heaped with mountain snow drifts ... the landscape will lose its melancholy bleakness and acquire a beauty of its own, when Mother Earth, like her children, shall have put on the fleecy garb of her winter's wear.[32]

However, for Nath presently living in Salem, the winter did not offer the same allure and magic as it had in Maine.

My Dear Sister

Salem's winter weather was damp, cold, and gray. He was trapped in this old home and missed his mother and sisters. His thoughts often turned to them, and he reminisced about his glorious days with them which were now gone. Thinking of Louisa drifted him toward melancholy. He admitted to himself that he was the cause of any upset between them due to his teasing or annoying her. Therefore, he wrote to Louisa an affectionate and somewhat contrite letter:

> Dear Louisa—I have received two letters from you for which I say under great obligations. I did not know Mother had been so unwell as to require a nurse. I am glad that she is recovering. All your friends in Salem are in tolerable health. I think you have improved in your hand writing very much…I wish very much to see you all and though you and I could never keep the peace when we were together, yet I believe it [ ]most always my fault …[33]

Nath continued in the letter expressing his loss of living his dream country life. Mournfully, he wrote, "But I shall never again run wild in Raymond, and I shall never be so happy as when I did, … I remain your affectionate Brother."[34]

The passing of time did not ease Nath's lamentations and he was getting on his relatives' nerves. Although moving back to Salem was not his choice, Nath was a sixteen-year-old invader who disrupted his grandmother's ordered house and life. His annoyances pushed his relatives to lose their patience from his unrelenting resistance to his studies, his constant grumblings about his job, and his lack of self-discipline. He proved to be a handful for the Mannings.

Although Nath missed his family terribly, he did not want them returning to Salem. He was holding onto the hope that he could one day return to his family and restore himself to the life he had lost. It must be considered that at fourteen or fifteen years of age he did not have the maturity to be separated from his mother. Also, the planning for a new house and a move to Maine permanently had taken two years. He was only given a few months to enjoy it. In his mind, it was unfair that his mother and sisters were able to continue in their new home when he had been ripped out of it. He advised Louisa, "I hope Mother will upon no account think of returning to Salem and I don't much want you to come either."[35]

Nath's counsel was not heeded. Louisa was sent back to Salem after only a year and a half residence in Raymond. Betsey and her frustrated relatives possibly decided that Louisa's presence in Salem will help improve her brother's unmanageable disposition. Also, Louisa would have an opportunity to enjoy childhood interactions with a variety of children her own age and continue her schooling. In the Spring of 1820, Aunt Mary Manning travelled up to Raymond to safely escort her young niece back to the Herbert Street house.[36]

Old Books with Candle

Chapter 4
Salem Is Home (1819-1821)

"I felt it almost as a destiny to make Salem my home ..."

—Nathaniel Hawthorne,
"The Custom House," Introductory
to *The Scarlet Letter*

"Dear Mother," Louisa wrote in her letter to her mother, "We arrived here on Thursday last after rather a tiresome journey ..."[1] For Louisa, the trip to the Manning's Herbert Street house in June of 1820 was an arduous and damp one. Aunt Mary Manning included her own note to her sister attached to Louisa's letter describing the journey home to Salem:

> Your daughter bore her journey extremely well. the first day we were out in a heavy shower of rain, and Thunder & lightning, when we got to Portland our clothes were considerably wet

yet through the blessing of Providence were but slightly affected with colds.[2]

The travel to Salem had included a stopover for Louisa and her aunt who noted in her letter, "our Friends were all delighted seeing her."[3]

When Aunt Mary and Louisa finally did arrive home in Salem, they experienced a surprisingly happy reunion. Aunt Mary immediately noticed a difference in her nephew. She commented in her letter to Betsey that "Nathaniel is well and is even more pleased than I expected he would be, with having his sister with him, they are both much pleased with being together."[4] The older brother, repentant of the teasing to which he had subjected his younger sister, was extremely happy to be with Louisa. He had an ally, one to commiserate with when his relatives annoyed him or when his days of study and work became too intolerable for his impertinent soul.

Louisa's presence and light-hearted demeanor added a gaiety to the Manning house that had been missing since her departure months earlier. She brightened the home and her brother's attitude. Nath's memories of the lonely long months of his life shared only with older relatives briefly faded into the shadowy corners of the old place. Louisa had begun to rescue Nath's spirits with her pleasant ways, temporarily minimizing his doleful complaints. Time would tell if Louisa's presence would permanently improve his outlook. For Louisa, she had her brother again, and she easily settled back to life in the first home she had known.

Louisa lost no time in arranging social occasions for herself. There were rounds of visits with her relatives Mary Dike, who was her Aunt Priscilla's stepdaughter, and Aunt Rachel

Forrester, a favorite Hathorne aunt who was her father's sister. Long walks sauntering around the village streets with Mary and her father, John Dike, or her friends Abigail Moriarty and Louisa Hawkes pleasantly passed the hours during sunny and warm summer afternoons. Social appointments, evening visits, and engagements like birthday parties and listening to orations by Uncle Dike often occupied Louisa's time.

When free moments allowed, she shared them with her brother, relishing the opportunity for her to have him all to herself. Louisa wrote to her mother on July 4th, "Nathaniel delivered a most excellent Oration this morning to no other hearers but me."[5] She was happy to spend hours with her brother, especially on his birthday, and he shared the time with much gratitude, a special treat for Nath who realized how lonely his day would have been without her.

Momentarily, Nath exhibited a new energy and ambition to focus on some interests of his own. Unfortunately, this did not include his studies! Nath dreamed up a plan to launch his own publication. This endeavor was the future author's youthful attempt as a writer, editor, and journalist. Louisa was quite pleased to reserve some time scattered among her many social engagements to assist her brother in his literary pursuit. The two employed paper and pen, generously provided by the Mannings, to publish the newspaper for distribution. The final product was filled with Nath's and Louisa's written work as well as recent news about family members.

This simple publication was not such a far-fetched idea for the children to pursue. Family members lived in Raymond and Salem with other relatives, at times, travelling or making visits elsewhere. The newspaper was a reasonable attempt at keeping track of everyone in this large family. Louisa did whatever her brother needed to get the new edition off the ground. Nath, its fledgling editor, willingly included her poetry. It is not surprising that Louisa, who was always the pleasant and cheerful child in the family, composed a poem about sunshine for Nath's *The Spectator*.

"Address to the Sun"

Glorious harbinger of day,
When the Moon her course has run,
When all darkness fleets away,
Then we see thee, glorious Sun.

—Maria Louisa Hathorne[6]

Although Louisa enjoyed writing poetry, she did not concern herself with lofty aspirations of becoming a poetess or pursuing publication except in her brother's newspaper. Louisa was content to be a companion and content with her life. Contrasting her frame of mind, Nath was never satisfied with himself nor his life. He was looking for a missing piece, possibly the father he barely knew. There was a restlessness and a frustration which pushed him to continually search for an invisible, illusive entity that would offer satisfaction to his existence.

However, there was one thing that Nath was very clear about in his mind. He was seeking the means to eliminate the oppressions of his life, specifically Uncle Robert, his Manning relatives, and old Salem itself. At his age, the only possible solution for the removal of any perceived tyrannies

SALEM IS HOME (1819-1821)

may have been to run away. Many young sea hands had done exactly that hoping for escape and adventure far away from home. Nath's father spent his working life at sea. Nonetheless, Nath's father also died during a voyage, thus, never returning to his family and leaving them destitute. Nath understood that reality, a knowledge that may have prevented him from entertaining the idea of a seafaring life for himself. Writing seemed to offer him a path toward an emotional escape from his present condition. If Nath could not obtain the physical freedom he desired, conceivably, he could enjoy freedom of his mind and spirit, although temporarily, through writing.

Unfortunately, Nath's ambitions for his publication were short-lived. The endeavor faded along with the summer. With the demise of his newspaper, Nath had additional time to accommodate the real obligations of his life. Still, although fleeting, Nath's summertime newspaper provided him with his first experiences in the craft of writing. It was one of very few opportunities that truly gave him joy and satisfaction during this time.

The rebellious young man did not possess the insight at the time to understand that his education and office job may prepare him for adulthood and future employment. The Manning uncles voluntarily provided for Nath's physical needs and his schooling. They also diligently planned toward a productive adulthood for their fatherless nephew that would eliminate dependence upon his uncles or their money. Nath simply did not appreciate their efforts and behaved with resentment toward them. On the other hand, he did like the money he was earning at his job. He wrote to his mother that "my Salary quite convenient for many purposes."[7]

Louisa enjoyed totally different circumstances. Her life had flexibility with not much responsibility. When she was not involved in her extensive social activities, she read books and played games like battledore and shuttlecock,[8] a game like badminton. The culture of the times allowed more latitude with the female children in a family. Young girls may be allowed to attend school for a few years to learn to read, write, and have a familiarity with arithmetic. Such knowledge was handy for running a household as the traditional expectation for girls at that time was marriage. Domestic skills were what young girls of the day were expected to learn, and for Louisa, those skills came naturally. She enjoyed and took pride in those pursuits.

Louisa's family enrolled her in "Mrs. Curtis's school and also to Mr. Turner's dancing school, Uncle William wished me to go …"[9] She immersed herself willingly, planning to succeed in those endeavors. Louisa was completely cooperative and, thus, fared much better than her brother because she did not feel compelled. Nath did feel compelled. However, Nath also had been enrolled for the dancing lessons, which he surprisingly atttended.[10]

Thus, both children were well occupied in Salem with their various activities. Nath muddled through his study and work while his sister kept to her busy schedule. Louisa relished her days filled with her two schools and endless social engagements. The time passed quickly with new pleasant memories to reflect upon and write about to her mother. Sometimes Louisa was so tightly scheduled and busy that she did not have the time to write home regularly. She was apologetic writing to her mother at the first opportunity, "I should have

SALEM IS HOME (1819-1821)

written before but have been so much occupied that I have not had any time ..."[11]

When Louisa didn't write, Aunt Mary, who was the substitute mother, provided Betsey with updates on the children. Louisa's occasional fragile health presented challenges, and there were days she was unable to attend school due to illness. The demands of studies were such that her Aunt Mary sometimes needed to assist her. Nonetheless, Louisa persevered with her endeavors and succeeded with the help of her attentive aunt who wrote to Betsey:

> I believe M. Lo. make very good improvement at school, she is a pretty good girl. I have a great deal to do for her but it is so pleasant a task I should be sorry to be deprived of it. I have been telling her you must give her to me. I tell her one is enough for you, but she says no she had rather be Mothers than any ones else.[12]

For the most part, Nath was quite patient with Louisa, understanding that she was still a little girl whose mother was living a distance away. Louisa wrote to her mother explaining, "Nathaniel has not laughd [sic] at me quarreled with me or pestered me more than once or twice since I came up."[13] Apparently Nath was very content with having his little sister with him. Thus, he was determined to not aggravate her enough, as a brother easily could, that she would want to abandon him and return to her mother.

In certain infrequent ways, Nath was not an entirely disagreeable youth. He was careful in his treatment of Louisa, and he did develop the habit of writing to his mother each week while he lived in Salem. His mother was thankful, telling him, "I am glad you write every week, though we do not. we have so little to write of any importance, that it seems hardly necessary to send a letter every week."[14] Nath was cognizant of the lack of letter writing from his mother and sister, Ebe. As he waited to hear from them, he suffered disappointment when no letters arrived for him.

A few days earlier, he had written to his mother, "Yours of last week was not received. I supposed because it was not written."[15] He called their bluff but also continued writing his own weekly letters to them. Nath informed his mother of news about the family and, of course, noted some of his playful sister's activities of which he seemed to take delight. In one letter he amusingly informed his mother, "Louisa seems to be quite full of her dancing acquirements. She is continually putting on very stately airs, and making curtisies."[16]

Nath found Louisa's dancing quite fanciful as she lightly pranced on well-worn floorboards through scantily furnished rooms. Her youthfulness scattered a fresh and lively energy over the somber home and Nath's equally somber attitude. Louisa was engaged in the dancing, but on a serious note, she knew there was a ball scheduled for the autumn. She planned to be perfectly ready for the social event of her young life. Aunt Mary wrote to Betsey, "Nathaniel & Maria are in good health. M. holds out very well to go to school & dancing wich [*sic*] I think is a good deal this warm weather."[17]

The summertime school and dance lessons continued through the hot weather. An occasional cool breeze from the sea sometimes erased, for a moment, the listless summer air.

SALEM IS HOME (1819-1821)

All the while, Louisa enjoyed the time of her young life with a busy schedule, which included companionship with her girlfriends. Aunt Mary wrote to Betsey about a special occasion, "M. went with Mrs. M. invitation to bathe with Abigail as they have a large bathing tub in their house..."[18] The experience was a splendid event for a young girl of Louisa's age.

A bathtub, a particular luxury at the time, was most likely fashioned from tin or copper. It was moveable to be stored or set aside when not in use. There were no indoor pipes for running water in homes, so well water was heated in kettles on the stove and then transported and poured into the tub. It was a time-consuming affair, a fact that indicated Louisa was highly regarded by her friends to go to such lengths for her enjoyment. More common in the day, washbasins were used so that most people had sponge baths to bathe away the day's dirt and dust.

Her brother, on the other hand, was not impressed. He had plenty of opportunity to bathe in a more mundane manner suitable to his tastes. He preferred swimming solitarily in a quiet inlet along the seashore in refreshing cool waters. There, he was free to jump in and wash away the summer heat and dust after completing his daily responsibilities. The sunshine and gentle swish of the water along with the quiet natural surroundings served to soothe Nath and remove him temporarily from the drudgery of his life.

Louisa greatly enjoyed her stay in Salem, but her time there did not diminish her longing for the rest of her family in Maine, writing to her mother, "I want to see you all very much."[19] In Raymond were her kittens and chickens, her flowers and berries. Unfortunately, Louisa could not split herself in half to be in both places at once. She was enjoying splendid experiences in Salem, but there was always an emptiness in her heart for those in the other home she was missing. She cherished her memories of Maine, and the responsibilities she had imposed upon herself there remained on her mind:

> I have sent Jane a box of wafers I could not think of any thing else she would like, well you tell her I thank her for taking care of my flowers and kitten and ask her to continue it. Tell Peter the same about my chickens. do all my things grow well, flowers, kitten and chickens. have you had many berries this year? we have had a good many Grandmaam has just bought some huckleberries.[20]

Meanwhile, Betsey and Ebe passed their time with great satisfaction. Writing to her son, Betsey indicated, "the season has been very pleasant ..."[21] She led a satisfying life overseeing her property and planning busily for her Sunday school.

Ebe, as well, enjoyed her independence and was living the life that her brother coveted for himself. She had no constraints placed upon her as she took long walks in the woods to enjoy nature, avoid housekeeping, and equally avoid social interaction. Unless, of course, she wished it. Ebe enjoyed reading a substantial number of books, which she went to great lengths for a supply. In a letter to her niece written decades later, Ebe described her life at the time:

SALEM IS HOME (1819-1821)

> When we lived in Raymond ... I stayed nearly three years—three winters and two summers there. I like to recur to it now, and I think it was a good life for me, because I acquired the habit of careful reading. I read the Waverly novels as they came out for there was a good circulating library in Portland, twenty-five miles off and a stage went thither once a fortnight, by which I went and returned books. We had a good many of our own for those times; perhaps I had access to books enough; I read Shakespeare assiduously, as I might not have done, if more had been within my reach. Also, I wrote verses, which seemed to be very pretty and were extolled by an intimate friend, with whom I corresponded.[22]

Uncle Robert, in August of 1820, planned a visit to transport needed supplies to Betsey. This trip also included a surprise. Louisa had knowledge of it and was quite excited to tell her mother the news. She revealed in a letter, "Uncle Robert expects to set out to-day to go to Raymond, ... Uncle Robert has bought a dog to bring down to you, I think he is very pretty, he looks goodnatured ..."[23]

Although Louisa was aching to see her mother, she embraced her current situation and found positive things on which to focus without complaint. Sitting by herself, she wrote to her mother about her dancing lessons and mentioned in the letter, "I have got to go to dancing school this afternoon, I like it very much ... I am writing in the little bed room all alone; I sleep in the upper little chamber sometimes alone ..."[24] Louisa was proud of herself that she could now sleep alone without childhood fears of shadowy figures plotting to scare her out of her sleep. Although Louisa was growing up, she signed her letter as a reassurance to her mother, "I remain your affectionate daughter Maria Louisa Hathorne."[25]

In an August letter to Louisa, Betsey, the long-distance mother, had some instructions for her daughter:

> Aunt Mary says you are a pretty good girl. I hope you will endeavor to assist her all in your power, make as little trouble as possible with your clothes, you must wait upon Grandmama when you are at home, and be kind and obliging to all your friends, do not exert yourself to [*sic*] much with dancing ... belong entirely to Aunt Mary you must obey her as you would a Mother ...[26]

Softly, Betsey instructed Louisa to be kind, helpful, and obedient and cautioned her not to overdo her activities. Coincidently, Betsey wrote a letter to Nath that same day as well. In her letter to her son, however, Betsey surprisingly did not include any instructions for him that he must behave himself! She may have had little desire to discipline her only son. Also, she could have suspected that Nath held some resentment toward her for agreeing to send him back to Salem. Or she felt a tinge of guilt because she was living her new life at the cost of her son's happiness. With miles of distance between them, Betsey allowed the Salem relatives significant space in dealing with her son in whatever manner they saw appropriate. They were the ones living with him daily.

SALEM IS HOME (1819-1821)

Betsey included in her letter to Louisa a message for her sister, Mary, that her Sunday school endeavors were going well. She asked Louisa to, "tell Mary we continue the Sunday school yes and sucede [*sic*] very well, I am glad she is a going to send more books …"[27] Betsey was quite optimistic and encouraged by the response to her Sunday school program. These activities refute the tales about Betsey living a lonely, reclusive life, at least during these years. Launching a Sunday school program required Betsey to become involved and accepted in such a sparsely populated community. She proved herself to be a person who could take charge, plan, and succeed in an endeavor. She was productive and lived almost independently with some outside assistance from her brothers.

Louisa was occupied for weeks with the dancing school and preparation for the upcoming autumn ball. She had practice sessions several times during the week with dance instructor, Mr. Turner. She wrote to her mother explaining her numerous day-to-day activities. They were enough to keep any young girl occupied:

> Monday I went to Mr. Archers examination. Tuesday Louisa Hawkes came up to see Mary Dike. Wednesday I went to Abigail Wests party, Thursday I went to Aunt Forrester. Friday I went to Elizabeth Richardsons party. [Sat]urday I went into Aunt Ruth's that I [ ] not anytime to write.[28]

A thoughtful and conscientious student, Louisa took her lessons seriously and worked toward perfection. The young debutante also wanted to have the look of perfection with her apparel. Louisa wrote to her mother, "Aunt Forrester gave me my ball gown, it was plain India muslin …"[29] Louisa, along with her special dress, had been made ready for her first ball with assistance by one of her beloved Hathorne aunts.

Included in Louisa's extensive social life were parties with other young girls her age. At two of these gatherings Louisa estimated "there was twenty nine girls at Abigail Wests" and "twenty eight at Elizabeth Richardson's."[30] She commented about both social events in a letter to her mother, "I had a nice time."[31] Louisa's mother was far removed in Raymond so not available to encourage or even discourage her daughter in any of her pursuits. Instead, Louisa thrived under the protective guidance of her loving and maternal Aunt Mary.

A chilly autumn rain poured down onto the streets of Salem which forced Louisa to stay indoors. The dark day gave Louisa time to catch up on things such as writing to her mother. In her letter, Louisa detailed:

> I went to Abigail Moriarty's last evening and had a nice time. I walked over to Beverly Saturday [ ] noon with Sally and John Dike and Mary Dike came home with us, I was quite tired. we had dancing enough [ ]week we went Wednesday afternoon Thursday all day and Friday morning the last six weeks will begin tomorrow and I suppose Mr. Turner wants to learn us to dance well before [ ] ball …[32]

SALEM IS HOME (1819-1821)

Louisa always enjoyed a good walk on a sunny day and was fit enough to stroll a good length because the distance from the Manning house to Beverly was almost three miles.

She added in her letter that she anticipated that her aunt may come for a visit tomorrow. To everyone's surprise, Aunt Priscilla Dike and her husband John arrived unexpectedly that very day. There was no more time to write letters to her mother because Louisa and Aunt Mary had guests to entertain. Aunt Dike sometimes brought games for her niece and nephew, but Louisa anticipated that her generous aunt and uncle may bring *Aikens Geography* as Louisa had requested.[33] Louisa, therefore, may have spent the afternoon with tea and a careful browsing through the pages of a book with her aunts and uncle.

The time of year had approached when the leaves on the trees made their annual transition from summer green to autumn gold. After a few short weeks of stunning color across the landscape, the leaves broke away from their branches to gently cascade downward to the ground. Temperatures turned crisp, and the cool winds picked up crunchy brown leaves from the street to redistribute them elsewhere in windswept swirls. The cool presence of the Fall season offered a more comfortable temperature for Nath at his job and for Louisa at her intensive dancing practices.

While Nath felt no uplifting in his life with the change of season, the excitement for Louisa and her fellow young dancers swelled to the pinnacle of expectation as the date of the ball drew closer. Louisa, practiced, practiced, practiced, ensuring that her dance steps would be perfect. "Monday afternoon, Tuesday all day, Wednesday all day, Thursday forenoon from nine till after three in the afternoon and then Thursday night the ball.[34]

The intense practicing for weeks, the spins and turns, the curtsies and counting steps had been completed. The autumn ball was suddenly at hand. Louisa elegantly made her entrance into the ballroom that evening along with an array of adolescent girls and boys from her dancing school. She was confident in her dance steps and her personal presentation as she wore her lovely and stylish ball gown. This special occasion would become one of the most exciting events of Louisa's young life. She had attained young ladyhood, a picture-perfect young debutante, as she danced and danced the hours away in the ballroom until suddenly the clock turned to the early minutes of the next morning.

Surprisingly, her rebellious teenage brother attended the evening's social event as well.[35] Surely, they shared at least one dance together. This special occasion had nothing to do with necessary studies or work training but social niceties and children coming of age. For this purpose, once again, the relatives had stepped up to provide for their fatherless niece and nephew. The Manning uncles had paid for months of dance lessons for both Louisa and Nath. Aunt Forester assured Louisa was dressed in style with a new ball gown for the evening affair. Nath's apparel hadn't come by compliments of his aunt but that of Uncle Robert's wallet. The preparation for Nath's and Louisa's attendance at this special Salem ball was a family project for selected Mannings and Hathornes.

The season's ball was too soon a memory for those who attended. It had been a glorious evening of dance, ladylike curtsies, and gentlemanly bows among the young residents of Salem. Possibly the images in one's mind were set with the memory of the music of Mozart and violins in the air. Shortly thereafter, Louisa wrote to her mother, "the ball is over."[36] She then described the evening in her own words:

> I went at six or a little after; all the scholars marched into the room with the grand march, there was a good many there. Nathaniel went; I had a beautiful time and did not get home till after one o'clock. I felt tired enough two or three days after. I did not get up the next day till 10 oclock.[37]

Louisa's special evening of young elegance in the social world of nineteenth century Salem had come to an end in the early hours of the following morning. The memories of the experience would last forever.

After the conclusion of the fashionable ball season, Louisa had more time for playing games with her brother when he had a few free moments to spare. Aunt Dike meddled some to assure they had entertainment: "Aunt Dike has brought a pair of battledoors, so that Nathaniel and I can play now ..."[38] The doting aunt would be pleased when the children did play with them, batting a shuttlecock with a hand-held paddle in the Manning yard. Although the recipient of new games to play without demands of preparations for the ball, Louisa had time to realize she missed her mother and Maine even more: "I want to see you and Ebe and all the folks. give my love to all the folks ..."[39]

Louisa's homesick letter expressed almost an element of

urgency in the words. Aunt Mary sent a note to assure Betsey that Nath and Louisa were doing well:

> Your children enjoy very good health and behave very well. Our Family is all well … give my love to Elizabeth, Brother Richard & Sister Susan and all inquiring Friends, our Dear Mother desires to be remembered to you all.[40]

Although Louisa wanted to see her mother, there were no plans for a trip home. She was still enrolled in school and winter was approaching. Any travel would necessitate an arduous journey back to Raymond. It was decided, therefore, that Louisa would remain through the winter in Salem no matter how much she missed her mother.

She was not alone in the melancholic thoughts. Nath also missed his mother, and there was no option for him to return to her either. He wrote wistfully, "It has been near of a year now since I saw you."[41] The brother and sister shared the same homesickness, but neither was leaving Salem at least for the next few months. Nath was relieved that Louisa would be staying with him through the dreary Salem winter.

In late autumn, a dark shadow came to cloud Louisa's bright and playful life. Since her arrival in Salem, Louisa had been a close companion to her Uncle John Dike's daughter. They had spent many afternoons visiting or strolling around Salem together. However lately, "Mary Dike has been quite sick but is a little better now,"[42] Louisa wrote to her mother. The rally was short-lived as Mary Dike began experiencing increasingly difficult health problems. Less than three weeks after Louisa's letter was sent to her mother, Aunt Mary wrote to her sister Betsey with an unpromising update. She wrote of Mary Dike's condition, "she has been very much out of health nearly ever since Mr. Dike & Priscilla returned from the Eastmans and is now very low and not expected to continue long in this world ..."[43]

At the time, the influenza had been lurking in the Manning house as well as around town, but Aunt Mary wrote positively to her sister Betsey that "N. & M.L enjoy good health & spirits M has grown [ ] & taller since she came up, I do not recollect that she has lost her appetite one day since she came ..."[44] Fortunately, serious illness had not pressed itself upon the young Hathorne brother and sister, but Mary Dike would not survive to see the new year.

In late 1820 and early 1821, Louisa went to visit the Dikes while her Aunt Priscilla and Uncle John were mourning the death of Mary. Louisa visited to ease the burden of their broken hearts. In a departure from living with Nath for the past several months, as January came to a close, Louisa wrote to her mother that voluntarily, "I stay into Aunt Dikes now but I have not stayed all the time till yesterday."[45] Louisa was maturing, becoming more secure in visiting away from her immediate family, not only visiting away but sleeping away as well. After the crisis subsided, Louisa returned to the Manning house where her life settled back to normalcy. The Dikes would be forever grateful for the kindness and solace that Louisa had offered them during their bereavement.

Along with the sadness, in January Louisa took comfort in the small joys that came her way. There had been New Year's Day as well as her birthday a few days later. She opened some special gifts from her relatives. Nath, possibly using some of his salary that he earned in Uncle William's office, had given Louisa a book to enjoy. It was an appropriate present from one who read so often himself. Louisa wrote to her mother itemizing the special gifts she received including "a new tortoise shell side comb" from Uncle Robert.[46]

This birthday was special, marking Louisa's passage from childhood to adolescence but without her mother's presence. She wrote to her mother, "I have been up here seven months the first day of this month and I am thirteen years old ..."[47] She continued to miss everything in Maine: her mother, Ebe, her own home, and her friends. She longingly wrote to her mother, "I want to see you and Ebe and all my friends at Raymond very much so does Nathaniel and indeed, so do we all ..."[48]

Nath, too, had been counting the days, weeks, and months. His negative opinion of Salem had not changed even with Louisa's presence. He dreamed of the wilds of Maine, the hunting and fishing and sleighing in the winter, all without the encumbrances of responsibilities determined by Uncle Robert. Although uncles, Robert and Samuel, scheduled a visit to Raymond in March, there was no plan to take either Louisa or Nath with them on that journey.

Louisa's contented mood changed a few weeks after her thirteenth birthday. She was almost always an invariably affectionate and cheerful child. However, in a letter she sent to her mother in February of 1821, her characteristically affectionate and cheerful disposition was noticeably missing. Had Nath's behavior finally rubbed off on his sister? Louisa too had become disgruntled, but the reason regarded the matter of arrangements for Louisa's continued education in Salem. Louisa was very upset and even the presence of her brother could not cheer her:

> I have one complaint to make, Aunt Mary says that I must leave off going to Mrs. Curtis's at the end of this quarter, ... Abigail Moriarty goes to Mrs. Curtis's and now I know all the girls. I do not want to leave off don't you think I had better go to Mrs. Curtis's? ... this is the first complaint I have made in any of my letters, and I almost wish I had not made this one ..."[49]

Nath had been consistent in his complaining about his life in Salem, and suddenly Louisa was in revolt. In her mind, she had good reason to find fault. It was an understandable request considering her age. The family understood her feelings and the decision was made for Louisa to remain at her present school. All was settled to satisfaction, and Louisa was once again her smiling self.

Although Louisa stayed close to home in Salem spending her time with her aunts and grandmother and friends, Nath began to venture outside the precincts of his hometown. He took advantage of a trip to Boston as Louisa wrote to her mother, "Nathaniel went to Boston to the theatre yesterday and came back today ..."[50] Nath explained to his mother in a letter that he saw King Lear and that, "It was enough to have drawn tears from millstones. I could have cried myself ..."[51] Nath had developed a respect and interest for classic literature while reading the types of books he had read throughout his young life, especially Shakespeare. The trip to Boston gave him the chance to go out and begin to see more of the world and experience what it had to offer outside of books. The theatre brought to life a story that he had read in a book. However, no matter how fascinating Boston may have been, Nath, like Louisa, longed for Maine and their mother.

In his letter to his mother, Nath made plans for a future visit to Raymond in September, "I shall probably see you in September ... It is now going on two years since I saw you. Do not you regret the time when I was a little boy."[52] Two years was a long time for a teenage boy to be away from his beloved mother. For Louisa, now a teenager herself, she would soon reach the day that marked her one-year absence from her Maine home. It was a difficult time for both children. They needed to be educated, but this resulted in their separation from their mother. Betsey was enjoying her new life, which may have been good for her own well-being and mental health but two of her children were not with her.

In April 1821, Louisa wrote to her mother with some pleasant news, "Aunt Dike has taken a little girl her name is Abigail Tailor; Susan Town[ ] took her for her own and when she died she wished Aunt Dike to take her; she is eleven years old, I like her very well."[53] The Dikes once again had a young girl of their own in their home to care for and to love. However, this new addition to the family did not diminish the loving relationship the Dikes shared with Louisa.

Louisa often had frail health, which at times limited her activities. However, Aunt Mary assured Betsey once again that Louisa was faring rather well in Salem, although she was suffering from a cold for the entire month:

SALEM IS HOME (1819-1821)

> She has in general enjoyed very good health since she came to Salem and is not now and never has been since she came up so sick as she was when I was at [ ] if she should be very sick, I should be very desirous to have you come up. but I hope by the blessings of Heaven she will be soon restored to good health ... M.Lo's appetite is good and she has good relish for Play.[54]

Louisa's own letter written three weeks later may have been more reassuring to her mother. She wrote "I go to school now. I was just sick enough to stay at home and play."[55]

Louisa and Nath had been together for the better part of a year in Salem while their older sister, Ebe, had lived in Raymond with their mother. With the coming of Spring, a surprise arrived for them when Ebe came for a visit. Did they notice a difference in her? By this time, Ebe was nineteen years old. She was no longer the teenage child they remembered. Nath and Louisa were in the middle of their teenage years themselves. From their perspective, Ebe appeared like a grown woman.

The three Hathorne children were together once again after months of extended absence and separation. They were at last able to talk together and catch up on the news, play a game or two, take a long walk about town, or visit with friends or relatives. As spring turned into summer in June, Nath wrote a note to their mother, "I was very happy to see Elizabeth, but hope she will return to Raymond soon, because I know you must be very lonesome without her. She seems very well contented, but prefers Raymond to Salem"[56] He added, "I believe you were never before deserted by all your children at the same time."[57]

Betsey was temporarily alone without her children, but it would not be for any extended period. A few weeks after Ebe's arrival, Louisa, after her school term finished in July, was sent back to Raymond. She was extremely happy to return to her mother.

Ebe was by this time reaching marriageable age. It was time for her to take advantage of Salem, where there was so much more to offer a young woman. However, Ebe, like her brother, did not wish to be in Salem. For one reason or another Ebe, Nath and their mother seemed happier living elsewhere instead of in the Herbert Street house. Nath once wrote: "I do find this place, almost horribly 'dismal.'"[58]

Chapter 5
Separation (1821-1825)

"The world may well bless the memory of 'Uncle Robert,' that his liberality was unfaltering and that his estimate of the judicious course for his nephew's education was so correct."

—Horatio Bridge

Louisa had fully enjoyed her time in Salem with school and dancing and playing games with Nath and her friends. After Louisa left for Maine, Uncle Robert may have thought that Ebe would fare just as well as Louisa socially in Salem. However, Ebe had a different personality. She did not possess perpetually genial attributes like Louisa, who was constantly arranging a series of dates for visiting with family and friends. Ebe preferred controlling the interactions she had with others as well as how she spent her time, like taking long walks in town and educating herself privately with her books. In sum, she preferred to be left to herself, which was difficult living in the Manning house. Ebe favored the life that Raymond offered if she had been given the choice.

Nath did not live in the Manning house by choice either. His uncles required his presence for school and work, and he had little time to himself. Nath previously complained to his sister Ebe when she was still living in Maine that, "I have almost given up writing Poetry. No Man can be a Poet & a Book Keeper at the same time."[1] Although experiencing some very pleasant times in Salem, Nath felt dominated by his Uncle Robert and detested the plans and decisions being made for him. The rebellious boy had no interest in attending college, previously writing to Ebe that, "I do not think I shall ever go to College. I can scarcely bear the thought of living upon Uncle Robert for 4 years longer. How happy I should feel, to be able to say 'I am Lord of myself.'"[2] It was a rather naïve sentiment as Nath had not a thought about how he should earn a living to become the lord of himself.

Ebe was nearby to hear in person her brother's grievances regarding his formal education. However, she may not have been totally sympathetic because she valued learning. Uncle Robert had already paid for schools and tutors for his nephew. The most recent tutor was Mr. Benjamin Oliver, a lawyer, who was hired to prepare Nath for entrance into college. That preparation included lessons for the reluctant student in Latin, Greek literature, and other disciplines considered to comprise a classic education at that time. Nath enjoyed reading the classics in literature and discussing them with his sister, but he was not a disciplined nor conscientious student. Therefore, it was the hired tutor's charge to shape him into one, a thankless task with an uncertain outcome.

SEPARATION (1821-1825)

Ebe, an intellectual equal of her brother, was available to assist him with his studies. This may have been the reason she was brought back to Salem. In his uncles' minds, Nath no longer needed a playmate like Louisa to entertain him. He needed to be educated, and because of her own capabilities, Ebe was the better choice for encouraging her brother to address his studies. She would revel in any intellectual and stimulating challenge. With involvement in her brother's study, she had access to his tutor and his books. She was dedicated to her attention in assisting him, but this also may have given her an opportunity to further educate herself as well.

In the Manning house, Ebe's sleeping chamber was located on the second floor below Nath's on the third floor. For studying, they set up a basket system with a rope. They placed papers in the basket and raised and lowered the basket from one floor to the other, up and down, sharing the necessary materials.[3] It is unknown why they went to such lengths to study together in this manner. They lived in the same house and shared access to the same staircase, the same parlor, and the same relatives. Perhaps, since they were both night owls, they studied long after other family members were asleep. It may be possible they chose the basket system to avoid prowling around the house with books and papers in the middle of the night and potentially disturbing the elder relatives.

Nath had no choice regarding his Salem education, and the same was true about college. Uncle Robert made the decision that his young nephew should attend Bowdoin College in Brunswick, Maine. Nath continued to be very resistant to the idea of attending college. However, once the decision had been made, encouraging his acceptance of his uncle's directive

My Dear Sister

was the location of the college. The institution was less than thirty-five miles east of Raymond, where his mother was residing. Nath wrote to his mother, "I hope you will remain in Raymond during the time I am in college."[4] The last time Nath was sent away to school near Brunswick the outcome was quite negative. He lasted a few weeks. With this latest of his uncle's directives and proximity to his mother, possibly this time, school would work out more positively. Nath may have realized that if he had not begged to leave Stroudwater, he could have lived nearer to his mother for the past two years.

With a newfound resolution regarding his higher education, Nath wrote to his mother that he planned to spend nine months of the year at Bowdoin and "… then I can be with you 3 months out of the year."[5] The plan seemed so perfect. At the time, no one considered the possibility that

Bowdoin College, Brunswick, Maine

the arrangement may not last. Nath had the expectation that it would.

Upon thinking about it for a week, Nath wrote another letter to his mother deciding, "I am quite reconciled to going to college, since I am to spend the vacations with you. Yet four years of the best part of my life is a great deal to throw away."[6] Throw away! The remark confirmed what little regard Nath had for his own education and his uncle's efforts. It is no puzzle why Ebe could be critical of her brother at times, considering his lack of respect for the education she very much desired for herself.

Uncle Robert was extremely satisfied with his nephew's entrance into one of the foremost colleges in the country. Nath should have been well on his way to a successful future in college followed by a career after his graduation with such a prestigious preparation for which his uncle paid. However, neither Uncle Robert nor his nephew knew what challenges would need to be overcome to make that future a viable one.

Nath still lamented to his mother of his situation, "Oh that I was rich enough to live without a profession!"[7] Be that as it may, Nath was not rich. He apparently had thought something about his future employment and the need for a profession. He sprung his own idea of a profession on his unsuspecting mother, "What do you think of my becoming an author, and relying for support upon my pen?"[8] Nath's mother may have patiently held her breath upon learning that thought, but it was a better thought than if her son had decided to go off to sea. Uncle Robert would have winced in disbelief; the Manning brothers were businessman. They had followed in the footsteps of their own father who owned successful enterprises that continued long after his death. Most probably, Uncle Robert was preparing his nephew for a future like his own. The idea that Nath would someday become an author had not entered Uncle Robert's pragmatic and business-focused mind.

Nath did not know at the time that his future would indeed include employment in commerce. He did not know that his future also would be greatly enhanced by the friendships he developed at Bowdoin College. Nor did he know as an entering student in September of 1821 that Uncle Robert, "who supplied him with means to spend as liberally as any of his companions,"[9] in his gift of a college education would come in very handily in Nath's future pursuits. The ambitious Uncle Robert established the groundwork for the successful man that his unambitious nephew might one day become.

The college experience also brought for Nath, for the first time in his life, an environment devoid of women constantly at his side. His mother and Louisa were a few miles away, and most of his aunts and his sister Ebe were farther removed in Salem. Nath needed to learn how to survive without the support of his female relatives. Spending a year in Salem without his sisters and mother may have introduced him to life without them. However, there were always his aunts and a grandmother present in Salem. His sisters too needed to learn to live without him for a greater length of time. Each had four years to come to terms with the changing dynamics in their individual lives and familial relationships.

When Nath entered Bowdoin, Louisa and their mother supervised the family property in Raymond filling their time with domestic or church-related pursuits. Also, they retained

SEPARATION (1821-1825)

the hope that while Nath attended college, not so far away, he might surprise them with a visit from time to time. Miles away in Salem, Ebe occupied herself by reading, possibly visiting relatives or the library, and taking her much enjoyed walks. There was a void without Nath at home, but the Hathorne women adjusted and continued with their usual daily endeavors.

Nath, on the other hand, was suddenly thrust into a life influenced by the camaraderie of young men.[10] Would he be ill at ease in dealing with men? He did have the mentorship of male tutors when he was young and the attention of his several Manning uncles. Thus, in the absence of a father, he had learned enough from those other relationships to succeed in developing a few meaningful friendships among his fellow classmates. There was the risk, however, that he might purposely rebuff them like he did his Uncle Robert if they set boundaries or expectations he didn't like.

Alfred Mason was Nath's first college roommate. Having a roommate the same age as himself was certainly a pleasant change after sharing a room with his much older Uncle Robert. Unfortunately for the college buddies, a fire destroyed their dormitory building in 1822. The two friends stuck together and moved to a rooming house run by a Mrs. Adams for the interim. Nath seemed to take the interruptions in stride. The roommates returned to reside in room number nineteen through their second year of college after Maine Hall was rebuilt.[11]

Nath and Mason seemed to fare well together. It was through Mason that Nath was introduced to fellow classmate Horatio Bridge. The two became close friends, and during part of their last two years of college, Nath and Bridge resided in the same boarding house.[12] The close friendship that developed between Nath and Bridge during their college years lasted decades into the future.

Bridge understood his friend. He later wrote about Nath's Bowdoin experience:

> That Hawthorne, coming, as he did, from a family of exceptionally recluse habits, gained there his first practical knowledge of the world. It was not strange, therefore, that in his personal relations he formed few intimacies and rarely sought the friendship of others. Reserve was a prominent trait in his character, but it was the reserve of self-respect, not of pride or timidity. He discouraged advances in a negative way, and gave his confidence only to a few.[13]

Thus, his quiet and reserved personality did not deter Nath from developing a few solid friendships at Bowdoin. In the class one year ahead was his friend future President Franklin Pierce, and another close friend was future Congressman Jonathan Cilley.

The daily lives of Louisa and her mother, while still living in Raymond, were suddenly brightened when in January of 1822 Nath came for a visit during a break from his freshman studies.[14] One must think of the pleasure for all to be together again. Nath savored briefly the illusive freedom his home there offered him. He was a college man in Brunswick, but when in Raymond, he was once again that young wild boy searching for an unencumbered freedom devoid of responsibility.

Nath was also a mother's son and a devoted brother to his sister Louisa. He brought joy into their everyday lives simply by his presence. However, Nath was becoming his own person, perhaps a bit selfish, and he often was remiss in keeping in touch with his family. Lost was the weekly habit of writing letters to his mother. Louisa shared her disappointment in a letter to Uncle Robert complaining, "... we have not heard from Nathaniel since he went to Brunswick."[15]

Regardless of her brother's absence, Louisa was too young to realize at the time that this behavior was the prelude to many long separations from her brother. Sometimes these separations were by circumstance; others were by choice. Nath had begun choosing his friends and visiting other locales instead of seeing his family. The life patterns of their Hathorne childhood slowly and often painfully changed into life patterns of adulthood. Her brother was growing up. He was leaving his family behind and moving toward his new college friends for companionship. These friends knew him as "Hath."

Louisa immersed herself in household interests to occupy her time and looked forward to Uncle Robert's upcoming visit. She was "glad to hear that Uncle Sam was coming down with you and hope you will come soon. The weather is pleasant and the sleighing good here, ..."[16] Louisa closed her letter with, "We are all well and shall depend on seeing Elizabeth in the spring."[17] Plans were being made that some of the family may be together again in Maine, and Louisa was very excited about the prospect.

My Dear Sister

Two months later as the warm Spring sunshine served to melt the waning late season snow, Louisa wrote to her sister Ebe, who was still living in Salem. Louisa mentioned how she was looking forward to the approaching visit by Uncle Robert and Uncle Sam writing, "we have had beautiful weather for some time past but it now snows. we had May flowers on the 6 of April we have a whole tumbler full of them. I wish you could see them."[18] Not a word had arrived from Nath. Louisa aired her impatience to Ebe writing with an urgency:

> We have had no letter from Nathaniel for nearly six weeks since the College was burnt, we write to him but do not know whether he receives our letters, when you write do let us know when you heard from him.[19]

Nath had other things to do and new friends with whom to spend his time. He often delayed writing letters, leaving his family to wonder what he had been up to. They could surmise that perhaps he was studying, but that often was not the case. He was into mischief. Nath fully admitted that regarding his college education, he:

> was an idle student, negligent of college rules and the Procrustean details of academic life, rather choosing to nurse my own fancies than to dig into Greek roots and be numbered among learned Thebans ...[20]

However, he muddled through sometimes to the chagrin of his studious classmates by playing cards with his errant friends. He often skipped religious services, confessing to Louisa, "I am sometime afflicted with the Sunday sickness."[21] He further explained:

> My occupations this term have been much the same as they were last, except that I have, in great-measure, dis-continued the practice of playing cards. One of the students has been suspended lately for this offence, and 2 of our Class have been fined. I narrowly escaped detection myself, and mean for the future to be more careful.[22]

Nath wasn't interested in studying, but fortunately, his wayward behavior was not so serious as to have himself expelled from Bowdoin. However, it must be considered whether he was truly being careful or sneaking in a card game or two on the side. If Uncle Robert had any inclinations about this frivolous kind of college activity, he certainly would have been greatly disappointed in his nephew. This first experience living with men his own age, and without a female in his presence, especially no mother, sisters, or aunts, made it easy for Nath to frequent activities that detracted from his studies. A good game of cards with his chums was much more satisfying to him than a serious study in mathematics or science.

His friend Bridge remembered, "Hawthorne indulged in the usual convivialities of the period; but his sedate aspect and quiet manners prevented the appearance of any excess, even within the limited circle of his intimate associates…"[23] He enjoyed card playing and was known to have a glass of wine or two with his close friends, "but he rarely exceeded the bounds of moderation—never losing more money than he could readily pay, and never imbibing enough to expose himself to remark."[24]

Besides the card games, a cigar, or an occasional glass of wine, there were also more wholesome outdoor diversions nearby Bowdoin to occupy Nath and Bridge. These opportunities brought joy to Nath's nature-loving side and possibly awakened the pleasant memories of his earlier life in Raymond. He enjoyed the outdoors once again, not with his sisters as companions, but with his college friend. Walks in the pine forests and fields, watching the huge logs float downstream in the river:

> Formerly the college grounds and the land adjoining included a great area of pine forest, with blueberry bushes ... with foot-paths running deviously for miles under the shady trees, where, in their season, squirrels and wild pigeons might be found in sufficient numbers to afford good sport. The woodland gave a charmingly secluded retreat ...[25]

Nath enjoyed the gifts of nature he passionately adored with a friend he deeply trusted. His early companionship with his sisters was becoming secondary to the companionship of his male friends. His sisters had no inclination that there was a change in Nath's attitude toward them. They continued to believe Nath's priority was themselves and that it would always be that way.

Bridge fondly reminisced that near the Androscoggin Falls:

> In this brook we often fished for the small trout that were to be found there; but the main charm of those outings was in the indolent loitering along the low banks of the little stream, listening to its murmur or to the whispering of the overhanging pines.[26]

He also recollected:

> There was one favorite spot in a little ravine, where a copious spring of clear cold water gushed out from the sandy bank and joined the larger stream. This was the Paradise Spring ... of late years the brook has been better known as a favorite haunt of the great romance writer, and it is now often called Hawthorne Brook."[27]

During these pastoral walks in the woods, Nath and Bridge expressed their thoughts using literature and poetry. As they both "were leaning over the railing of the bridge just below the falls, listening to the falling water, and enjoying the beauties of the scene ..."[28] Bridge recited Shakespeare while Nath recalled his own previously composed verses:

> We are beneath the dark blue sky,
> And the moon is shining bright.
> Oh, what can lift the soul so high
> As the glow of a summer night ...[29]

My Dear Sister

Long walks with Bridge and the occasional diversions from study made college life bearable for Nath. It also seemed to open his mind more to the written word and the innate talent within him. He created poetry and stories as simply as with a pleasurable walk through the woods with his friend. The evolution of written words was becoming more and more a part of Nath's existence and his plan for himself.

Knowing his mother and Louisa were close by was the comfort Nath needed when he was packed off to college. Nath had no way of knowing that less than a year after he entered college his family situation would change. The time was quickly approaching when Louisa and her mother would need to make their departure from their Raymond home. As Betsey grew older life was proving to become difficult for her and her often ill daughter to manage. Betsey had been away from Salem for almost four years, and she may have missed her own elderly mother who was still living and residing in the Manning house. Circumstance and family ties were calling Betsey home from her years-long personal adventure in Maine. Therefore, the pair made plans to return to Salem to be cared for properly in the Manning home.

Ebe was extremely distressed with the prospect of her mother permanently returning to Salem. She understood that if her mother did return, Ebe would lose any opportunity to, once again, live in the Raymond she loved. She would also forfeit the chance to remove herself from all the meddling relatives who did not understand her desired way of life. Attempting to dissuade her mother from leaving Raymond, Ebe wrote a lengthy letter from Salem expressing in very clear terms to her mother that she:

was very sorry to learn that you intend to come to Salem but I presume your determination is fixed, & I <u>know</u> that in one week after your return you will regret your present peaceful home. Not all the pleasures of society, great as they <u>are represented</u> to be, can afford the slightest compensation for the tumultuous and irregular life which one is compelled to lead in a family like this. I wish I had remained in Raymond ...[30]

Forceful though it was in her expression, Ebe failed in the entreaty to change her mother's decision. By June of 1822, Betsey and her youngest daughter were brought back to Herbert Street. Ebe had wished to return one day to Raymond, but neither Betsey nor her family would ever return to live there again. Ebe later wrote, "...by some fatality we all seemed to be brought back to Salem, in spite of our intentions and even resolutions."[31]

In a sudden twist of fate, the Hathorne family's presence in Maine had disappeared. One may think that this turn of events would be a disaster for the reluctant student. However, Nath quickly adjusted. In lieu of traveling to Salem to visit his family, on occasion, Nath instead decided to visit with his college friends in Maine. He wrote home to Louisa, "I am invited by several of the students to pass the vacation with them. I believe I shall go to Augusta, if Mother and Uncle R. have no objections. The stage fare will be about $5, and I should like about $10 dollars as spending money."[32]

Bridge later wrote to describe Nath's college experiences at Bowdoin. He recorded that his close friend "... was not studious in the general acceptation of the term, but he devoted much time to miscellaneous reading,"[33] outside the course of studies. Not surprisingly, Nath read many books and preferred the humanities and languages, especially Latin. His letters home sometimes had Latin scattered here and there among the news.[34] Nath joined the Athenaeum Society with friends including Bridge, Chilley, and Pierce. By doing so, he gained access to the volumes of books in the Athenaeum library.[35]

One must consider if Nath and Bridge's future accomplishments were foretold by an ancient fortune teller who they occasionally visited. In a time worn cottage set deep in the pine forest near Bowdoin, this mysterious sorceress gleaned, "from the tea leaves in a cracked cup or from a soiled pack of cards, evoked our respective destinies."[36] Bridge reminisced, "She always gave us brilliant futures, in which the most attractive of the promised gifts were abundance of gold and great wealth of wives."[37]

Whether the fortune teller was speaking of only Nath and Bridge or their college friends as well, it is true that several among their friends and classmates proved to become quite successful. Horatio Bridge advanced in the U.S. Navy. Alfred Mason became a physician while John S.C. Abbot a minister and George B. Cheever a theologian. Some eventually entered politics like Jonathan Cilley who was elected a congressman. Franklin Pierce became a soldier rising to brigadier general in the United States Army, with service during the Mexican War, a congressman, and most notably President of the United States.[38]

While Nath rubbed elbows with aspiring men destined

SEPARATION (1821-1825)

for future prominence, his family waited to hear from him. Louisa, occupying herself with visiting friends and relatives, hoped to receive a letter postmarked from Brunswick and bearing the signature of her only brother. For the unsuspecting sister, a letter did arrive but brimming with quite a mischievous intent. Nath, always the reluctant student, thought more of getting away from school rather than excelling in it. In this letter to Louisa, he devised a plan to free himself from school before the end of the school term. He wrote to her:

> I am in a terrible hurry to get home, and your assistance is necessary for that purpose ... it is so long since I saw the land of my birth that I am almost dead of homesickness, and am apprehensive of serious injury to my health if I am not soon removed from this place.[39]

The errant student feigned homesickness to make a good case for himself. He knew he could not pull off the escapade alone and required outside assistance for this latest of blunders. Nath solicited the help of his amiable sister, Louisa. Desperate to leave school, he requested his sister to make up an excuse that his mother was sick or his uncle needed him—an audacious lie!! He wrote to Louisa instructing her:

> In order to effect this, you must write me a letter, stating that mother is desirous for me to return home, and assigning some reason for it. ... You must write immediately upon the receipt of this,

My Dear Sister

and I shall receive your letter on Monday; ... If you are at a loss for an excuse, say that mother is out of health ...[40]

He then threatened in a post-script writing, "If I do not get a letter by Monday, or Tuesday at farthest, I will leave Brunswick without liberty."[41] Nath pushed further with dramatic desperation in his words writing, "Haste, haste, post-haste, ride and run, until these shall be delivered. You must and shall and will do as I desire."[42] Innocent Louisa, his devoted sister, was called upon to become his co-conspirator. The outcome of those solicitations to Louisa is unknown. It is known that Nath finished the school term.

Nath was fighting a battle raging in two conflicting directions about what he wanted for himself. His family desired that he should remain the "Nath" of his youth. They wanted to keep him home forever. His friends expected he was now the college man who they knew as "Hath." He sought to spend more time with his friends but also wanted to be near his family again, just on his own terms. Nath seemed to want it both ways. While away from his family he was negligent with his own letter writing, but he thrived on the news of home no matter how trivial. His sisters, as well, longed to hear from their brother, but his letters to them became less frequent. He appealed to Ebe for any news that she could include in her letters that she sent to him:

> You ought to give me a more particular account of yourselves and all that concerns you, as, though it might appear trifling to others, it

would be interesting to me. I suppose Louisa has by this time returned from Newberryport, and gives herself the airs of a travelled lady.[43]

Nathaniel's inner conflict would remain for years until something happened to force him to decide. In contrast, Louisa suffered no conflict. She was content with her life and enjoyed her relatives and friends who, in turn, adored her. If an invitation was given to her and her health permitted, she gladly accepted. Sometimes that meant a short travel away from home. There were no real demands placed on Louisa. The expectation was that she would eventually marry.

Ebe knew what she wanted. Her intellectual pursuits, including reading, writing and studying, would take precedence over social interactions. However, she had difficulty obtaining her desired lifestyle living in the Manning house. She explained the problems she was encountering in a letter written prior to her mother's move back to Salem. Ebe was not happy with the treatment she was enduring in the Herbert Street house:

> I wish I had remained in Raymond. I am obliged to visit every day and all day, because if I am half an hour at home, my ears are assailed by long and severe lectures, which may be just, but are certainly most injudicious & ill-timed ... If I attempt to converse with any one of the family, if I ask the slightest question, a reproof is invariably joined with the answer I receive. Bodily Labour comprises their only idea of intellectual

and moral excellence, and an angel would fail to obtain their approbation ...[44]

Ebe, by this time, was twenty years old, and like her brother, she wanted more say in her life, even though the Mannings were wholly supporting her. Similar to their dealings with Nath, the relatives were losing patience with Ebe. It is not known what exactly the Mannings wanted for Ebe. Perhaps they were frustrated because she was not in any way close to marriage. She was still going out and visiting, so she hadn't given up on her friends. However, her outside visitations may have been an escape from what she was hearing at home:

> If I remain at home, the whole family express their astonishment at my "moping in the house when the weather is so fine," & if I go out two days in succession, I am, with equal justice and elegance, accused of "spinning street yarn." If I do, I am blamed for devoting my attention exclusively to one person, who unfortunately never happens to be the right one. I shall never be able to give satisfaction to them, yet I believe all this is done and said in kindness, & that they really feel a great deal of solicitude for my welfare ...[45]

Thus, while Louisa was happily engaged in pleasant social calls, Ebe struggled at home, and Nath edged along with his education. Bridge, years later, described his friend during those college years with such terms as "quiet and most amiable,"

SEPARATION (1821-1825)

and "his manner self-respecting and reserved."[46] Nath's time at Bowdoin, however, was not without his dalliances.

Close to their graduation, Nath and Bridge became the founding members of an impromptu society called "The Navy Club."[47] It was formed from graduates who were not selected to speak at the commencement exercises. Each member of "The Navy Club" had a title with Nath being "Commander," Bridge, the lowly "Boatswain," a student noted as D.D. was the "Commodore," and the most jovial personality served as "Chaplain."[48] The group declined membership of their club to any of the best students in the graduating class, and they proceeded to party through graduation week. Not only did Nath avoid the prospect of ever speaking at graduation, but he also refused to have his silhouette cut along with the rest of the graduating Seniors. Bridge followed his friend in avoiding such artistry.[49] This regrettably resulted in the young profiles of these later famous men being lost to history.

Nath's Uncle John Dike came to visit him at Bowdoin prior to his college graduation in 1825. Together, they returned to Raymond for a visit, which should have brought joy to Nath's heart. Instead, the visit commenced as bittersweet and devolved into disappointment. Nath had loved his home there, and his youthful reminisces were indelible in his mind. To him, Raymond was home. By 1825, the "home" that Nath had fondly remembered no longer existed. His mother and sisters had left the house that was especially built for them and were again living in Salem. In addition, Nath felt no familial warmth from the Maine relatives nor any remnant of comfort with the familiarity of the locale.

My Dear Sister

It had become a different place to him. Nath wrote to his sister Ebe that he:

> Received but little pleasure from my visit to Raymond and do not desire to return there again. Uncle Richard seemed to care nothing about us, and Mrs. Manning was as cold and freezing as a December morning.[50]

Nath quickly came to the realization that there was no longer any reason for him to return ever again. The Raymond of his happy childhood memories and of his dreams to return had vanished forever.

Following that visit with his nephew, Uncle Dike spoke in very complimentary terms to the family about Nath's talents. Nath was somewhat disturbed at the glowing revelations as he did not concur with his uncle's elevated estimation of his abilities. Writing from Brunswick to Ebe, Nath considered what was said about him. He attempted to downplay the compliments because at the time, Nath was very pessimistic about the prospects for his future. He believed more in Uncle Robert's estimation of him as his being nothing more than ordinary:

> The family had before conceived much too high an opinion of my talent and had probably formed expectations, which I shall never realize. I have thought much upon the subject, and have finally come to the conclusion, that I shall never make a distinguished figure in the world, and all

I hope or wish is to plod along with the multitude. I do not say this for the purpose of drawing any flattery from you, but merely to set Mother and the rest of you right, upon a point where your partiality has led you astray. I did hope that Uncle Robert's opinion of me was nearer to the truth, as his deportment toward me never expressed a very high estimation of my abilities.[51]

As far as Nath's college performance, Uncle Robert's estimation was truer to the course. Nath graduated eighteenth in a class of thirty-eight.[52] In light of his inclination for avoiding studies, status in the middle of the graduating class may be considered an accomplishment. However, some of his friends fared much better. Both Pierce and Henry Wadsworth Longfellow ranked among the highest in their respective classes. Nath finished his college career as an average and undistinguished student. Yet, to the pleasure of Uncle Robert, his nephew had graduated. To the pleasure of Louisa, Ebe, and their mother, Nath returned to live in the Manning house.

For the first time in more than five years, the Hathorne family was once again living under the same roof. There was no fanfare trumpeting in Nath's heart as he returned to his mother and sisters. He was overcome with a gloom in his disposition. He had no job prospects, which was unusual for a college graduate at a time when very few men had the opportunity for a college education. It appeared that Nath's life had returned to what it had been when he was four years old. He was a widow's son supported by his maternal relatives, sleeping in a dimly lit upstairs room. However, Nath brought back with him four years of experience at college, where he had earned the true friendship and bond of men who had been his classmates.

Throughout his lifetime, Nath nurtured and valued those college friendships. At times, his friends were available when he most needed them to offer hope amidst despair. Upon leaving college, he and Bridge agreed to correspond with each other. They playfully decided upon a new signature for each when writing letters. This was not a whimsical college promise soon to be forgotten once the graduates went their separate ways. Nath and Bridge honored their agreement out of true friendship.

Nath chose the name "Oberon," a significant choice when one considers his love for the classics and Shakespeare. Oberon was a medieval king of the fairies and a character in Shakespeare's play, *A Midsummer Night's Dream*. Bridge chose the common yet noble name of "Edward."[53] Of English medieval origin, the name combines the meaning of *prosperous* and *protector*. Bridge would, in future years, become a very uncommon person both prosperous and, as a military man, a protector of citizens. For Nath, only the passing of time would serve to prove if ever he would become an equal to his capable friend Bridge.

Upon graduation, Nath was released from his Uncle Robert's directives. In turn, his uncle was free to get on with his own life. In 1824, Uncle Robert, at the age of forty, married Rebecca Dodge Burnham. Nath was still attending Bowdoin at the time. The unappreciative nephew did not attend the wedding, writing to his aunt:

SEPARATION (1821-1825)

> I sincerely sympathize with Uncle Robert, and the family, in the pleasure they must feel at the approaching event. I wish that it were possible for me to be present, in order that I might learn how to conduct myself when marriage shall be my fate.[54]

This slight must have been noticed by the family, but there is no surviving record of a response. Nath simply missed the wedding. Surely, Louisa and Ebe had attended. They both loved their uncle and often expressed their feelings toward him in letters they wrote. In one letter Ebe sent when she was sixteen years old, she wrote an endearing mention to her Uncle Robert:

> I am commissioned, with a large stock of loves and tendernesses, and good wishes, &c &c &c &c &c &c &c &c &c &c, but I always omit everything of this kind; it is enough to say that we are all well, and I hope you are the same. I remain, &c & &c &c &c &c &c E.M. Hathorne.[55]

Years later, Nath would mention in his story "Sylph Etherege" a character who was "an orphan ... under the guardianship, and in the secluded dwelling of an old bachelor uncle."[56] Could this have been a reference to his own uncle who looked after his fatherless nieces and nephew for years? Nath gave no specific mention or credit to Uncle Robert who did so much for him. There was simply the use of a bachelor uncle in one of his stories.

My Dear Sister

In contrast to Nath's disregard, Uncle Robert remained a favorite of Louisa's. After his marriage, his wife, Rebecca, became a favorite of Louisa as well. During the subsequent years, Robert, free from the constraints of being a surrogate father, had time to devote to his own wife, children, and outside interests. Robert Manning became a noted pomologist, specializing in fruit trees of which he planted several on his property on Dearborn Street in Salem. His own son, also named Robert, later followed in his footsteps.

Nath and his family still were not free of the need to depend on Manning hospitality and money. Nath was in no position to support his mother and sisters and believed that he was someone without any significant attributes, talents, or saving graces. He had no employment but desired to be a writer. His uncles had paid for his education, yet his family apparently did not push him to obtain gainful employment, if nowhere else, then in the family business. Family letters do not indicate whether his uncles had tried to pursue his employment somewhere. If they had, the prospect failed. The relatives may have concluded this phase about a writing career would be short lived and Nath would agreeably enter the world to earn a living. However, commerce or entrepreneurship held no interest to him. Nath enjoyed literature and, therefore, made no plans for himself other than writing.

Nathaniel's friend, Bridge, encouraged him on this subject of authorship, especially during their long woodland walks at college. Bridge held his own optimistic thoughts that Nath may eventually become successful at writing and later wrote:

On such occasions I always foretold his success if he should choose literature as a profession. He listened without assenting, but, as he told me long afterwards, he was cheered and strengthened in his subsequent career by my enthusiastic faith in his literary powers.[57]

Those special literary powers that Bridge observed in his friend would not easily be coaxed out for others to appreciate. Sometime near his graduation, Nath changed the spelling of his last name from Hathorne to Hawthorne. He may have wished to distance himself from the dreaded and cursed past of his Hathorne ancestors regarding the Quakers and the Salem witch delusion that weighted heavy on his mind. However, he gave his friend Bridge a simpler explanation. He added the "w" back into his name after he noticed certain ancestors had used it "and he had merely resumed it."[58]

His sisters followed his lead and changed the spelling of their names, adding the "w" as well. Eventually, letters written to Betsey from her children were addressed as "Hawthorne." It is not known if this was her choice or her children's. There is the possibility that in Betsey's own heart she forever remained, as on the day she was married, Mrs. Hathorne. However, the aspiring young author from that time forward became known as Nathaniel Hawthorne.

Dearborn Street house, Salem, Massachusetts,
built by Robert Manning for his sister Betsey Hathorne

Chapter 6
Solitude (1825-1837)

"I doubt whether so much as twenty people in the town were aware of my existence."

—Nathaniel Hawthorne

Regardless of their name change to Hawthorne, Nathaniel and his sisters' blood remained the once accursed Hathorne blood. They may have tried to distance themselves from the heritage of their birth, but the legacy of their ancestors was fixed stubbornly close to them. Nathaniel was a lonely figure prone to solitude. This tendency was further amplified and solidified the moment he returned to Salem after his graduation.

Ebe possessed the same tendencies in her personality. However, her journey into an almost total seclusion would take much longer, a very slow process that developed over a period of several years. She eventually would inch her way from simply avoiding socializing when she could to a selective seclusion to a semi-seclusion that equated to an almost hermit like existence. Nathaniel had pointed to the Hathorne side of the family for his own personality leanings toward seclusion:

> I had always a natural tendency (it appears to have been on the paternal side) toward seclusion; and this I now indulged to the utmost, so, that, for months together, I scarcely held human intercourse outside of my own family; seldom going out except at twilight …[1]

Added to the scenario was their mother. Betsey had enjoyed four years of near independence in Raymond. When she returned to Salem, her adventure ended abruptly, returning her to a state of dependency as in prior years. Thinking defeatedly, there was nothing more for her future but widowhood and ill health. With this realization, Betsey might have given up and decided to withdraw from life. If this was the case, she could have inadvertently taught her children to withdraw from life and its challenges by her example. Thus, Nath and Ebe's leanings toward seclusion could have been a combination of Hathorne tendencies compounded by a learned behavior from their mother. For the most part, Louisa did not seem affected to any great extent.

Sequestered in the "haunted chamber"[2] of his youth, Nathaniel commenced his arduous journey to transform himself into the writer he had long aspired to become. Ironically, this dark room, often his prison, may have provided him a comfort zone, a refuge from a world into which he was not ready to enter in active citizenship. There, he mulled the curses,

Quakers, and witches that whirled in his head. He thought of his ancestors and Salem. He remembered his detailed observations of the people he saw during his travels to Boston or places farther from home. Before him arose another journey, a very personal and extended undertaking which would prove to be a difficult one. He must determine for himself how to weave all those snippets of information he had gathered in his mind and turn them into interesting and unique stories.

Nathaniel's impending genius would eventually sort his ideas into a creative framework. However, he was hampered by his solitude and his state of mind at the time. He may have been despondent, depressed, or discontented with his present situation. He had completed his education but was trapped at home while his college friends were all venturing out into the world. Nathaniel had retreated into the rafters of the family home and largely stayed there. However, Nathaniel had one focus, and that was his desire to be a writer. He was determined to reach his goal.

However, his decision forced him to once again be dependent upon Manning money. This was his own choice. He had not pursued entering the outside world to make a living like his college friends. He may have concluded that working at a job would distract him from his writing. He, therefore, chose instead to lock himself away in his singular pursuit toward creativity and invention. For this reason, any escape from the Salem he despised eluded him, but he remained there with a purpose.

Escape eluded Ebe as well. Living in the Manning house with all its varied residents had been a challenge for her since she returned from Raymond. During subsequent years, the house had begun to empty, and eventually her life there was somewhat eased. She did what she wanted for the most part and essentially chose to stay home. She was satisfied with her relatives' continued willingness to support her. As a female member of the family, she was not required to obtain any kind of employment because the family had the expectation for her eventual marriage. However, at a young age, Ebe proved to be an unconventional woman. Most young women of that time accepted the prospect to marry, run a household, and bring forth children. Ebe was not inclined to follow convention and pursued her own path.

Therefore, except for family obligations in which she often preferred limited or no involvement, her time was her own. Ebe may have believed that her brother's time was her own as well. She established herself in the family hierarchy as a helper to her brother, which was an acceptable undertaking for a sister to pursue. She had all the time in the world for his writing pursuits. The brother and sister, similar in personality, were uncommonly close. They understood each other more than anyone else in the family, and their strangely magnetic relationship continued for years.

This mutually agreeable companionship, although symbiotic, came at a great cost. Ebe did hold a certain grip on her brother. She was possessive where he was concerned and wanted him to herself. She never wanted nor expected her brother to develop an outside existence, and unlike Louisa, Ebe did not wish one for herself either. It is possible that Ebe dreamed up a notion that she and her brother should spend their lives living in seclusion and jointly experiencing an intellectualism centered around their writing together. She drew

SOLITUDE (1825-1837)

Nathaniel closer to the confined order of her desired lifestyle. It was an easy task considering Nathaniel's own inclination toward seclusion.

Years later Ebe described Nathaniel's daily routine during those solitary lonely years of his life:

> His habits were as regular as possible. In the evening after tea he went out for about one hour, whatever the weather was; and in winter, after his return, he ate a pint bowl of thick chocolate (not cocoa, but the old-fashioned chocolate) crumbled full of bread ... In summer he ate something equivalent, finishing with fruit in the season of it. In the evening we discussed political affairs, upon which we differed in opinion ...[3]

Sometimes, however, Nathaniel did leave the house during daylight for long, solitary walks that led him to the nearby ocean or a quiet pond or inlet. There, he enjoyed nature in its most pristine form. At times, he recorded in his journal a description of his experiences while walking about town or to the seaside locales he enjoyed. Writing of one of these excursions to north Salem on a pleasant summer afternoon he jotted down his thoughts:

> Beautiful weather, bright, sunny, with a western or northwestern wind just cool enough, and a slight superfluidity of heat ... I bathed in the cove, overhung with maples and walnuts, the water cool and thrilling. At a distance it sparkled

bright and blue in the breeze and sun. ... I strolled slowly through the pastures, watching my long shadow making grave, fantastic gestures in the sun.[4]

There is not much known about Louisa in the years when Nathaniel lived in the same house with her. Few letters exist to document her activities because her immediate family were all living together in one place. For her, life seemed to be established as it had been by enjoying visits, reading, domestic undertakings, and occasional travels to other hamlets nearby. Her demeanor had been consistently cordial, helpful, and reliable since she was a child. As she matured, her innate social and caregiving skills along with her even-tempered personality caused her to be surrounded and loved by family and friends.

Louisa's life was one of delightful companionship, and as a result, she often was presented with invitations. Ebe wrote to her Aunt Mary Manning in 1827 mentioning:

> Maria [Louisa] has had an invitation to pass the winter in New York with Mrs. Wyeth, and the next summer in Syracuse, with Mrs. Archer, but chooses to remain at home, at least for the present ...[5]

Louisa's sociability extended toward Nathaniel's college friends whenever their presence served to grace the sparsely decorated parlor of the Manning house. One such friend was Horatio Bridge:

SOLITUDE (1825-1837)

> I was charmed with the quiet and refined manners of Mrs. Hawthorne, and with the pleasant and lady-like bearing of her younger daughter.[6]

Louisa was that younger daughter, and her sociability and friendly manner caused the guests that visited her family's home to remember her for a long time. Louisa's sister, Ebe, on the other hand, was largely unseen. Bridge mentioned:

> The elder daughter—who Hawthorne often said had more genius than himself—I never saw until after his death.[7]

This was over a time span of forty years!

Nathaniel's solitary existence stretched further into his future as solemn days extended to weeks, months, and finally years. Three years had passed, almost a thousand days since his graduation, when Nathaniel attempted to be published in 1828. Although a man of little means, he paid $100, a hefty sum, to have his story, *Fanshawe*, published anonymously.[8] Writing the book after graduating from college, Nathaniel set his story at fictitious Harley College, fashioned after his alma mater Bowdoin College. The heroine of the story, the dark eyed and lovely eighteen-year-old Ellen Langton, possessed similarities to his own sister Louisa who was just about the same age as the character, Ellen, when Nathaniel wrote the story. Much like Louisa, Ellen was a cheerful spirit imbuing a sense of happiness upon those around her.

Nathaniel may have modelled his main character in the story, Fanshawe, after himself. Nathaniel often took solitary walks, no matter what the weather and often did so at night. Fanshawe's personal habits seemed to reflect exactly that of the author's:

> He was still the same solitary being, so far as regarded his own sex; and he still confined himself as sedulously to his chamber, except for one hour—the sunset hour—of every day. At that point, unless prevented by the inclemency of the weather, he was accustomed to tread a path that wound along the banks of the stream ...[9]

Unfortunately, Nathaniel's book, *Fanshawe*, did not gain notable popularity through his own fault. The book was newly in print when, after seeing the published product, Nathaniel was greatly dissatisfied with his work. In haste, he frantically proceeded to gather any copies of his book that could be found and destroyed them. For the immediate future, the money Nathaniel had paid for publishing his book had been wasted. Disheartened at this point, Nathaniel abandoned book writing. He concentrated his efforts on the writing of short stories like "Alice Doane" and "Susan Grey." It was this short story genre where Nathaniel's writing abilities would slowly enter the literary spotlight. The opinionated Ebe later commented about her brother's short stories, "There was much more of his peculiar genius in them than in 'Fanshawe.'"[10]

Although Nathaniel successfully published a story here and there, he did not earn enough income to support himself, let alone, his mother and sisters. Although now adults, none of them had struck out on their own whether by employment

SOLITUDE (1825-1837)

or marriage, including Ebe and Louisa, who were no nearer to their independence than himself. Betsey suffered chronically ill health which may have exacerbated her reclusive state of mind. Nath and Ebe, to different degrees, were following in her footsteps. Louisa was twenty years-old, and the family still held hope she may marry. At this point, they may have given up the idea for Ebe. It could be questioned if Ebe had become a caregiver for her mother during this time. However, considering her strong-willed personality and her lack of domestic leanings, it is doubtful. Louisa was innately a caregiver, so she more likely took on such responsibilities when her own health permitted.

By this time, Uncle Robert had been largely responsible for Betsey's family for twenty years. Although married with a young family, he dutifully retained his duties toward his sister. Therefore, Uncle Robert built a new cozy little house next to his own on Dearborn Street for Betsey's family. Once again, moving out of the old Manning homestead in 1828, the Hawthornes settled into another new home built especially for them. The residence offered a quieter location than Herbert Street, where the family businesses had been conducted. Nothing changed, however, for Nathaniel or his family beyond the street address and its further distance from the center of town.

As usual, Louisa took charge of domestic matters for her larger extended family. Sometime during the following year she cared for her two young cousins, Uncle Robert's children who lived next door. While their parents, Robert and his wife Rebecca, visited outside of Salem, Louisa, who was in her early twenties by this time, proved quite capable with

131

the children. In addition to caring for them, Louisa also kept a watchful eye on Uncle Robert's prized fruit trees in his pomological garden on his property. As when she was a child, Louisa immersed herself in domestic responsibilities, this time for her special Uncle Robert, his children, and his home.

In addition to her activities associated with tending small children and trees, social niceties kept Louisa well occupied. In one instance, she entertained a favorite aunt, Mrs. Dike, for an afternoon of pleasant conversation. Louisa excitedly described the news in a letter to her Aunt Rebecca. She wrote that her Aunt Dike's visit was something "wonderful to tell" and explained that the days flew by so fast with a "shortness of the time must be my excuse for the matter and manner of this letter …"[11]

The two small Manning cousins filled up Louisa's busy days. The children indulged her with their love and impish behaviors. It was a reminder that merely a few years earlier Louisa had been the loving impish child. Louisa, as the substitute parent, played with her small cousins and at times, comforted them. Little Robert Manning, with worry about his parents' long absence, asked Louisa in a concerned voice, "they shall come home to see me."[12] He had thoughts that his parents had set off for a land far away and he might never see them again. His parents had travelled to Maine, but to a small child, it may have seemed the other side of the world. His sister Maria, who was slightly older, tried to assure him, "They have not made their visit yet."[13] Little Maria expressed the confidence that her parents had not run off forever but would return home unharmed to them.

SOLITUDE (1825-1837)

As the years went by, especially for Louisa and Ebe, an interaction was maintained with their cousins. Ebe corresponded with her Manning cousins for many years until her last days. Had the dislike Nathaniel held toward his Uncle Robert filtered down into his feelings toward his uncle's children? There may have been an understood civility between them, and possibly, they did like each other. Years later, one of Nathaniel's younger cousins would step up to intervene for Nathaniel in a very tragic situation.

It was very evident that Louisa shared a mutual devotion with her cousins. While caring for the children, Louisa wrote to their mother, Rebecca Manning in June of 1829, providing her an update on the children and the family, "The children have been very good ever since you left home and talk about Father and Mother often ..."[14] Louisa asked of Rebecca to, "Remember us as affectionately as possible to Uncle Richard and Aunt Susan and tell them how much pleasure it would give us to see them here ..."[15]

Louisa had continued a warm affection for her aunt and uncle in Raymond, Maine. This contrasted with Nathaniel whose frosty impression of them during his 1825 visit led him to avoid contact with them all together. In subsequent years, the association with the relatives in Maine had diminished. Uncle Richard died, his wife, Susan, remarried, and the house that had been built for Nathaniel's mother in Raymond had changed hands.[16]

Thus, the Raymond that Nathaniel and his sisters fondly remembered no longer existed for any of them. Eventually, interest between the two sides of the Manning family in Salem and Maine faded into nothing. The lives of Nathaniel, Ebe, and Louisa centered almost entirely within Salem once again. It seemed they were indelibly established and permanently affixed to the village of their birth.

The summer season sometimes offered Nathaniel a welcome respite from his self-imposed seclusion as he traveled about or outside New England with one of his uncles, primarily Uncle Samuel. The trips provided a warm weather sojourn away from Nathaniel's somber writing chamber and equally somber life. His uncles may have tried to devise ways to pry Nathaniel out of his writing chamber and into a life in the working world, teaching him a little about business along the way. They surely maintained hope that one day he would obtain employment since the Manning's paid for his college education and had planned for his future self-sufficiency. By 1828 during Nathaniel's travels with his uncles, he had already seen New Haven, Connecticut, and returned there a year later.[17]

As always, Louisa waited for Nathaniel's letters, posted during his travels, from places she might never see in her lifetime. She eagerly read the details of his trips, imagining what he saw through the descriptive words she read. In August 1831, she read of her brother's visit with Uncle Sam to New Hampshire. The traveling pair spent some time at the tavern owned by a family friend. Nathaniel wrote a lengthy letter to Louisa explaining:

> One of Uncle Sam's old acquaintances keeps the tavern at Concord, so that it was like the separation of soul and body to get him away.[18]

Apparently, Uncle Sam enjoyed his visit, perhaps a little too much, such that it was difficult for him to resume his journey. After departing from the tavern, the two travelers explored the Shaker Village in Canterbury. Nathaniel, seemingly, was attracted to the lifestyle there and wrote, "I spoke to them about becoming a member of the Society, but have come to no decision on that point."[19] Possibly he was teasing Louisa about joining or actually entertaining a plan for himself to run away from Salem forever as he had always dreamed. This experience may have planted an idea in his head because a few years later Nathaniel would endeavor to join an agrarian-based community.

Nathaniel's travels provided him with topics and experiences for developing some of his future stories. He later wrote "Sketches from Memory" about the White Mountains and Mount Washington in New Hampshire. In his story "The Canal Boat," Nathaniel described what may have been the details of a trip on a canal boat on the Erie Canal in upstate New York: "I embarked about thirty miles below Utica, determining to voyage along the whole extent of the canal at least twice in the course of the summer."[20]

These summer sojourns interrupted the four long and uneventful years that Nathaniel lived in the Dearborn Street house. Life did not improve there with the passage of time. Nathaniel still could not afford to support himself by writing. His mother's health was not improving, thus requiring the family to vacate the Dearborn house and return once again to the security of the Manning house on Herbert Street in 1832.[21] Realistically, the cost of supporting an entire house for the four of them may have determined another move was necessary. In and out, back and forth, the old family homestead stood to offer a haven of last resort to the Hawthornes from whatever plights they may endure. Once again, Nathaniel found himself in the dark upstairs chamber, trapped in the all-too-familiar prison of his youth.

It was a different house by this time, one no longer bursting with aunts and uncles, grandparents with three small children running around. Some of the former residents had already died like Grandmother Manning, Grandma'am, in 1826; others married over the years and moved out. The emptiness of the dark, old home added to its dreariness. Nathaniel's mother was experiencing progressively worsening illness and seclusion. Ebe, at thirty years of age, was increasingly preferring to spend her time inside the house. Both she and Louisa remained unmarried. And Nathaniel sequestered himself. trying desperately to become an author.[22]

Louisa, and perhaps a friendly pet, were the only beings capable of spreading a little sunshine into the darkness that seemed to always pervade the old place. Uncle Robert had good reason to build a house for his own family to live on another side of town. He created a sanctuary for his family with lovely gardens and fruit trees that offered a bright pastoral setting for raising his own children, removed from the bleakness of the Manning homestead where he had grown up.

Although it appeared that Nathaniel's life after his Bowdoin graduation was one of drudgery and loneliness, there were some bright spots. His summertime travels offered many experiences for him in destinations both close and farther from home. In his journal, he often recorded detailed observations including weather and descriptions of a variety of

SOLITUDE (1825-1837)

people that he had encountered during his travels. On a trip to Boston, he wrote:

> I rode to Boston in the afternoon ... It was a coolish day, with clouds and intermitting sunshine, and a pretty fresh breeze ... We stopped at the Maverick House ... The bill of fare for the day was stuck up beside the bar ... the company ... seemed to be merely Sunday gentlemen,— mostly young fellows ... One, very fashionable in appearance, with a handsome cane. ... There were girls too, but not pretty ones ... Most of the people had smart canes and bosom-pins ...[23]

At home, there were pleasant moments when he dined with his sister Louisa at tea every day and occasionally visited his mother whenever she ventured out of her chamber to see him later in the afternoon.[24] There were also welcome times of fun and sociability for both Nathaniel and his sister Louisa among their friends.

Louisa and Nath befriended and socialized with a few contemporaries in Salem. Most notably were David Roberts and Horace Conolly, the adopted son of Susanna Ingersoll, whose house later became the setting for *The House of the Seven Gables*.[25] Susanna had inherited the house long before it would acquire fame, and there, she lived a rather lonely life. However, after taking guardianship of the young Conolly, she doted on him and paid for his education at Yale where he studied theology.[26]

At the old Ingersoll house, Nath and Louisa met those

My Dear Sister

friends for social card games and pleasant conversation. It was not a long distance to arrive at the not-yet-famous house. Louisa and Nathaniel may have walked there together down Herbert Street crossing Derby Street. After a stop at the wharves to notice the noisy activity, they continued to Turner Street. The old gabled Ingersoll house stood near the end of the street close to the water.

This small group of friends formed a "club" reminiscent of Nathaniel's college days with each of the members of this club having a title. They chose to be royalty. Along with Susanna

Susanna Ingersoll home, Salem, Massachusetts, the setting for Hawthorne's *The House of the Seven Gables*

Ingersoll often included in the games, "Hawthorne was the Emperor, Louisa, the Empress, Conolly, the Cardinal, and Roberts, the Chancellor."[27]

Eventually, Nathaniel grew to dislike Conolly for his loud and irresponsible ways. Years later, he wrote to Louisa complaining that Conolly, "treated me very ill during my visit to Salem—not inviting me to come and see him, and being otherwise intolerably rude. He is a real blackguard—which I have no hesitation in saying to you."[28] Although Louisa remained on cordial terms with both Roberts and Conolly, she married neither.

These card games, like his daily walks about Salem, provided a small escape from Nathaniel's lonely life. Also, as in his youth, a dark and rainy day offered its own diversions for comfort to the aspiring author as he wrote:

> Pleasant is a rainy winter's day, within doors! The best study for such a day, or the best amusement,—call it which you will,—is a book of travels, describing scenes the most unlike the sombre one which is mistily presented through the windows.[29]

Reading books remained an important part of Nathaniel's life, and he received much enjoyment and escapism from this favored pastime. It provided the struggling author with a refuge from the daily drudgery he endured. Books transported him to another time and another place away from his current reality. His sisters, no doubt, read on rainy days too. For more than twenty years, the Manning book collection had been the faithful, although silent, companions for the Hawthornes.

No matter the small pleasantries that Nathaniel enjoyed, he believed that he lived an inconsequential existence. His Bowdoin friends were going places in their careers; yet, he was going nowhere. He had neither a profession, a career, nor success. Franklin Pierce was elected to the New Hampshire House of Representatives serving from 1829 to 1833. He then commenced serving in the United States House of Representatives. Horatio Bridge practiced law for several years before entering the United States Navy in 1838.

Nathaniel, for the present, had to be satisfied with the summer travels that added a little interest to his monotonous existence. In some places, the beautiful scenery lifted his spirits and the local folklore intrigued him. In about 1833, he visited Swampscott, a town located about 4 miles from Salem. He was nearing the age of thirty, and there he experienced the first pangs of love. Nathaniel had become smitten with a young woman who worked in a local shop. The tender feeling may have been mutual. Her name was Susan, and "She gave him a sugar heart, a pink one, which he kept a great while ..."[30]

Susan was a pleasant inspiration; however, this inspiration did not become more than an infatuation, certainly not Nathaniel's wife. He immortalized her, however, in a story that he wrote titled "The Village Uncle."[31] The object of Nathaniel's fascination, whom he called the "Mermaid," was:

> a slender maiden, though the child of rugged parents, she had the slimmest of all waists, brown

SOLITUDE (1825-1837)

hair curling on her neck, and a complexion rather pale, except when the sea-breeze flushed it.[32]

Nathaniel's longing for such a lovely being "... kindled a domestic fire within my heart, and took up her dwelling there ..."[33] It was easy to fall in love while the sea breezes combed through one's hair on a warm and sunny New England day.

At some point in his travels Nathaniel arrived on Martha's Vineyard, a lovely island off the coast of Cape Cod, Massachusetts. In one of his stories, "Chippings With a Chisel," he noted, "Passing a summer, several years since, at Edgartown, on the island of Martha's Vineyard ..."[34] However, there was no success of a romance for Nathaniel to carry home with him to Salem. He returned the same solitary young man that he seemed destined to remain.

Nor is there any record of romance for Ebe who seemed to have no inclination for matters of the heart. In addition to her solitary nature, Ebe knew the grief caused by her father's death. She may have decided to spare herself such interminable loss. Louisa took advantage of opportunities to travel short distances, but there are no records of any budding romances for her during those trips either. Louisa seemed happiest near her mother. It is possible that the separation when she was twelve years old for her schooling may have caused her to never want to leave her mother. Louisa could venture away for a few days, but otherwise, she preferred to stay close.

Apparently, Louisa did not take trips with Nathaniel. She did, however, travel to visit girlfriends or relatives. During the summer of 1835, Louisa set off by herself to Newberryport to visit some friends. Louisa was in her mid-twenties by the time of this adventure. In a letter she sent to her mother, she wrote:

> I did get here in good order <u>bag</u> and <u>baggage</u>... You know the stage had not arrived when I went up to the Coffee House on Saturday, when it did come in the first place, I saw Mr. Micajah Lunt, to my great satisfaction, as he, of course, took me immediately under his protection which made the <u>long journey</u> much pleasanter.[35]

Everyone enjoyed Louisa's company, even Mr. Lunt, during the bumpy stagecoach ride. Louisa's visit in Newberryport with her now married girlfriend turned out splendidly as she wrote her mother saying:

> Susan and I have got to go down in town this forenoon to make some calls. She is the same as ever and I feel very much at home with her and her husband and we can see the girls whenever we choose.[36]

Louisa questioned her mother about things happening at home, "How do you and Elizabeth get along without me?"[37] It was a fair question because Louisa was the Hawthorne to answer the front door, invite in guests, or handle the activities for running the household.

Betsey had two children absent from her home at one time. Louisa was in Newberryport, and Nathaniel may have been busy with his summer travels. Louisa inquired in her letter

SOLITUDE (1825-1837)

to her mother, "have you heard from Nathaniel since I left home?"[38] Louisa informed her mother that she would "not stay a very great while however, on account of Nathaniel's coming home. I may not write again before I come home. So do not be anxious about me let me hear from you if any thing is the matter."[39] As always, Louisa looked forward to seeing her brother.

Nathaniel, although not publicly well known for his writing, had been experiencing some success with the publication of his short stories. Although many anonymously, between 1828 and 1837, he wrote pieces for *The Token* and had contributed to the *New England Magazine* and the *Knickerbocker* among other publications. His stories included "The Seven Vagabonds," "Sketches from Memory," "The Gentle Boy," "The Mermaid," "Young Goodman Brown," "The Man of Adamant," and "Alice Doan's Appeal," among others.[40] He also had written his novel *Fanshawe*, which he had quickly destroyed. In his journal written on or after October 25, 1836, he had noted, "In this dismal chamber FAME was won."[41] There was no explanation or what he might have been referencing. Possibly, he was becoming more confident with his profession, experiencing merely wishful thinking, or simply jotting an idea for a story. For the present, it seemed Ebe may have been correct in her appraisal that the short story was where her brother held his greatest writing strengths and opportunities.

At thirty-two years of age, Nathaniel was offered one such opportunity in early 1836, eleven years after his college graduation. He had obtained employment, although briefly, as a poorly paid magazine editor in Boston. This position should have made him extremely happy. He was getting paid to write, and he was a distance from Salem although not very much on either count. During his tenure in Boston, he often solicited Ebe in Salem to help him with writing for Samuel Goodrich's publications including the *American Magazine of Useful and Entertaining Knowledge*, requesting her to "Concoct, concoct ..."[42]

At home in Salem, Ebe industriously contributed and fulfilled her brother's many requests. This is exactly what she wanted for her life, writing with her brother. In the Manning house, she may have isolated herself by locking herself in her chamber to concentrate like her brother had done. There, she wrote contentedly, seizing upon the opportunity to continue writing with Nathaniel in whatever capacity she could. She may have left her writing chamber briefly for short daytime walks to the Atheneum to borrow books as she had done since she was a girl. An evening walk in the shadows made by a full moon could clear her head to write anew the next day. The outside world soon was erased as she returned inside home to write alone.

Nathaniel certainly had no problem asking Ebe for help. It could be questioned whether he fully appreciated her efforts. Ebe dutifully continued with the work anyway. Nathaniel did depend on her, and Ebe derived a degree of satisfaction from the work. She dared to dream her dream of a life devoted to collaborating with her brother as partners in writing. Ebe would never willingly relinquish her grip even into the years to come, no matter where Nathaniel's life took him.

While Ebe received letters from her brother asking for her help with his writing, Louisa received letters filled with his

SOLITUDE (1825-1837)

grumblings regarding the burdens of his life in Boston. He complained to her of being overworked and underpaid:

> Dear L. I am so busy with agents, clerks, engravers, stereo type printers ... —and the devil knows what all—that I have not much time to write.[43]

Louisa continued to be the sister with the sympathetic ear. Nathaniel knew she would listen to him and understand.

Nathaniel was struggling with writing for low wages and without appreciation in Boston. The experience could give any aspiring writer anxiety, and Nathaniel was not immune. By the summer, Nathaniel had met with defeat. He was forced to return home after futilely hoping he would be paid in full for his work. His mother and sisters were content that they had Nathaniel with them at home. However, Nathaniel was despondent by this point, feeling himself a failure, especially in relationship to the success of his college friends. Living in the Manning house and unemployed, he was greatly discouraged about writing prospects. As he retreated into the upstairs chamber, he was trapped into an all-too-familiar dark existence, where he was incapable of escaping his dependence on the Mannings and incapable of leaving Salem.

Horatio Bridge, always supportive and loyal, attempted to boost his friend's morale in person and in his letters. He would address them "Dear HATH," not as the idyllic "Oberon" from college days, but as, his friend. In an October 1836 letter, Bridge offered encouragement:

145

> I have a thousand things to say to you ... You have the blues again. Don't give up to them for God's sake and your own, and mine, and everybody's. Brighter days will come, ...[44]

A few days later Bridge wrote to his downtrodden friend again. This time his words were firm, saying:

> I have just received your last, and do not like its tone at all. There is a kind of desperate coolness about it that seems dangerous. I fear that you are too good a subject for suicide, and that some day you will end your mortal woes on your own responsibility.[45]

Bridge seemed increasingly concerned about Nathaniel's state of mind. This would not be the last of his letters of encouragement. Two months later, he wrote again to Nathaniel on December 25, 1836, offering advice:

> DEAR HAWTHORNE.—On this Christmas day I am writing up my letters. Yours comes first ... At all events, keep up your spirits till the result is ascertained; and my word for it, there is more honor and emolument in store for you, from your writings, than you imagine. The bane of your life has been self-distrust. This has kept you back for many years; ... I have been trying to think what you are so miserable for. Although you have not much property, you have good

health and powers of writing, which have made, and can still make you independent ..."[46]

Bridge had good reason to be optimistic. Unknown to Nathaniel, this steadfast friend had secretly written to publisher S.G. Goodrich, inquiring about how to expedite the publication of Nathaniel's book of short stories. Nathaniel had waited a long time without success for his book to be published. He had initially submitted the stories to the publisher in 1830, six years earlier. To help his friend, in 1836, Bridge fronted the $250 guarantee for publishing the book. Bridge required only that Nathaniel not be told about his involvement in the guaranty.[47] Goodrich wrote to Bridge in coldly blunt terms, "The publication will be solely for the benefit of Hawthorne; he receiving ten per cent on the retail price—the usual terms."[48] Goodrich, it appears, was not very confident regarding the book's prospects.

Shortly after Bridge had executed this publishing arrangement, he carefully opened a sealed document, which had been entrusted to him by Nathaniel for safekeeping in 1824. It was a college prank, an accord between friends. However, Bridge had no knowledge of its contents. Instructions were given to keep the envelope sealed until the specified day of November 15, 1836. Bridge quickly scanned the words. It was a contract, but more accurately a bet, made between Nathaniel and his college friend, Jonathan Cilley. The contract, signed by Cilley, read:

> If Nathaniel Hathorne is neither a married man nor a widower on the fourteenth day of

My Dear Sister

November, One Thousand Eight Hundred and Thirty-six, I bind myself, upon my honor, to pay the said Hathorne a barrel of the best old Madeira wine.[49]

The other side of the contract was signed by Nathaniel promising to owe Cilley said wine if Nathaniel had indeed married before the agreed upon date. Bridge may have chuckled about the silly bet. Nathaniel hadn't married, and thus, Cilley owed his friend the Madeira wine. Bridge wrote to Nathaniel a few weeks later, "I doubt whether you ever get your wine from Cilley. His inquiring of you whether he had really lost the bet is suspicious … Cilley says to me that if you answer his interrogatories satisfactorily, he shall hand over the barrel of old Madeira."[50] Unfortunately, a year later their friend Cilley was dead from a duel, the result of political intrigue.

Nathaniel would later immortalize his college friend in his story "Jonathan Cilley":

> On the 23d of February last, Mr. Cilley received a challenge from Mr. Graves of Kentucky … The challenge as accepted, and the parties met on the following day. They exchanged two shots. … and Mr. Cilley fell dead into the arms of one of his friends … Alas, that, over the grave of a dear friend, my sorrow for the bereavement must be mingled with another grief—that he threw away his life in so miserable a cause![51]

SOLITUDE (1825-1837)

Early in 1837, Bridge wrote to Nathaniel with words of confidence for the future:

> So your book is in press, and will soon be out. Thank God the plunge will be made at last. I am sure it will be for good.[52]

The book was titled *Twice-Told Tales* and was a collection of Nathaniel's short stories that were written during the preceding few years. Bridge did not tell his friend about his involvement until several months later. Their long walks at Bowdoin into the thick Maine forests to hear the words of a fortune teller seemed a lifetime ago. However, the hopes and dreams of those youthful days were coming to fruition for Nathaniel Hawthorne. Bridge wrote later about his friend that, "The cloud had lifted at last, and he never afterwards wholly despaired of achieving success as a writer."[53]

Another Bowdoin graduate, Henry Wadsworth Longfellow wrote to Hawthorne after reading *Twice-Told Tales*. He expressed optimism that Nathaniel had finally found his career as a writer and author after almost a dozen years of solitary quest. Longfellow closed his letter to his friend with, "I hope to hear from you again soon; and to what other literary plans you may have … with many thanks for your kind remembrance."[54]

Before any such literary plans were made, Nathaniel was invited to visit Bridge at his Augusta, Maine, home, "When you come, make your arrangements so that you can stay two or three months here. I have a great house to myself, and you shall have the run of it."[55] This invitation was one that

My Dear Sister

Nathaniel gladly accepted. He packed some luggage for the trip and left his dark upstairs chamber. He exited the threshold of the Manning house, where he had entered and departed many times during the chapters of his life. He left his mother and sisters at home, and he left ghostly old Salem to join his dear college friend. It seemed Nathaniel may be taking his first steps out of the darkness of his life to a brighter future.

Both still bachelors, the two men shared a month together nurturing the friendship from their college days long past. They discussed their plans and dreams, enjoyed each other's company, and looked toward to the future. Bridge fondly recorded years later that:

> To this irregular household Hawthorne came to spend a month with me; and doubtless it was a pleasure to him—as it certainly was a great one to me—that we could thus enjoy a few weeks' reunion, without ceremony and without restraint.[56]

Nathaniel also recorded the visit in his journal on July 5, 1837, the day following his birthday, "Here I am, settled since night before last with B—, and living very singularly …"[57]

Nathaniel, finally achieving some success, looked back on the years of his youth without resentment or regret. He had a more favorable and objective attitude, with some newly gained maturity, as he put into words:

> Meanwhile, strange as it may seem, I had lived a very tolerable life, always seemed cheerful, and

enjoyed the very best bodily health. I had read endlessly all sorts of good and good-for-nothing books, and, in the dearth of other employment, had early begun to scribble sketches and stories, most of which I burned. Some, however, got into the magazines and annuals; but, being anonymous or under different signatures, they did not soon have the effect of concentrating any attention upon the author.[58]

By 1837, Nathaniel had embarked on a new path. The somber darkness that haunted his life seemed to be fading and replaced with a brightened outlook. He had dreamed about and struggled toward this goal for a dozen years. After the publication of *Twice-Told Tales*, he reminisced:

> I was compelled to come out of my owl's nest and lionize in a small way. Thus I was gradually drawn somewhat into the world, and became pretty much like other people.[59]

While visiting at the Bridge mansion, Nathaniel mused, writing in his journal:

> Then here is myself, who am likewise a queer character in my way, and have come to spend a week or two with my friend of half a lifetime,— the longest space, probably, that we are ever destined to spend together ...[60]

My Dear Sister

Nathaniel had a feeling that his life was about to advance, "... for Fate seems preparing changes for both of us. My circumstances, at least, cannot long continue as they are and have been; ..."[61]

Life would not be as it had been for Nathaniel. His first book was in print and published under his own name. Nathaniel was grateful to Bridge for facilitating the publication and changing the course of his life. Several years later the dedication in the "Preface to the Snow Image" was to his friend Horatio Bridge Esq., U. S. N.:

> On you, if on no other person, I am entitled to rely, to sustain the position of my Dedicatee. If anybody is responsible for my being at this day an author, it is yourself. I know not whence your faith came; but, ... it was your prognostic of your friend's destiny, that he was to be a writer of fiction.[62]

Slowly and most cautiously, Nathaniel had begun to break away from the magnetic pull of his relatives and the vise grip of his sisters and mother. His two sisters would soon come to the unpleasant realization that their brother preferred being with other people rather than them. He enjoyed the company of his friends who offered camaraderie, moral support, and at times, outright assistance. Very shortly, however, Nathaniel would learn that in Salem there lived a lovely young woman named ... Sophia.

Part 2

A Life to Fruition

Nathaniel Hawthorne,
1851, Thomas Phillibrown, engraver

Chapter 7
Cupid's Arrow (1837-1842)

"Love, whether newly born, or aroused from a death-like slumber, must always create a sunshine, filling the heart so full of radiance, that it overflows upon the outward world."

—Nathaniel Hawthorne,
The Scarlet Letter

Louisa, quite affable within the precincts of Salem, may have already been reacquainted with the three Peabody sisters, Elizabeth, Mary, and Sophia. Many years before, the younger version of the Peabody and Hathorne children had played outside together as small children. Elizabeth Palmer Peabody reminisced years later about the encounters:

> We used to play with the Hawthorne children ... Nathaniel Hawthorne I remember as

a broad-shouldered little boy, with clustering locks, springing about the yard.[1]

During those younger years, it is doubtful the Peabody sisters made any lasting impression on the athletic little boy. He was the same age as Elizabeth Peabody but two years older than her sister, Mary. In addition, Nathaniel was four years older than Louisa and five years older than the youngest Peabody sister, Sophia. The age difference was such that becoming close friends with the much younger neighbor girl may not have been a probability.

Sophia, debilitated with severe headaches throughout her childhood, was a frail child. Of consequence, she may have spent much of her adolescent years indoors.[2] Sophia also had been moved in and out of Salem with members of her family as circumstances required, including a stay in Cuba with her sister. Nathaniel, when not living in a Manning house, had not resided in Salem at all. He spent several months of his youth in Maine at the family home in Raymond and four years as a college student at Bowdoin College in Brunswick. For a brief segment of employment, Nathaniel had resided in Boston. The remaining years of his young adulthood in Salem had been spent in hiding in the Herbert Street or Dearborn Street houses.

Therefore, it is not surprising that the paths of Nathaniel Hawthorne and Sophia Amelia Peabody had not crossed in recent years. They both had resided in Salem in their respective homes, which coincidently were situated relatively close to one another. However, they remained strangers, leading separate lives and reaching adulthood without a passing thought of the games they once had played as children. Their two families, although respected citizens of Salem, lived for the most part in their individual universes that may have rarely intersected. The time was approaching where certain conditions might press for both families to make contact once again.

Many years had already passed since Nathaniel and his sisters had reached marrying age. Louisa seemed happiest living with her mother. Ebe apparently had no plans to attach herself to a husband. The sisters preferred staying at home and having Nathaniel at home with them. Ebe especially had her own designs regarding her brother. She never wanted him to marry at all, once saying, "He will never marry, he will never *do* anything; he is an ideal person."[3] Ebe expected her brother to spend his time writing without any interfering social encumbrances. She expected him to stay home with *her*.

Thus, unsolicited matchmaking was not something that Nathaniel was troubled with by either of his sisters. However, he was a grown man and having a serious personal relationship had crept into his thoughts at times. His previous infatuation with the lovely young lady in Swampscott, Susan, was intense but short-lived. Nathaniel had certainly thought about marriage someday. There was the challenge with his college friend Cilley regarding marriage. Yet, for Nathaniel, now in his early thirties, no lasting romance, no devoted woman at his side, no marriage had been sewn into the fabric of his life. The two Hawthorne sisters were quite content in thinking that Nathaniel's status as a fervent bachelor would continue. In their minds, there was no reason for any change. Things had changed in the intervening years for Nathaniel. He had grown to be:

My Dear Sister

the handsomest young man of his day, in that part of the world. ... He was five feet ten and a half inches in height, broad-shouldered, but of a light, athletic build ... His limbs were beautifully formed ... His hair, which had a long, curving wave in it, approached blackness in color ... His eyes were large, dark blue, brilliant, and full of varied expression ... His complexion was delicate and transparent, rather dark than light, with a ruddy tinge in the cheeks.[4]

Someone was going to fall in love with him, and at his age of thirty-three years, it was about time. It's interesting to note that his father's life ended at that age. Now at that same age, his son's life may have been about to begin.

In Salem, there must have been at least one or two of the local young ladies who may have noticed Nathaniel, including Elizabeth (Lizzie) Palmer Peabody.[5] Thus far, there was no young maiden who had caught the attention of his brilliant eyes for him to marry her.

Bridge remembered the personal strengths and characteristics of his friend, describing Nathaniel:

> With rare strength of character, had yet a gentleness and an unselfishness which endeared him greatly to his friends. He was a gentleman in the best sense of the word, and he was always manly cool, self-poised, and brave. He was neither morose nor sentimental; and, though taciturn, was invariably cheerful with his chosen friends; and

CUPID'S ARROW (1837-1842)

there was much more of fun and frolic in his disposition than his published writings indicate."[6]

Although it took several years, Nathaniel finally experienced the success of published authorship with his book *Twice-Told Tales* published under the new spelling of his name, "Hawthorne." In addition, his demeanor had undergone a magical metamorphosis, transforming him into a mysterious and eye-catching gentleman. He seemed to have more confidence to thrust himself forth into the real world of Salem and beyond, to stretch the perimeters that once bounded his life.

Nathaniel's journey toward marriage began with Lizzie Peabody who had noticed certain stories in *New England Magazine*. She later reminisced, "It was not until 1837 that I discovered that these stories were the work of Madame Hawthorne's son."[7] Lizzie possibly thought that Ebe, the Hawthorne she considered brilliant, might have written the stories. Nathaniel's frequent solitary long walks about Salem led people to believe he had nothing to do with his time. No one would suspect that he had been diligently writing stories for the past dozen years in the upstairs chamber in the old Manning house.

Lizzie had great difficulty persuading the Hawthornes to visit the Peabody home, and it took some time for that to happen. Louisa would have enjoyed visiting socially with the Peabody family. However, it is unlikely that Nathaniel and Ebe were excited and, therefore, dragged their respective feet dreading the visit entirely. Added to the dread was the location of the Nathaniel Peabody home. Located on Charter

Street in Salem, the house was so closely set next to the Old Burying Point Cemetery:

> It gives strange ideas, to think how convenient to Dr. P——'s family this burial-ground is,—the monuments standing almost within arm's reach of the side windows of the parlor,—and there being a little gate from the backyard through which we step forth upon those old graves ...[8]

One of those old graves belonged to the infamous Hathorne ancestor, John, who "was the witch-judge. The stone is sunk deep into the earth, ... other Hathornes lie buried in a range with him on either side."[9] Also buried in this same cemetery was Martha Corey, a victim Hathorne sent to the

Headstones of Hathorne family members at
Old Burying Point Cemetery, Salem, Massachusetts

gallows for witchcraft in 1692. Whatever the reason for the long delay, whether the ghosts of cruel ancestors or wronged victims, simple superstition or lack of desire to visit, Louisa, Nathaniel, and their sister Ebe finally arrived at the front door of the humble Peabody home.

The Peabodys were comfortable but not wealthy. They had lived in various houses depending on their relocations over the years in and out of Salem. Nathaniel Peabody had been a doctor and then a dentist whose practice ebbed and flowed with the Salem economy.[10] He and his wife, Elizabeth, who taught school in their home, adequately raised their children, three daughters as well as three sons, Wellington, George, and Nathaniel.[11]

On a cool late autumn evening when hints of the coming chills of winter could be felt during the late hours, the mysterious Hawthorne trio stood like shadows at the Peabody door. The two sisters, cloaked in darkness accompanied by their brother, were cordially invited to enter the Peabody home. Lizzie, who had been the Peabody sister to answer the door that evening, was the first to witness the three mysteriously enchanting Hawthorne faces. Lizzie motioned them to sit and make themselves comfortable. When the opportunity arose, Lizzie excused herself for one moment and quietly scurried up the stairs, careful not to fall flat in her haste.

She headed to the chamber occupied by her invalid sister Sophia. Lizzie stormed in, practically breathless, to encourage Sophia to come down to meet the special guests. Excitedly Lizzie pronounced:

My Dear Sister

O Sophia, you must get up and dress and come down! The Hawthornes are here, and you never saw anything so splendid as he is,—he is handsomer than Lord Byron![12]

Lizzie was indeed impressed with Nathaniel but Sophia, suffering from ill health for most of her life, refused to see him. She calmly assured Lizzie that he will call again, and therefore, there would be another opportunity to meet him. Sophia had no interest in dealing with men for romantic involvement or marriage. She knew that with her fragile health she may never meet the demands as a wife and mother regardless of any romantic dreams she may have had in her head. There was no urgency to meet anyone, handsome or not.

Lizzie, regaining her composure as she left Sophia's chamber, calmly descended the stairs. She returned gracefully to the parlor to entertain the Hawthornes and possibly to fall a little in love with the handsome and compelling Nathaniel. She was also drawn to Ebe:

> With her black hair in beautiful natural curls, her bright, rather shy eyes, and a rather excited, frequent, low laugh, looked full of wit and keenness, as if she were experienced in the world; there was not the least bit of sentiment about her, but she was strongly intellectual.[13]

Lizzie, well-read and travelled, would have been attracted to Ebe's intelligence and intellectuality. Ebe, in turn, would find in the Peabody sisters women who were far more

CUPID'S ARROW (1837-1842)

educated and interested in education than most people of her time.

Lizzie also noticed that Nathaniel:

> was very nicely dressed; but he looked, at first, almost fierce in his determination not to betray his sensitive shyness, which he always recognized as a weakness. But as he became interested in conversation, his nervousness passed away; and the beauty of the outline of his features, the pure complexion, the wonderful eyes, like mountain lakes reflecting the sky,—were quite in keeping with the "Twice-Told Tales."[14]

Gathering her impressions regarding the youngest of the Hawthornes, Lizzie noticed, "There was nothing peculiar about Louisa; she seemed like other people."[15] This may have been the reason that Louisa was so well-liked and loved by all of those who knew her. Louisa was easy to be with; she exhibited no mystery; she was what she showed to others. Louisa may have softened the sharp edge of her sister Ebe's rather cool and collected personality. Louisa's mellow presence may have enhanced the aura of the quiet and reserved nature of her suddenly handsome and alluringly attractive brother.

The other Peabody sister, Mary, also met the Hawthorne guests that evening. The visit left her in awe. The visit left all the Peabody's in awe as word spread about the evening and the mysterious Hawthornes, especially the newly-found author, Nathaniel. There was much astir in the Peabody family. The stirring swirled as Nathaniel became more acquainted with Lizzie Peabody. For the lonely and private man, he was becoming comfortable, or curious, about the Peabodys. He had enjoyed his initial conversations with the sisters and decided to continue where he left off, or he was simply fulfilling his promise that he would return. He was drawn to return. Was it fate stepping in to orchestrate an impending change in his life that he perceived during his last sojourn with his friend Bridge?

Nathaniel's latest visit to the Peabody home was markedly different than the ones before it. Lizzie and Mary's younger sister made an appearance to meet the man that had so enthralled her sisters. The encounter turned almost mystical and dreamlike. Angelic, as if softly descending from a cloud and dressed in white, the third sister airily floated down the stairs of the Peabody home. Breaking the heavenly silence, Lizzie introduced her sister to Nathaniel with the words, "My sister, Sophia."[16] The angel had a voice, "a low, sweet, voice"[17] which carried lightly through the air as the three sat in conversation.

Immediately, there was a magical interaction transpiring between the two strangers who had just been introduced. For Nathaniel, it was Sophia whom his eyes were attracted to, "he would look at her again, with the same piercing, indrawing gaze."[18] He was fixed on her features, studying her every word and move. Her beauty captivated him, and he was enchanted by her charm. Fate was stepping in, at last, to change Nathaniel's life. He was possibly falling in love.

Sophia too sensed something she had not experienced before in her life. This emotion may have frightened her. She realized of her guest:

that his presence, from the very beginning, exercised so strong a magnetic attraction upon her, that instinctively and in self-defense as it were, she drew back and repelled him.[19]

Nearing the end of the visit, Nathaniel offered to escort Lizzie to the Manning house the next evening so that she could visit with his sisters and asked, "Miss Sophia, won't you come too?"[20] Sophia quickly rebuffed him saying, "I never go out in the evening, Mr. Hawthorne."[21] In earnest, Nathaniel replied almost longingly, "I wish you would!"[22]

Fate possibly could have been thwarted that evening, but fate was strong enough to persist. Perchance, it was Nathaniel who was strong enough. If Sophia wasn't going out to the Hawthorne's home, then Nathaniel would visit the Peabody house. He had good reason to return after his introductory visits. There was foremost his pursuit of Sophia, but her brother George was also home after his return from New Orleans. The time with George would be short lived. Sophia had already lost her brother, Wellington, and then in 1839, she lost George too after a long struggle with his health.

Lizzie developed more than a fondness for her literary guest, but Nathaniel was interested in her sister. This caused Lizzie to ponder about the emerging relationship that Sophia was developing with him. Lizzie, who introduced them, thought to herself, "What if he should fall in love with her!"[23] Was it possible that Nathaniel could really fall in love with Sophia? Lizzie knew that Sophia, ill since childhood, may not be interested in marriage. That may not preclude the frail angel of a woman from winning Nathaniel's fragile and delicate heart.

My Dear Sister

As the months passed, the Peabody sisters made a unified effort to be friendly with the Hawthorne family while the Hawthornes reciprocated. Cordial hand-written notes flowed between the two houses. For Louisa, the three Peabody sisters were new companions. Ebe's interests, although she was largely self-educated, aligned with those of the Peabody sisters, who also were uncommon for their intellectual pursuits. Ebe sought them out for intelligent interaction and discussion. Ebe wrote to Sophia:

> This is the first opportunity I have had to thank you for those beautiful flowers, or for the volume of Carlyle, which I am reading with delight … When Mary is at home I hope for many delightful walks with your mother and with her. If it is good weather tomorrow evening, will you not come and spend it with us?[24]

Ebe was, by this time, slipping slowly into her own solitary world. Nathaniel revealed:

> But my sister Elizabeth is very witty and original, and knows the world, in one sense, remarkably well, seeing that she has learned it only through books. But she stays in her den, I in mine: I have scarcely seen her in three months.[25]

Apparently, days and weeks could pass when Ebe was not seen at all during the day. If she did make an appearance, it might be at night when she stepped out from the shadows of her own chamber. Solitarily lurking about after sunset, Ebe would sometimes roam the corridors of the dimly lit Manning house. In the shadowy darkness, she also occasionally ventured outside to silently grace the desolate Salem side streets as she walked by the dim light of an evening moonlight. It would be difficult to discern the rustle of her cape as she walked about from the fluttering of an old owl's wings. While her brother finally broke out of his isolating behavior, Ebe was increasingly choosing to live in her brother's former world of grays and shadows and darkness.

Sophia was successful in nurturing a pleasant rapport with Nathaniel's mother and Louisa by visiting with them at the Manning house. She wished that she could develop a better relationship with Elizabeth. On one of Sophia's visits to the Hawthornes, "Elizabeth did not know I was coming, I thought I should not see her."[26.] To Sophia's surprise, Ebe did leave her chamber to visit with her, "There now! Am not I a privileged mortal?"[27] thought Sophia. Ebe:

> Received me very affectionately, and seemed very glad to see me; and I all at once fell in love with her. I think her eyes are very beautiful, and I liked the expressions of her taper hands … she urged me to stay so much, as if she wanted me … I think I should love her very much. I believe it is extreme sensibility which makes her a hermetess. It was difficult to meet her eyes; and I wanted to, because they are uncommonly beautiful.[28]

My Dear Sister

At the outset, there was an opportunity for an amiable friendship between Sophia and Ebe. Sophia certainly made the effort. Initially, Ebe was cordial to Sophia, inviting her, "I have delayed answering your kind note, in the hope of a change in the weather, that I might be able to propose a walk ..."[29] Ebe did enjoy her walks and regardless of her slow withdrawal from the world in general, she continued her walking. However, over time, Ebe, realizing her brother's growing affection toward Sophia, had begun harboring some resentment toward the object of his heart. Ebe began to view Sophia as a rival for her brother's attentions. For some time, Ebe had been comfortable thinking her brother had long ago made the decision to forgo marriage and stick with his family. That was before he met the lovely Sophia. Suddenly the situation had changed, and Ebe's family hierarchy was in jeopardy.

Nathaniel finally found a reason to jump off the fence he had been sitting on since his college days. For years, he had been torn between attempting to balance the demands of his family and the companionship with his friends. What was happening now was no simple companionship with friends. Nathaniel realized balancing would no longer work for him. He was forced to act, decide on a change, and Sophia was the reason for this deliberate change. Nathaniel needed to loosen the grasp that his relatives had on him to move forward to possibly create a new life for himself with the woman he was growing to love.

Ebe was certainly astute enough to understand that Nathaniel was becoming his own person. He had his own plans for his life, which possibly meant pushing Ebe and the family aside for another woman! For years, Ebe had helped Nathaniel with his studies and his work, gathering books and materials, writing together. She increasingly felt threatened that her long-held plan of writing with her brother may disappear. She was not willing to share her brother with anyone outside the family either, especially a beautiful and talented young artist like Sophia. Ebe knew that Sophia could conceivably take Nathaniel away from her entirely.

Therefore, Ebe was determined to prevent that scenario from occurring. In her state of mind, she would have disliked any woman that Nathaniel chose, but it was Sophia that he did choose. Ebe never wanted her brother to find himself a wife, and she had no plans to take Sophia into her heart. Her intense dislike and resentment for Sophia festered and years later, Ebe confessed to the Manning relatives:

> I might as well tell you that she is the only human being whom I really dislike … I could have lived with her in apparent peace, but I could not have lived long; the constraint would have killed me.[30]

Ebe was not successful in sabotaging the relationship that had developed between her brother and Sophia. However, in the deepest and darkest fault in her heart, she wished for it. Most probably *no* sister of Nathaniel's could have interfered with the blossoming romance that was Nathaniel and Sophia's. Thus, Ebe was left to reconcile herself to the realization that she could not stop her brother from loving Sophia. Notwithstanding, Ebe had no intention of making life easy for Sophia in the Hawthorne family.

My Dear Sister

Nathaniel had once written in his journal, "A man tries to be happy in love, he cannot sincerely give his heart, and the affair seems all a dream."[31] He was now in love and trying to be happy, but there were obstacles that he and Sophia needed to overcome. They had, thus far, surmounted or at least partially restrained familial interference, but the current economic environment presented another challenge. The financial panic and depression that hit in 1837 crushed the publishing sector, and further challenges would remain for years. It was a difficult time to be in love. Although Nathaniel was fortunate to have his first book, *Twice-Told Tales*, in print, the prospect of monetary gain appeared almost impossible. Money was tight for the Mannings, and Nathaniel was a self-employed and impoverished writer. It was not the best of circumstances for two people to be planning a future together.

The lovers carried through by rejoicing in simple pleasures. One evening in the Peabody parlor, Sophia sketched the face of her beloved onto paper, forming an outline, defining the contour of his face, his eyes, his mouth until a true likeness appeared. In another sketch, Sophia produced a rendering of the "Gentle Boy." Nathaniel included it in a special edition, *The Gentle Boy: A Thrice Told Tale* which he lovingly inscribed:

TO MISS SOPHIA A. PEABODY
THIS LITTLE TALE,
TO WHICH HER KINDRED ART HAS
GIVEN VALUE,
IS RESPECTFULLY INSCRIBED
BY THE AUTHOR[32]

CUPID'S ARROW (1837-1842)

Nathaniel ignored the gravestones and ghosts of the old burying ground next to the Peabody house and continued to return to see Sophia. Memories of the place lingered with him, and decades later, he based the setting for his story, "Dr. Grimshawe's Secret" on that very house. For the present, however, the strong attraction between Nathaniel and Sophia endured beyond the travails of their lives. Within a year or two, Nathaniel made his marriage proposal. However, with her years of infirmity, Sophia was hesitant. She agreed to Nathaniel's proposal contingent upon her recovering from her illness. She made a proposal of her own, "If God intends us to marry, He will let me be cured; if not, it will be a sign that it is not best."[33] Acting with prudence and generosity, Sophia placed her betrothed's well-being before her own. The engagement was between the lovers alone and kept secret from the families. This secret, especially, was carefully concealed from Nathaniel's mother and his two sisters.

In addition to Sophia's concern about her own strength were the perceived reactions that may be exhibited by the Hawthornes. Would they ever accept her as Nathaniel's wife? Nathaniel, however, was either much more optimistic about the resolution of tension with his family or ignored the issue entirely. He tried to encourage Sophia in a letter he wrote to her:

> I think I can partly understand why they feel cool towards you; but it is for nothing in yourself personally, nor from any unkindness towards you, whom everybody must feel to be the lovablest being in the world. But there are some untoward

circumstances. Nevertheless, I have faith that all will be well, and that they will receive Sophia Hawthorne into their heart of hearts. So let us wait patiently on Providence, as we always have, and see what time will bring forth.[34]

Providence was a long time coming from Nathaniel's own relatives. The Peabodys, on the other hand, were much more gracious. Sophia's sister Lizzie interceded for the two love birds. She may have been in love with Nathaniel herself, but she gracefully put Nathaniel's and Sophia's happiness first. Lizzie successfully had entreated through George Bancroft, the Collector of Boston, an appointment for Nathaniel which resulted in a position as "weigher and gauger in the Boston Custom House."[35] Thus, in 1839, Nathaniel left Sophia and Salem to work and save money.

While apart, Nathaniel in Boston and Sophia in Salem, the two shared numerous letters. To protect their privacy, years later Nathaniel noted in his journal, "I burned great heaps of old letters, and other papers, a little while ago … The world has no more such, and now they are all dust and ashes."[36] However, a handful of their letters had survived. In one letter, Nathaniel had written to Sophia describing their special romance, "Nothing like our story was ever written, or ever will be; but if it could be told, methinks it would be such as the angels might take delight to hear …"[37] The love smitten writer often addressed his letters with endearing terms such as, "My Dearest", "Best Beloved", "Dearissima" and "Belovedest" while closing with "God bless you" or "you sinless Eve."[38]

Sophia returned his love in equally poetic words. As she

CUPID'S ARROW (1837-1842)

reflected on the past year, she wrote on the last day of December in 1839:

> I cannot tell you how much I love you ... My love is not in this attitude,—it rather bends forward to meet you. What a year this has been to us! ... It has proved the year of our nativity. Has not the old earth passed away from us?—are not all things new? YOUR SOPHIE.[39]

New Year's seemed a special time for Nathaniel as well. In his story "The Sister Years," he mused:

> Last night, between eleven and twelve o'clock, when the Old Year was leaving ... The New Year ... waiting for the signal to begin her rambles through the world. The two were own sisters, being both grand daughters of Time; and though one looked so much older than the other, it was rather owing to hardships and trouble than to age, since there was but a twelvemonth's difference between them.[40]

Nathaniel was lonely and missed the one person who gave him true happiness. He recorded in his journal in February of 1840 about his dreary days at the Boston Custom House:

> I have been measuring coal all day, aboard of a black little British schooner, in a dismal dock at the north end of the city ... Sometimes I

descended into the dirty little cabin of the schooner, and warmed myself by a red-hot stove ... But at last came the sunset, with delicate clouds, and a purple light upon the islands; and I blessed it, because it was the signal of my release.[41]

For Nathaniel, the work in Boston became a tedious burden. It was a dirty and uncomfortable job in a dirty and uncomfortable environment. A month later he wrote in his journal:

> I pray that in one year more I may find some way of escaping from this unblest Custom House; for it is a very grievous thraldom. I do detest all offices—all, at least, that are held on a political tenure.[42]

Nathaniel did escape the Boston Custom House a year later when he was forced out of his job. He found himself without a source of income, which put pressure on his and Sophia's plans to marry. Nathaniel had his savings that he was carefully setting aside for his marriage. Making a tenuous decision, he used the entirety of his savings to either invest or loan $1,000, a substantial sum, to George Ripley for a transcendental communal experiment in West Roxbury called Brook Farm.[43] Nathaniel had hoped that this investment would allow Sophia and he the resources to marry and offer a place to reside after their marriage. Nathaniel moved to Brook Farm in 1841 to live his dream. He spent his days performing strenuous work, tending to vegetables, milking cows, and chopping wood. There was no time to read the newspapers nor write stories.

A few months earlier in 1840, Sophia had moved with her family to Boston. As a result, there was a short time when Sophia and Nathaniel were both living there and could frequently share time together. It was a special time because Nathaniel and Sophia were removed from the stress of the Hawthorne relatives. However, after Nathaniel lost his job at the Custom House, he had little option to stay there and support himself. His investment in Brook Farm, according to his calculations, would be helpful. Therefore, Nathaniel, residing at Brook Farm, was removed from Sophia in Boston. He was also removed from his sisters in Salem.

Therefore, Sophia was not the only woman in Nathaniel's life who missed him while he lived at Brook Farm. Ebe, annoyed yet devoted to her brother, spent her time collecting copies of his stories. Writing to Lizzie Peabody, she mentioned, "… I had been cutting out his articles in order to make a volume. I regret as much as you do that he would not be prevailed upon to collect them himself."[44] Ebe did the collecting for her brother just as she often had involved herself in his work. She had no intention of letting go of any part of him. She hoped that the distance between her brother and Sophia would cool the romance and then Nathaniel would come running home to his family and to her.

Ebe and Lizzie Peabody, similar in education and intelligence, spent their lives in study. However, they spent them differently. Lizzie went out into the world to educate children. Ebe stayed home to educate herself. Regarding Nathaniel, both women held certain desires which may or may not have been compatible. Ebe wanted her brother to stay at home with her to accomplish boundless literary pursuits. Lizzie may have dreamed of marrying him. Ebe and Lizzie reacted with contrasting responses to Nathaniel's devotion to Sophia.

Louisa was almost inconsolable during her brother's tenure at Brook Farm and worried about his welfare. She wanted to see him, even if it meant on his own terms. Each day, she looked forward to receiving letters from him and endured utmost disappointment every day when a letter did not arrive for her. In May of 1841, Nathaniel did write to Louisa from Brook Farm a rather starry-eyed letter writing that:

> This is one of the most beautiful places I ever saw in my life ... Once in a while we have a transcendental visitor, such as Mr. Alcott; but generally we pass whole days without seeing a single face, save those of the brethren.[45]

Louisa, the sister interested in his everyday needs, took to sewing to occupy her thoughts. She fashioned a special work shirt for him. Nathaniel appreciated the gift that she had so carefully sewn and wrote to her, "The thin frock which you made for me is considered a most splendid article, and I should not wonder if it were to become the summer uniform of the community ..."[46] For Louisa, knowing that her brother liked the gift was all the affirmation she needed.

Nathaniel had described in his letters to Louisa the real work he was accomplishing. It was not the writing of whimsical tales with his pen but laborious farm chores. The letters he received from the family at home were a pleasant respite from the endless and tiring work. He missed receiving frequent letters from Louisa and instructed her, "When you write to me (which I beg you will do soon), direct your letter to West Roxbury ..."[47]

Reading letters from home satisfied Nathaniel, but Louisa wished to see her brother's *face*. Wishing him to come to Salem for a visit, she became quite agitated when he did not arrive. One small consolation was that she could gaze upon the new painting of her brother's likeness. She wrote to him:

> It is a comfort to look at the picture, to be sure; but I am tempted to speak to it sometimes, and it answers never a word; and when mother looks at it, she takes up a lamentation because you stay away so long and work so hard.[48]

His image in the painting was no substitute for the real living and breathing brother and son who was decidedly absent from Salem. Louisa commented in her letter to Nathaniel about the portrait, writing:

> The color is a little too high, to be sure; but perhaps it is a modest blush at the compliments which are paid you to your face. Mrs. Cleveland says it is bewitching, and Miss Carlton says it only wants to speak. Elizabeth says it is excellent.[49]

Louisa playfully continued in her letter that, "It has one advantage over the original,—I can make it go with me where

My Dear Sister

I choose!"[50] Playfulness aside Louisa reminded her brother how she missed him writing, "But good as it is, it does not by any means supply the place of the original, and you are not to think that you can stay away any longer than before we had it."[51]

The following month, Nathaniel received another letter from Louisa, addressed "Dear Natty." She had grown very weary of his absence and scolded him harshly:

> I had not written before, because we had been looking for you every day; and we do most seriously object to your staying away from home so long. Do you know that it was nine weeks last Tuesday since you left home?—a great deal too long.[52]

Louisa had been counting the weeks; her world revolved around her family and especially her dear brother. She softened her tone farther into her letter and expressed her concern for his well-being. She was very distressed that the farm work may be too demanding for him writing:

> I cannot bear to think that this hot sun is beating upon your head … What is the use of burning your brains out in the sun, when you can do anything better with them? Ebe says she thought you were only to work three hours a day for your board, and she cannot understand your keeping at it all day."[53]

CUPID'S ARROW (1837-1842)

If Nathaniel wasn't coming to visit her in Salem, then Louisa considered traveling to see him at Brook Farm. She became interested in taking a trip into the country to visit him and asserted, "I am bent upon coming up to see you this summer..."[54] Understanding the urgency in her words, Nathaniel followed with a visit to Herbert Street to appease his perturbed relatives and quiet Louisa's scolding words.

Weeks passed with another void of letters from Nathaniel. Louisa wrote again in August:

> Dear Natty, I have waited for a letter from you till I am tired and cannot wait any longer. And I have been to the post-office and received the same answer so often, that I am ashamed to go any more. What do you mean by such conduct,—neither coming, nor writing to us? It is six weeks to-day since you left us, and in all that time we have heard nothing from you...[55]

These may not have been Louisa's sentiments alone. Her words may also have reflected the thoughts of her mother and Ebe. Louisa admonished her brother, "We do not like it at all... Mother is very vehement about it."[56] Nathaniel was choosing to live his own life outside of Salem although his mother and sisters were tugging determinedly to draw him back to them.

Upon reading this letter, Nathaniel decided that it was time that he saw his family again if for no other reason but to calm them down. He wrote to Sophia telling her that he planned to spend a few days in Salem. Since Sophia was living in Boston, Nathaniel would travel there to see her:

My Dear Sister

> I do long to see our mother and sisters; and I should not wonder if they felt some slight desire to see me. I received a letter from Louisa a week or two since, scolding me most pathetically for my long absence. Indeed, I have been rather naughty in this respect ...[57]

Besides the demands of his relatives, Nathaniel also had other distressing worries on his mind. It became apparent to him that the investment in Brook Farm, one which took up his entire savings, was not the opportunity that he had hoped. Dashed were his plans to bring Sophia there after their marriage. He wrote in August 1841:

> It is extremely doubtful whether Mr. Ripley will succeed in locating his community on this farm ... We must form other plans for ourselves; for I can see few or no signs that Providence purposes to give us a home here. I am weary, weary, thrice weary of waiting so many ages.[58]

Defeated and disgusted with the Brook Farm endeavor, he wrote in his journal during September 1841, "One thing is certain. I cannot and will not spend the winter here. The time would be absolutely thrown away so far as regards any literary labor to be performed ..."[59] His mindset had changed as he decided to forsake Brook Farm and spend his time devotedly pursuing his writing once again. With some luck, he could write enough to support a wife because there was a good possibility he would never recoup his investment.

Another stumbling block had to do with Sophia. From the beginning of their romance, Sophia's fragile health had been a question in her mind. She was not entirely convinced that she was healthy enough to become a wife and did not want to burden her beloved with her chronic and uncontrolled health issues.

The suffocating situation with Nathaniel's mother and sisters looked to potentially make their marriage difficult. The possible demise of Brook Farm left Nathaniel without an occupation, money, or a place to live, jeopardizing his marriage plans. Although beset with these troubles, the two lovers persevered with their dreams. There were hurdles set before them, but they continued toward their future together.

First, they set a date for late June of 1842 for their marriage. Secondly, they looked with the assistance of friends to find a future residence in Concord. Then, perhaps the most difficult third hurdle, Nathaniel waited until a month before the planned wedding date to inform his relatives. After his visit to see his mother and sisters, Sophia followed with a genial letter to her future sisters-in-law. Nathaniel with much gratitude wrote to Sophia, "Dearest Heart, Your letter to my sisters was beautiful,—sweet, gentle, and magnanimous; ... If they do not love you, it must be because they have no hearts to love with, ..."[60] He added, "They will love you, all in good time, dearest; and we will be very happy."[61]

Nathaniel presented an optimistic tone to his Sophia, promising her that one day all would be well. This sentiment was not echoed by his sister Ebe who was fuming. She understood the obvious outcome of losing her brother to the artistically talented Sophia. Ebe did not want this marriage

My Dear Sister

to happen. The time had come for Ebe to let her thoughts be known. A month before the planned wedding, she penned an acerbic return letter to Sophia stating:

> Your approaching union with my brother makes it proper for me to offer you my assurances of a sincere desire for your mutual happiness. I hope nothing will ever occur to render our future intercourse other than agreeable, particularly as it need not be so frequent or so close as to require more than reciprocal good will, if we do not happen to suit each other in our new relationship.[62]

Blunt as it was, the letter unmistakably indicated Ebe was not planning any coziness between herself and her future sister-in-law. Poor Sophia! Not yet married to her beloved Nathaniel and there were already pressing in-law problems to overcome. Ebe continued her letter to Sophia in her characteristically straight forward manner:

> I speak thus plainly, because my brother has desired me to say only what was true: though I do not recognise [sic] his right to speak of truth, after concealing this affair from us so long. But I believe him when he says that this was not in accordance with your wishes, for such a concealment must naturally be unpleasant, and besides, from what I know of your amiable disposition, I am sure you would not give us unnecessary pain. It was especially due to my mother that

she should long ago have been made acquainted with the engagement of her only son: it is much more difficult to inform her of it at this late period, with only a few weeks to prepare her feelings for his marriage.[63]

However, three weeks later, Ebe had a change of heart, at least for the moment, that was documented in a letter. Possibly Sophia showed the first letter to Nathaniel after which he spoke to Ebe regarding its caustic and cruel content. Whatever the reason, Ebe wrote again to Sophia attempting to smooth things over by writing another letter. Not surprisingly, Ebe dragged Louisa into the situation as well:

> Neither are my sister and myself wanting in that sisterly affection to which you feel that you are entitled, and which it will be a source of great happiness to us to find returned. I deeply regret that I said any thing in my note to give you pain; if we can all forget the past, and look forward to the future it will be better. The future seems to promise much happiness to you, for certainly I think your disposition and my brother's well suited to each other ...[64]

Although Ebe's objection to her brother's prospective marriage was unsettling to him, Nathaniel had dreaded more his mother's reaction to the news. He did not want his impending marriage to be received with her disappointment, sadness, or pain. He already had enough tension dealing with Ebe's reactions. His mother had been familiar with the Peabody family since her children were young. Would this marriage really have been so dreadful for her? In the end, Nathaniel's visit with his mother went far better than he expected. He wrote from Salem to Sophia to tell her:

> Scarcely had I arrived here, when our mother came out of her chamber, looking better and more cheerful than I have seen her this some time … Foolish me, to doubt that my mother's love could be wise, like all other genuine love! And foolish again, to have doubted your instinct … It seems that our mother had seen how things were, a long time ago; … My sisters, too, begin to sympathize as they ought; and all is well.[65]

Nathaniel's mother appeared to be completely accepting of her son's marriage to Sophia. On the other hand, Mrs. Peabody, Sophia's mother, experienced her own personal trepidations about her daughter's wedding. She kept her feelings to herself. She liked Nathaniel well enough, but she feared that she was losing her daughter. After some thought and waiting until after her daughter's marriage, Mrs. Peabody eventually overcame her fears and wrote to Sophia confiding:

> I set myself aside and thought only of the repose, the fullness of bliss, that awaited you under the protection and in possession of the confiding love of so rare a being as Nathaniel Hawthorne … I have not lost her, but have gained a noble son.[66]

CUPID'S ARROW (1837-1842)

Apparently, all was reasonably ready for the wedding to take place in late June. A date had been set and relatives informed. Just prior to the wedding day, Sophia suffered another attack from her severe headaches. This forced a delay to the wedding to allow her time to recover. She also needed to believe that she was indeed well enough to become the wife of Nathaniel Hawthorne. Her groom took it in stride.

He wrote to her, "I will even be happy, if you will only keep your heart and mind at peace. I will go to Concord tomorrow or next day, and see about our affairs there."[67] It was a wise choice to plan to move away from Salem. Nathaniel and Sophia, as husband and wife, would have the opportunity to settle into their own marriage without interference. They could live their own life and decide when and where to visit the relatives. Nathaniel added to his letter a postscript:

P.S. I love you! I love you! I love you!
P.S. 2. Do you love me at all?[68]

The days passed, and once again, Sophia felt well. The new wedding date, July 9, 1842, had arrived for a quiet ceremony taking place at the current Peabody residence, 13 West Street in Boston, where Sophia's sister, Lizzie, had opened a bookshop. Sophia, dressed for her wedding on a warm New England day, proceeded to the Peabody parlor in a heavenly-like promenade to stand next to Nathaniel. The marriage ceremony was officiated by Reverend James Freeman Clarke, who pronounced the couple man and wife after the marriage vows were taken.

Sophia's family was present for the simple ceremony, including Lizzie who quietly kept her thoughts about Nathaniel to herself. Nathaniel's family was noticeably absent. Ebe frowned upon the marriage so that was an obvious explanation for her to avoid attending the wedding ceremony. She had lost in her aggressive pursuit to stop it. With that, she also lost her long-standing dream. Nathaniel's mother may not have been well enough to travel or in her state of seclusion unprepared to tolerate a trip to Boston, even for her son's wedding. But why would Louisa not attend? Had Louisa the same misgivings as Ebe, or was she merely standing aside while her headstrong sister was consumed with anger and frustration? If Louisa didn't share Ebe's disposition, being often ill, she may not have been well, prohibiting her from traveling to Boston. Perhaps she felt torn. For the bride, who already had a somewhat strained relationship with certain of her new in-laws, their obvious absence from the wedding ceremony may have been a welcome relief.

After the ceremony, the wedding guests bid farewell to the newlyweds and watched as the carriage slipped away, carrying the bride and groom from Boston toward their new residence in Concord twenty miles away. Sophia Hawthorne suddenly experienced neither fatigue nor headache from all the excitement of the wedding day and was overcome with a new sense of well-being.

Marriages.

At Boston, on Saturday morning last, by Rev. James Freeman Clarke, Nathaniel Hawthorne, Esq. to Miss Sophia Amelia Peabody, daughter of Dr. Nathaniel Peabody.

"Marriages," *Hill's New Hampshire Patriot*,
Concord, New Hampshire, July 14, 1842

CUPID'S ARROW (1837-1842)

The couple arrived at the Ripley house in Concord, built in 1770 by the grandfather of Ralph Waldo Emerson with a view overlooking the Concord River. They would make their stay in that house some of the happiest years of their lives. Nathaniel mentioned their arrival that day in his story, "The Old Manse." He wrote, "Nor, in truth, had the old Manse ever been profaned by a lay occupant until the memorable summer afternoon when it entered as my home."[69] It was a mention noting that the previous residents had often been religious ministers whose residence was referred to as a *manse*. This included the home's first resident, Reverend William Emerson, Sr.

The house had been prepared for their arrival with fresh flowers adorning the well-worn home and emitting pleasant summer floral fragrances into the air. Sophia was truly grateful to Elizabeth Hoar for her efforts pertaining to the move to Concord. She wrote in a letter to Mrs. Caleb Foote, a friend in Salem, "The agent of Heaven in this Concord plan was Elizabeth Hoar; a fit minister on such an errand, for minister means angel of God. Her interest has been very great in every detail."[70]

Although Louisa had not attended his wedding, Nathaniel did have her on his mind. As Sophia was busy unpacking wedding gifts and settling into the house, he wrote to Louisa the very next day following his marriage. He didn't express any hurt feelings or reproachful attitude for her absence from the wedding. However, he was careful in his letter to make sure that Louisa, his mother, and Ebe understood he and Sophia were extremely happy:

My Dear Sister

Dear Louisa

The execution took place yesterday. We made a Christian end and came straight to Paradise where we abide at this present writing. We are as happy as people can be, without making themselves ridiculous, and might be even happier, but as a matter of taste, we chose to stop that at this point.[71]

Chapter 8
Louisa Visits! (1842-1845)

"... the sunny days seemed brighter and the cloudy ones less gloomy ..."

—Nathaniel Hawthorne,
Fanshawe

Throughout his life Nathaniel always could share his thoughts in letters to Louisa. Writing a letter to her after his marriage may have been an easier one for him to compose. Louisa carefully opened the envelope, postmarked from Concord and focused on each of her brother's words, "Sophia is very well, and sends her love."[1] Then Louisa understood what appeared to be an invitation for her:

> We intend that you shall be our first guest (unless there should be a chance visitor) and thus beseech the honor and felicity of your presence, sometime in August. New married people, I

189

believe, are not considered fit to be seen, in less time than several weeks.²

Nathaniel was extremely content with the former parsonage that he had rented for his first marital home. He was equally happy about his marriage as he wrote to Louisa:

> I know you will be delighted with our home and the [ ] [ ] scenery; and I have a confident hope that you will be delighted with ourselves likewise. I intend to improve vastly by marriage—that is, if I can find any room for improvement …³

Either due to his extreme happiness at his marriage or his success at publication, Nathaniel seems to have developed a

The Old Manse in Concord, Massachusetts

degree of self-confidence which bordered on the fringes of arrogance. It was a contrast to his depressed disposition while living in the dark and dreary Manning house, where he believed he held no appreciable talents or future. Nathaniel then added in his letter to Louisa an assurance that his marriage will not lessen his love for his own family:

> I promise myself few greater pleasures than that of receiving you here; for in taking to myself a wife, I have neither given up my own relatives, nor adopted others. Give my love to mother and Ebe.[4]

Such assurances from her brother may have been comforting to Louisa. However, on the other hand, Sophia had her own thoughts regarding a visit from Louisa. Sophia was aware of the uphill struggle she might face to win the hearts of her reluctant in-laws. Was congeniality at all possible? The new bride hoped their knowledge that Nathaniel was happily married may in some way ease the strain and sway the forlorn Hawthorne women to accept her.

Setting in-law problems aside, for the present, Nathaniel and Sophia enjoyed their life together. Money, however, was extremely scarce with little to be had for taking care of necessities. The newlyweds made do with what was available to them. They enjoyed the summer months which offered beautiful pastoral surroundings about their home. The boughs of the willow trees whisked with a summer breeze while elms and maple trees offered cool shade. The orchards in seasonal turns supplied ample amounts of apples, peaches, cherries, and pears. Wild grape vines climbed about the property, zig-zagging their way around rock or a fallen branch. Nathaniel delighted in his garden while watching his green peas and summer squash mature. The river behind the house supported beautiful pond lilies and water lilies, keeping company with an adequate stock of fresh-water fish.[5] Nathaniel rejoiced in the bounties of the property he referred to as the Old Manse, "I relish best the free gifts of Providence."[6]

The newlyweds had meals prepared from whatever foods the property offered them with occasional meat from the butcher.[7] A fresh fish from the river was served with the luscious bounties of summer fruits and vegetables. Their earthly needs were simply met provided by their natural surroundings. Nathaniel, middle aged at his marriage, made an entry into his journal dated August 5th, where he pondered the joys in his life:

> Happiness has no succession of events, because it is a part of eternity; and we have been living in eternity ever since we came to this old manse.[8]

Ralph Waldo Emerson, George Prescott, Henry David Thoreau, and Ellery Channing[9] had come and gone as the weeks of summer passed in Concord. Missing was a visit from Louisa who was supposed to have been the newlywed's first guest. Mr. & Mrs. Hillard had also visited and wished for Louisa to visit them as well. Nathaniel sent a message to Louisa suggesting she visit with the Hillards prior to boarding the stage at Earle's Coffee House:

LOUISA VISITS! (1842-1845)

> Mrs. Hillard has requested me to beg of you to come to their house, on your way to Concord; and I think it an excellent arrangement ... Do not, on any account, fail to take advantage of her invitation; ... She wished me to ask you to stay all night; and you can if you choose.[10]

Louisa did visit her brother in Concord at least three times while he was living at the old manse but there is not much known about most of her visitations. Ebe made very infrequent visits to see her brother during their lifetimes, and little is known of those visits as well. After some nudging from her brother, with his letters of instructions for her,[11] Louisa packed her luggage taking a train and stagecoach to Concord during the early autumn for her first visit. It was a pleasant time of year to travel when summer nights began to cool sooner, the moon rose a bit earlier in the sky, and on certain days, there was a hint of crisp Autumn air. The early turning of a leaf to a bright yellow or gold signaled the time for a welcome change of season.

Louisa enjoyed seeing her brother spending her days picking berries or cutting flower arrangements with Sophia. There were walks through the orchards and into the woods to hear the summer songbirds and the waters flowing and gurgling in the nearby river. It was all reminiscent of Louisa's days living in Maine with her brother more than twenty years earlier. They were children then, but the fondness between them had been sustained in the intervening years. Now in adulthood, there was not only her beloved brother but the addition of a sister-in-law. Louisa and Sophia quickly cultivated a closer

193

relationship, which became more than that of sisters-in-law. They developed a sisterhood, perhaps with Sophia's guidance, a kinship, like what Sophia enjoyed with her own Peabody sisters. The common focus of their affections, however, was their mutual love for Nathaniel.

During the first summer, Henry David Thoreau who owned a boat "built by his own hands" and named "Musketaquid" sold it to Nathaniel who renamed it "Pond-Lily."[12] Nathaniel found great enjoyment with his boat and "made a voyage in the Pond-Lily all by myself yesterday morning and was much encouraged by my success in causing the boat to go whither I would."[13] He was following in his father's and grandfather's path. Not captaining large ships on the ocean as they had done but successfully commanding his own small rowboat on the nearby river. It became a favorite pastime for him to idle away summer hours. A month later he noted, "My chief amusement has been boating up and down the river."[14]

A coolness filled the air with the first hints of the coming change in season. Orchards laden heavy with fruits and gardens once full of vegetables showed signs that their bounty was being used up or stored for future consumption. The green leaves on the trees turned to the golden, red, and orange colors of autumn. They floated to the ground to dry up, turn brown, and crunch under someone's footsteps to be mashed into nothingness. The warmth of summer disappeared with days growing shorter as each twilight passed. Enter the cold and crispness of a season that would signal at its end the coming of winter.

To some the season may have been one for reflection yet sometimes remorse. It was the reminder that life's cycle eventually turns and may come to an end. The flowers disappeared as annuals faded to nothingness and perennials became buried deep underground, settled for a long winter's sleep. The trees became unclad skeletons to remain such until clothed with new leaves during the next spring. For some, it could be a dreary time with days of diminished sunshine followed by long, dark and frosty evenings, a time of coldness and gloom.

There was a death; its announcement arrived for Nathaniel in the form of a letter from Louisa in October 1842. Nathaniel immediately responded in a return letter to her, "My dear Sister, I have just received your letter,"[15] referencing, " the sad intelligence of Uncle Robert's death."[16] Nathaniel did not plan to attend the funeral excusing himself with, "if there were a little more time, I would certainly be present at the funeral ..."[17] Perhaps there was too short notice for Nathaniel to travel to Salem. The letter was a day or two in transit. It would be a few more years before the telegraph became viable for quicker communication. Uncle Robert's funeral may have been imminent enough to make it impossible for Nathaniel to arrive in time. Then too, Nathaniel, in his younger days, loathed Uncle Robert's persistent efforts for his education. Although now happily married, there could be a lingering resentment from his childhood, harboring a little of that young selfishness and ungratefulness he had exhibited in his younger years toward his devoted uncle.

As he had not attended his Uncle Robert's wedding, Nathaniel also chose not to attend his uncle's funeral. He easily excused himself in his letter to Louisa saying that he "cannot, at present, leave Concord. ..."[18] It was a hollow excuse to be absent for the funeral of the man who had sacrificed his own youth to care for his sister and her three fatherless children. Uncle Robert had made the dedicated effort to educate Nathaniel and ensure his nephew's success in the future. Nathaniel apparently was blinded to understand those efforts and kindnesses even as a grown man.

As Nathaniel's mother, sisters, and the many Mannings in Salem mourned Uncle Robert, winter's harsh coldness blanketed New England. Louisa, Ebe, and their mother shared a solemn Thanksgiving dinner in Salem while the Hawthorne newlyweds remained in Concord, dining alone for their first holiday dinner together. Regardless of the weather, for them everything was a special event including their first Thanksgiving dinner. It was simple fare but a joyful occasion for Nathaniel and his wife. Nathaniel wrote to Louisa the next day in a lengthy letter, clearly missing her presence, "We wished for you at dinner yesterday-there being nobody but our two selves ..."[19] He teased Louisa in the letter mentioning her lack of writing to them, asking her, "Why should we write, more than you?"[20] And asking her, "Why don't you write, at least once in seven centuries, and tell us how you are and what is going on?"[21]

Nathaniel hadn't outgrown his need for news from the family although he was similarly negligent in his letter writing to Louisa. He made his own excuses for their lack of correspondence, "Sophia would have written before now; but her household duties keep her busy ..."[22] Of course, there were the preparations to be made for their Thanksgiving dinner cooked on their newly acquired stove, "She made a pumpkin pudding and some pumpkin pies by the mere force of instinct—having never been taught; and they would have done credit to an old pastry-cook …"²³ The centerpiece of their humble feast was a turkey that "weighed but five pounds, but was very good, and I carved it in first rate style. Sophia read the directions from Miss Leslie's house book."²⁴

Nathaniel completed his lengthy letter to Louisa and then prepared to go out that day with Sophia to, "dine with Mr. Emerson."²⁵ He told Louisa that "Sophia intended to have written half of this letter … but she has had no time to write a line."²⁶ Nathaniel signed the letter cordially, "Your affectionate brother, N.H."²⁷ He, however, before he signed his name, revealed to her his true feelings regarding personal letters saying, "I do abominate letter-writing."²⁸

The winter months of frigid temperatures and ever deepening snow settled upon the two lovebirds. Winter is usually harsh in New England, and this first winter of their marriage proved the same. Nathaniel spent the season writing in his upstairs study, which was decorated with:

> The sweet and lovely head of one of Raphael's Madonna's and two pleasant little pictures of the Lake of Como … a purple vase of flowers, … My books (few, and by no means choice; for they were chiefly such waifs as chance had thrown in my way) stood in order about the room, seldom to be disturbed.²⁹

A small desktop adjacent to the fireplace served to rest Nathaniel's pen when his writing ceased for the day. That desk bore the impression of each stroke of Nathaniel's pen during his residence in the "Old Manse." The face of his desk holds the memories of his many sketches, some never to be completed or read by any other human eyes. Yet, it was also witness to the many tales that would one day make Hawthorne a household name. As the sunshine streamed in to brighten the old worn desk, the author found his words. The study window overlooked a Revolutionary War battlefield while the Concord River flowed past in silence. The ever-prevailing pastoral scene outside caused the author to occasionally break his intense thought to momentarily enjoy the historic yet bucolic view before he sat to write down his next thoughts.

The Old North Bridge (restored) over the Concord River, Concord, Massachusetts

The economic environment had been poor for several years, and Nathaniel was not optimistic about obtaining gainful employment. However, he was happy with his present situation writing to Louisa, "I am very well contented to remain here."[30] This was his paradise although he was continually short of money. He had his loving new wife, his rented abode in which to live with her, and an abundance of time to write in his study. As he had done in Salem after his college graduation, Nathaniel settled in, this time with Sophia to create a daily routine. There is something comforting about a daily routine, and Nathaniel wrote each morning uninterrupted.

Afternoons included a dinner meal with Sophia after which Nathaniel, also, "Every day I trudge through snow and slosh to the village, long into the post-office, and spend an hour at the reading room ..."[31] He returned home as the winter's afternoon sun bid farewell to the sky. Then closed the day with "our beautiful long evenings from four o'clock to ten ..."[32]

The first winter following their marriage was coming to an end, when in March, Nathaniel travelled to Salem to see his relatives. He shared some positive news with Sophia that "I found our mother tolerably well; and Louisa, I think, in especial good condition for her ..."[33] However, regarding his sister Ebe, little had changed in her attitude, and Nathaniel wrote to Sophia that Ebe had "not quite thawed."[34]

It was not the lingering winter chill that Nathaniel had indicated about Ebe but instead her continued defiance regarding his marriage to Sophia. Ebe had neither reconciled herself to her brother's taking a wife nor to the reality that her brother suddenly had his own life. He softened the situation to Sophia by adding in his letter to her:

My Dear Sister

> They speak of you and us with an evident sense that we are very happy indeed: and I can see that they are convinced of my having found the very little wife that God meant for me ... In short, they seem content with your husband, and I am very certain of their respect and affection for his wife.[35]

Nathaniel's marriage and departure from Salem may have been a turning point which accelerated Ebe's journey into further isolation. She didn't get to keep her brother to herself, and she withdrew further into her reading and her studies. Although she still walked often about town, made short visits elsewhere or to her brother, such activities were less frequent. In another few short years, Ebe's isolation and solitude would become increasingly pronounced and ultimately permanent.

Spring had arrived as the fruit trees flowered in light pinks and white. Light sweet scents of blossoms filled the air. A welcome break in Nathaniel's writing offered a slight variation to temporarily alter his set routine, as Sophia wrote to her mother:

> I went into the orchard, and found my dear husband's window open; so I called to him, on the strength of the loveliness, though against the rules. His noble head appeared at once; and a new sun, and dearer, shone out of his eyes on me.[36]

One late afternoon, Sophia entered her husband's upstairs study, looking out one of the windows facing the Concord

River. She removed her wedding ring as daylight turned to dusk and walked over to where "The study had three windows, set with little, old-fashioned panes of glass, each with a crack across it."[37] She began to etch into the thick glass with the diamond of her ring inscribing her thoughts on the windowpane. The words read, "Man's accidents are God's purposes. Sophia A. Hawthorne, 1843."[38]

Nathaniel approached her lovingly, took the ring, and added his own words to the window, "Nath. Hawthorne, This is his study, 1843."[39] It was a dialogue, a dance, of sweet, unsaid words between husband and wife. Sophia closed the conversation as she etched in the glass, "Inscribed by my husband at Sunset April 3, 1843, In the Gold Light d S.A.H."[40] The inscriptions that Sophia and Nathaniel etched into the glass of the study window transcend time and silently remain today as a remembrance of the love and adoration they held for each other.

Nathaniel continued with his daily routine, spending a part of each day upstairs alone in his study. The habits of his youth had continued into adulthood as he ventured to write. However, writing for the sake of writing could not be his only pursuit. Searching for a means to support his family required that he send out inquiries for writing assignments for which he would be paid. Eventually some solicitations and responses were received in return. Sophia wrote to her mother that:

> Mr. Hawthorne received a letter from James Lowell this week, in which was a proposal from Mr. Poe that he should write for his new magazine, and also be engraved to adorn the first number![41]

My Dear Sister

There was hope of writing assignments with the prospect of receiving a future payment of much needed income.

As the season quickly turned into summer, Sophia and Nathaniel renewed their wish for Louisa to visit them again. Traveling was easier in the warmer months with longer days providing more light and improved weather. They, therefore, had only a short time to convince Louisa to come during the brief yet pleasant New England summer. In early September, Nathaniel wrote to her with instructions and a revelation that the Hillards would not be available for her to stop there as she had done the prior year.[42] Within the next weeks, Louisa had arrived for a visit.

The pleasant autumn soon turned to a typically harsh and cold winter. December provided its requisite amount of New England snowfall. This season also brought anticipation as the Hawthorne's awaited the birth of their first child. The couple lived a life of frugal solitude, yet at the same time, they appeared to thrive. When their cook, Mary, had gone away to Boston, Nathaniel took over some of the household responsibilities. Being the first to arise in the morning, he "kindled fires in the kitchen and breakfast-room … the tea-kettle boiled, and potatoes were baked and rice cooked …"[43] The two ate their modest breakfast before Nathaniel removed to his study to write. Often, he insisted that Sophia sit with him to assure she received some needed rest although she sometimes ventured to walk with him to town.

Their poor financial situation did not minimize their joy in the celebration of their second Christmas together as a married couple in 1843. Their dinner was rather sparse fare by today's standards but, "On Christmas day we had a truly Paradisiacal dinner of preserved quince and apple, dates, and bread and cheese, and milk."[44] After which, the New Year brought the expectation of a blessed addition to their family. During the evenings, warmed by their two stoves, the expectant parents occupied themselves by reading literature. Sophia wrote:

> My husband has been reading aloud to me, afternoons, and evenings, Macaulay's Miscellanies, since he finished Shakespeare.[45]

Nathaniel had read aloud since his childhood, often to his mother and Louisa. During the years that followed those youthful endeavors, he developed a tone, an intonation, an expression that was magical to Sophia's ears and heart. She wrote, "His style is perfectly clear."[46]

It was to Louisa that Nathaniel wrote announcing the birth of his first child on March, 3, 1844:

> Dear Louisa, You and Elizabeth are aunts, and our mother is a grandmother to a little girl, who came head first into the world at ½ past 9 o'clock this morning, after being ten awful hours in getting across the threshold.[47]

He added that "Sophia had a terrible time, but is now quite comfortable and perfectly happy."[48] Such was the joyful news that should have been well accepted by all who knew them. Then came the pronouncement that was cause for alarm in the precincts of Salem. In the postscript to his letter, Nathaniel informed his family of the name for his newly-born red-headed baby girl, writing, "We had a name already—Una! Is not it pretty? Una Hawthorne. Una Hawthorne!! It is very pretty."[49]

Nathaniel loved the name Una possibly for the reference to the heroic Una in the epic poem *Fairie Queene* by Edmund Spenser.[50] The story was a favorite of his since childhood. Some in their circle of family and friends did not share in enthusiasm for the name. Nonetheless, Nathaniel and Sophia named their daughter Una, choosing John L. O'Sullivan, to be her godfather.[51] The hours in Nathaniel and Sophia's days were filled with caring for their newborn daughter and adoring their firstborn child. Sophia wrote to her mother: "I have no time-as you may imagine ... My husband relieves me with her constantly, and gets her to sleep beautifully. I look upon him with wonder and admiration."[52] Nathaniel was thrilled to have a daughter and his pride in her clearly glowed from the words he wrote to his friend Horatio Bridge:

> I am happy to tell you that our little girl is remarkably healthy and vigorous, and promises, in the opinion of those better experienced in babies than myself, to be very pretty ... I flatter myself she will be the prettiest young lady in the world. I think I prefer a daughter to a son.[53]

Nathaniel was entranced by his daughter. He visited his mother and sisters in April and wrote:

> When I got to Salem, there was great joy, as you may suppose ... Mother hinted an apprehension that poor baby would be spoilt, whereupon

I irreverently observed that, having spoiled her own three children ... she averred that it was impossible to spoil such children as E—and I because she had never been able to do anything with us ... I do not understand that I was quite such a miracle of precocity, but should think it not impossible, inasmuch as precocious boys are said to make stupid men.[54]

Louisa, thirty-six years old by this time, visited her brother in August of 1844. She, of course, was ready to meet little Una. After her arrival at Nathaniel's home, Louisa sent a letter to her mother describing her trip which was filled with "my adventures."[55] Louisa had first traveled to Lynn with every seat taken when a kind gentlemen offered her his place as he nobly stood "all the way to Lynn."[56] Traveling from Lynn to Boston, she then boarded the train for the rail depot at Concord. From there travelling by stagecoach, she arrived at Nathaniel's house where, "he came to the door to receive me, glad enough to see me."[57] The brother and sister looked forward to a fine visit together.

However, Louisa had not been introduced to her little niece. Sophia had gone to Boston, "taking Una of course, so that I have not seen the wonderful baby yet."[58] Sophia planned to return home in a few days. Thus, a rare opportunity was offered to Louisa to have her brother all to herself for several days. She was free to spend her time as decades earlier when Nathaniel recovered from his injured foot and similarly as the year they spent together in Salem for their schooling. The pair easily fell into a comfortable routine, enjoying each other's companionship. During these delightful days with her brother, Louisa wrote to her mother "in the mean time we are making out grandly."[59]

Nathaniel proved his abilities in the kitchen. Louisa described that, "he is very handy, makes the fire and sets the table."[60] She had an inclination that "Nathaniel cooked all day yesterday, when I got here he had just done his dinner and washed up the dishes."[61] Her brother also seemed to have developed some creativity in his meal preparing, inventing a special concoction he called his "hotch potch."[62] Louisa explained that it was "a collection of all the fruits he could get stewed, sweetened and spiced with great genius.[63]

Much, if not all the edible fare, the delicious fruits and vegetables, were harvested from the grounds of the "Old Manse" or sources nearby. The river offered a good supply of fish for Nathaniel to catch and cook. Louisa mentioned that Nathaniel, "prides himself greatly upon his cooking and talents for housekeeping."[64] However, Louisa too was adept at kitchen duties and planned to "make a pumpkin pie or some apple dumplings, or something of that kind."[65] When her brother, "proposed to wash the dishes," she offered to complete that task herself.[66]

They lived in harmony, yet with Louisa's presence or not, Nathaniel kept to his writing routine. Louisa occupied herself by tidying up the house and mending her brother's clothes. It was a tranquil domestic scene for the author but one whose wife was out of town. What kind of impression was this? Louisa teased, "Nathaniel wonders what the neighbors will think to see him send his wife away in the morning, and receive another lady in the afternoon, ..."[67] Any eyebrows raised from the local townspeople would return to normal once Sophia arrived home with the baby in her arms. Louisa wasn't thinking about hiding indoors until Sophia arrived home either. True to form, she planned to "go about while I am here."[68]

Nathaniel, one possessed with thoughts of curses and ghosts of the Hathorne past, had mentioned to Louisa that the "Old Manse" may be haunted with ghosts. There had been several previous residents living in the house, some already long dead, but Louisa saw enough to decide for herself on this ghostly matter. She reported to her mother, "I have seen no ghosts."[69] There were, however, very real uninvited residents in this well-worn house. These were the kind that run wild in the night making pitter patter noises from one end of the house to the other as they scurry to find morsels of food carelessly dropped to the floor. "We are overrun with mice which are not so bad,"[70] Louisa wrote. The mice were not something that caused her any concern, and she was "glad that I came now, for it seems to be the best time."[71] For Louisa, it was one of few opportunities that she took advantage to visit with her brother when he lived outside of Salem after his marriage. And by coincidence, for a few days, she had her brother entirely to herself, except for the mice …

Following Louisa's visit, summer colors transformed to paint a vibrant New England autumn. Too quickly, it had faded into a cold and gray December when Nathaniel saw Louisa during his visit to Salem. Unsurprisingly, the Christmas season at the Manning house was as bleak as ever. The anticipation of entering his former home may have brought foreboding thoughts and memories of unhappy years to Nathaniel's mind. It was not only he who experienced the home's perpetual air of

207

darkness and doom. Louisa also found the place overly vacant, as Nathaniel wrote to Sophia, "Louisa complains of the silence of the house; and not all their innumerable cats avail to comfort them in the least."[72] The Manning home had remained as dreary a place as Nathaniel remembered, and with the scarcity of residents, it seemed all the worse.

His mother and sisters pressured Nathaniel to stay in Salem at least through Christmas day, but Nathaniel refused them their wish because he missed Sophia and Una. Writing to his wife, addressing the letter, "Sweetest Phoebe," he explained:

> My only festival is when I have you ... The time spent away from you is unsubstantial,—there is nothing in it; and yet it has done me good, in making me more conscious of this truth. Give Una a kiss, and her father's blessing. She is very famous in Salem. We miss you and her greatly here in Castle Dismal.[73]

Winter eventually surrendered its bitter coldness to a sunny, warm spring when college friends Horatio Bridge and Franklin Pierce came for a visit to Concord in May of 1845. Sophia noted that while her husband was cutting wood:

> Mr. Bridge caught a glimpse of him, and began a sort of waltz towards him. Mr. Pierce followed; and when they reappeared, Mr. Pierce's arm was encircling my husband's old blue frock. How his friends do love him![74]

LOUISA VISITS! (1842-1845)

Aside from the pleasant visits, Nathaniel was in dire need of some occupation that paid better than writing so that he could adequately support his new family. His friends with political connections, namely Bridge and Pierce, maneuvered to find Nathaniel an appointment in a political position that would pay him a salary. Those politics often provided hurdles that needed to be negotiated and took time.

Unfortunately, too, Nathaniel was owed money for his written work, and in turn, he was unable to satisfy his own debts. Two years earlier, he had written in his journal on March 31, 1843, "... the magazine people do not pay their debts; so that we taste some of the inconveniences of poverty. It is an annoyance, not a trouble ..."[75] However, Nathaniel now had a small child to support. Suddenly, the annoyance he previously wrote about of not being regularly paid had become a real trouble for him. Although he could provide food on the table and shelter, Nathaniel Hawthorne admitted that his family was living an impoverished existence.

Also, "There is owing to him from Mr. Ripley and others, more than thrice money to pay all his debts ..."[76] The financial situation was further complicated by the manse's owner, "Mr. Ripley, resuming possession of the former abode."[77] Nathaniel and his family, were obligated to quickly vacate the "Old Manse" and obtain alternate housing on short notice so that Ripley could move back. Where could the Hawthornes go, and how would Nathaniel pay the rent? Sophia would live anywhere to be with her husband and child. She wrote to her mother:

209

Unceiled rafters and walls, and a pine table, chair, and bed would be far preferable with him, to an Alhambra without him even for a few months. He and Una are my perpetual Paradise; and I besieged Heaven with prayers that we might not find it our duty to separate, whatever privations we must outwardly suffer in consequence of remaining together ...[78]

Sophia knew that she must find a new residence for her family as quickly as possible. She solicited the assistance of her sister-in-law, Louisa, for temporarily moving into the Manning house. Sophia had thought that her small family could move into the old kitchen for the time being, where the rent may be less than if they lived in the Manning parlor. However, Louisa, acting in the best interest of her brother and his family, informed Sophia that Mr. Manning, being unhelpful, "would ask as much for the kitchen as for the parlor; so we will have the parlor. So now I shall have a very nice chamber, upon whose walls I can hang Holy Families, and upon the floor can put a pretty carpet."[79]

Sophia was thankful and optimistic for the potential roof over her family's head. She was also happy that her family would remain together and not be forced to live in separate dwellings. However, she also knew with whom she would be living—her reclusive mother-in-law and her icy, cold sister-in-law, Ebe. Sophia was secure in her love for her husband, and she had a fond relationship with Louisa. She optimistically hoped for the best, although, she hardly had any choice.

Thus, as in previous difficult times in his life, Nathaniel

LOUISA VISITS! (1842-1845)

once again crossed the threshold of the Manning house during the autumn of 1845; once again in poverty. There Nathaniel attempted to continue with his writing. He wrote to Bridge after his return to Salem:

> Here I am, again established in the old chambers where I wasted so many years of my life. I find it rather favorable to my literary duties, for I have already begun to sketch out the story for Wiley & Putnam ...[80]

Salem Custom House, Salem, Massachusetts

Chapter 9
Transition (1845-1852)

> "...for me to be beyond measure thankful and blest to find shelter anywhere with my husband."
>
> —Sophia Hawthorne

Like a repetitive nightmare that invades one's slumber, Nathaniel was once again writing in the familiar dim upstairs room. The adjustment was easier for him as he simply fell back into the former habits of his youth. There was a familiarity to him, which he accepted, and settled into the "haunted chamber, for thousands upon thousands of visions have appeared to me in it; and some few of them have become visible to the world."[1] Thus, occupying himself, he diligently worked on his collection of stories to be titled *Mosses from an Old Manse*.

Sophia had a more difficult time. She was obliged to adjust to living in one room, a contrast to the large colonial style house in Concord where she enjoyed the run of the property with her husband. As Sophia tried to cope with this situation,

Louisa and Ebe remained somewhere else in the house with their mother and the pet cats. It was a quiet scene offering little serenity for Sophia while tempered with an intense undertone of stress.

With her husband absorbed in writing, Sophia passed her time caring for their daughter Una and other domestic duties as well as arranging Nathaniel's wardrobe:

> I have almost arranged his wardrobe for a year to come, so that he can begin all over new again. He never lets me get tired. He arrests me the moment before I do too much, and he is then immitable; and I cannot obtain grace to sew even an inch more, even if an inch more would finish my work.[2]

There was good reason for Nathaniel's attentiveness to Sophia. During a time when their life was totally in flux, living in meager rented rooms with no real promise of steady income, Sophia and her husband joyfully expected their second child.

It was no surprise that the living arrangements at Herbert Street quickly became unaccommodating and stifling for Sophia. She also worried about the health of their very young daughter, Una. Since they were living in such close quarters with the oft-ill Hawthorne women, Sophia feared, "Madame Hawthorne and Louisa are too much out of health … I do not like to have Una in the constant presence of unhealthy persons."[3]

The situation became intolerable for Sophia. She was

lodging in a gloomy house with her in-laws and enduring an environment where the kitchen was not a place that she could call her own. There was plenty for her to miss from her life in Concord such as cooking in her own kitchen, walking with her husband along a country road, or wandering outside among the orchards and gardens of the Old Manse. Sophia needed to relieve the unbearable strain, and her only escape was to flee with Una to visit the Peabodys in Boston. This brought "only one solitary drawback, and this is the occasional absence of my husband, should he enter his official station before we return to Salem."[4]

Nathaniel had been awarded a political appointment as Surveyor of the Custom House in Salem. Therefore, stocked with a new black broadcloth suit with satin vest, he was ready to enter new employment which paid a handsome twelve hundred dollars a year.[5] With this employment, Hawthorne suddenly had the means to adequately support his growing family. Uncle Robert would have been extremely pleased if he had lived to enjoy the personal satisfaction of his hard-fought endeavors.

Nathaniel left the Manning house following his wife to Boston by May of 1846. Springtime was busy for him and his family. He had temporarily moved to Boston, had a new well-paying job in Salem, and his collection of stories, *Mosses from an Old Manse*, was published and released. These events were followed by a blessed one on June 22, 1846, when Nathaniel and Sophia welcomed their second child, a son, to their family. Announcements were made, but unlike the response regarding Una's name, there was no discussion about the new baby's.

My Dear Sister

Possibly to avoid any unwelcome remarks or because the parents simply had been unable to decide, several months passed before the new Hawthorne baby was given an official name. Sophia wrote of her little boy, "As to Baby, his cheeks, eyes, and limbs affirm enormous well-being ... he is modelled on a great plan in respect to his frame."[6] Over the years, there would be many pet names that Nathaniel used for his little offspring including "old boy," "the little man," the Black Prince" and "old gentleman."[7] However, at present, after much delay and discussion the baby was finally named Julian.

Moving back to Salem for his job at the Custom House required new housing. Neither Nathaniel nor Sophia would consider returning to the Manning House. They resolutely would not live there. From the brief experience Sophia had with the place, she shared her husband's feelings entirely. Therefore, the Hawthornes moved to temporary quarters on Chestnut Street in Salem. Living there, Nathaniel focused on his family and his new job. He may have implied about his position in his story "The Intelligence Officer," describing the character as "A grave figure, with a pair of mysterious spectacles on his nose and a pen behind his ear, was seated at a desk, in the corner of a metropolitan office."[8] Nathaniel could have been that grave figure seated at a desk in the Salem Custom House.

Louisa was delighted her brother had returned because they once again resided in the same town. This offered the opportunity for her to conveniently visit with her young niece and nephew at the Chestnut Street house and sometimes to care for them as well. One cool November evening, Louisa and the housemaid Dora arrived to babysit the infant Julian and the toddler Una.[9] The parents had gone to visit with Ralph Waldo Emerson at Mr. Howe's home that evening. For Sophia and Nathaniel, it was, "the first time we have spent the evening out since Una was born."[10] The outing offered a pleasant reprieve from the attentive parents' duties at home. There was no worry as the children's loving Aunt Louisa was in charge for their every need.

By September of the next year in 1847, Nathaniel and Sophia found another more suitable home in Salem. They excitedly moved into a large house, rented for $200, at 14 Mall Street.[11] Nathaniel had written to Sophia before their marriage concerning his own relatives, optimistically stating that they will all be happy together after their marriage. The conclusive test for this was about to commence. With this move to Mall Street, it was planned that Nathaniel's mother, Louisa, and Ebe would be moving in with them!

Although Nathaniel was taking care of his entire family, the situation could possibly result in disaster. Louisa might not have presented any problem to Sophia; they seemed to enjoy each other's company. What about her mother-in-law and Ebe? Nonetheless, Sophia was seemingly as optimistic as her husband regarding the new residents. She wrote to her own mother about the arrangements for Mrs. Hawthorne living with them:

> It will be very pleasant to have Madame Hawthorne in the house. Her suite of rooms is wholly distant from ours, so that we shall only meet when we choose to do so. There are few people

> in the world whom I should like or would consent to have in the house even in this way; but Madame Hawthorne is so uninterfering, of so much delicacy, that I shall never know she is near excepting when I wish it; and she has so much kindness and sense and spirit that she will be a great resource in emergencies.[12]

Surprisingly, considering the often-tense history with her in-laws, the time spent living on Mall Street worked out rather well. Regarding her sisters-in-law, Sophia wrote, "Elizabeth is an invisible entity. I have seen her but once in two years; and Louisa never intrudes."[13]

Nathaniel, not Manning money, had become the true provider for the Hawthorne family. The situation was also improved for Sophia with her position as the mistress of the house. She was not a guest nor boarder in the Manning home, living at their mercy and under their house rules. She had authority in the Mall Street house and had given careful thought to the living arrangements. She planned to keep her own family on one floor and selected the rooms for the parlor and sleeping quarters. She particularly liked that, "The house is single in depth, and so we shall bask in sunshine all the winter."[14] The devoted wife rejoiced too that her husband had his own study for writing on an upper-level floor. Most of his previous studies were located upstairs, and he seemed to prefer that location. She mused, "it will be to me a Paradise of Peace to think of him alone and still, yet within my reach."[15]

Sophia extolled positive thoughts toward her mother-in-law and rejoiced that:

It is no small satisfaction to know that Mrs. Hawthorne's remainder of life will be glorified by the presence of these children and of her own son. I am so glad to win her out of that Castle Dismal, and from the mysterious chamber into which no mortal ever peeped ...[16]

Sophia contrasted her mother-in-law's bedroom in the old Manning house as one where, "the sun never shines," to her chamber at Mall Street, "Into these rooms in Mall Street it blazes without stint ..."[17]

The Mall Street house, Salem, Massachusetts

My Dear Sister

Regardless of the sunshine teeming through the windows of the Mall Street house, the disposition of one member of the household hadn't changed. Ebe may have been contented to live in the same house as her brother once again. This time, however, Nathaniel's wife was included in the package. Ebe, although very pleasant to the children, underhandedly worked to challenge Sophia's authority. If there was an opportunity to afflict Sophia, Ebe took advantage of the situation.

In one telling incident, Sophia was firm that her children were not to be given candy indiscriminately. In defiance, Ebe offered some candy to her niece Una with total disregard of Sophia's directive, remarking, "Oh never mind; your mother will never know!"[18] However, Sophia did learn of the incident and quickly addressed the situation to deny Ebe from getting away with such tactics. Sophia banned Una from visiting her Aunt Ebe's chamber.[19] More than five years had passed since Nathaniel happily married Sophia, yet Ebe never reconciled herself to the union. She relentlessly continued to fight a particularly individual and subversive battle against her sister-in-law Sophia. All the while, Ebe was being housed and fed by her dutiful brother, Nathaniel, who happened to be Sophia's husband.

Ebe characteristically stayed to herself in her room, avoiding most contact with her sister-in-law. However, when Sophia left with the children for a summertime visit to her family in Boston, Ebe took the opportunity to come out of hiding while no one else was around. She had retained her old owl habits shuffling through the lonely corridors of the Mall Street house or strolling outdoors in the evening as she had done at the Manning homestead. She appeared within eyesight of her brother at a very late hour and startled him. Nathaniel wrote to Sophia:

> I went into the little room to put on my linen coat, and, on my return to the sitting-room, behold! A stranger there,—whom dost thou think it might be?—it was my sister Elizabeth! I did not wish to risk frightening her away by anything like an exhibition of wonder; and so we greeted each other kindly and cordially, but with no more *empressment* than if we were constantly in the habit of meeting ... Perhaps she will now make it her habit to come down and see us occasionally in the evening.[20]

During the following months, little is known about life in the Mall Street house. Nathaniel was occupied with supporting his family. Sophia was free to raise her family or pursue her art or possibly take a pleasant walk about town as Louisa was home to watch the children. Louisa enjoyed many hours a day with her beloved niece and nephew, and they loved her for the attention. She planned to sew "a new gown and a new bonnet"[21] for Una's doll. Louisa, unlike her purposely sequestered sister, was always available to help when Sophia needed a hand. Louisa did so willingly. The time living with her brother's family on Mall Street was one of contentment for Louisa. She had her family together again, all in a sun-filled house with her brother available where she could visit with him during afternoon tea or in his study.

Nathaniel's mother, although elderly and frail, was

comfortable during this time. She could take pleasure in watching her grandchildren play in the side yard as Julian "swung with Una on the gate, and looked out upon the wonder of the passing world …"[22] Betsey had reached an age where she outlived most of her own relatives. Her parents had passed away long ago as well as brothers and sisters. Whatever joy she mustered came from her own progeny who were all living in the Mall Street house with her.

Nathaniel, devoted to his family, also was a devoted friend to such men as Franklin Pierce and Horatio Bridge. He had developed a professional friendship with another Bowdoin college alumnus, the poet Henry Wadsworth Longfellow. Hawthorne had heard about an intriguing story set in Acadia in Canada from his old card-playing acquaintance, the now Reverend Horace Connolly.[23] Nathaniel had no interest in the writing such a story. Strangely, Nathaniel had written in his journal in 1837, an idea for a story, "A young man and a girl meet together, each in search of a person to be known by some particular sign … At last some casual circumstance discloses that each is the one that the other is waiting for."[24] In the ten years since he wrote down that idea, he may have decided that writing this type of romanticized story was not of interest to him. Nathaniel therefore suggested Connolly's Acadia story to Longfellow who did take up the task. The result was Longfellow's time honored and celebrated epic poem *Evangeline*, "finished on Longfellow's fortieth birthday" in 1847.[25]

The story solidified their friendship as Longfellow, a professor at Harvard, wrote to Hawthorne in February of 1848 inquiring if Hawthorne would stop by in Cambridge sometime to visit. He also offered to repay a debt saying, "Perhaps

I can pay you back in part your generous gift by giving you a theme for story in return ..."[26] Longfellow did not forget that he was offered the story of Evangeline because Hawthorne had directed the opportunity to him.

The poet and the author remained in touch. A few months later in November of 1848, Hawthorne planned a visit with Longfellow, writing to him:

> I will gladly come on Thursday, unless something unexpected should thrust itself into the space between. Thoreau is to be at my house ... I shall take the liberty to bring him with me, unless he have scruples about intruding on you. You would find him well worth knowing; he is a man of thought and originality ...[27]

At Mall Street, Nathaniel led a contented life, busy with his work and family. He was a devoted and loving father who marveled at his children while watching them grow. They grew far too quickly as he wrote:

> But the days and the years melt away so rapidly that I hardly know whether they are still little children at their parents' knees, or already a maiden and a youth ... The future too soon becomes the present, which, before we can grasp it, looks back upon us as the past ...[28]

Nathaniel also enjoyed playing with his children, and his talents at writing allowed him to play with them in the letters he wrote to them when they were apart. When Una and her mother were visiting relatives in Boston, Nathaniel wrote a loving letter to Una, breathing life into his daughter's little doll as if she was actually a living thing:

> Your dolly wants to see you very much. She sits up in my study all day long, and has nobody to talk with. I try to make her as comfortable as I can, but she does not seem to be in very good spirits. She has been quite good, and has grown very pretty, since you went away ...[29]

Familial contentment turned somber in 1849. The year was one of misfortune and trauma for the Hawthornes. At best, it opened a door that perhaps may never have been opened if not for the changes that took place in their lives. Due to political deception, Nathaniel lost his position at the Salem Custom House after three years of employment. Therefore, his means to support his family had disappeared. He no longer had any paycheck, and the outlook was disheartening. Sophia, when she heard the news of his dismissal, was not upset in the least. She happily exclaimed to him, "Oh, then you can write your book!"[30]

Nathaniel was hardly in any position to write a book; he had seven mouths to feed and keep a roof over their respective heads. However, Sophia knew that the family would be kept in a positive monetary position. She had planned for such an occurrence and had her own secret resource. Being her normal frugal self, from years of counting pennies, Sophia had carefully saved during her husband's tenure at the Custom House. She set aside from the household money and stashed "a large pile of gold in the drawer of her desk. This drawer she forthwith with elation opened, and triumphantly displayed to him the unsuspected treasure."[31] Nathaniel, relieved of the possibility of being totally ruined thanks to his prudent wife, set to writing his book.

One crisis was avoided; another commenced. A few weeks later Nathaniel's mother fell gravely ill, and Sophia became the primary nurse to her sick mother-in-law. Nathaniel, for the most part, had the responsibility of watching their two young children. It appeared that Louisa and Ebe were either too frail themselves at the time or too distraught to care for the toddlers. So as the family crisis unfolded in the Mall Street house, Nathaniel's work on his new romance was put aside. He, the devoted father, tended to his family responsibilities. His son Julian later wrote of those dreadful days:

> Day after day, throughout the hot and sunny summer weather, Hawthorne sat in the nursery, or stationed himself at the window overlooking the yard, and watched them play and prattle before him; settling their little disputes, sympathizing with their little squabbles, listening to their voices, their laughter, and their tears; while, all the time, in the chamber above, his mother lay upon what all knew to be her death-bed.[32]

During their mother's critical illness, Nathaniel and his sisters took the opportunity to visit their mother at her sickbed. As the month of July came to an end, it was evident that Mrs. Hawthorne's life on earth was coming to an end. On July 29, 1849, Nathaniel wrote detailed and emotional entries in his journal to record forever the last few days of his mother's life. Times like these can force long forgotten memories to surface. It causes one to think and rethink past events and the emotions attached to those events even if they had occurred many years prior. By afternoon on that day, Nathaniel wrote:

> At about five o'clock I went to my mother's chamber, and was shocked to see such an alteration since my last visit. I love my mother; but there has been, ever since my boyhood, a sort of coldness of intercourse between us, such as is apt to come between persons of strong feelings if they are not managed rightly. I did not expect to be much moved at the time,—that is to say, not to feel any overpowering emotion struggling just then,—though I knew that I should deeply remember and regret her ...[33]

Nathaniel does not explain with specifics. It may be that his mother was so overcome with grief after his father's death that she was unable to show love to her son in a way he needed. Possibly, she could not parent him alone. Nathaniel may have harbored continued feelings of resentment or abandonment from when he was shipped off to Salem for school. Whatever the reason, large or small, details in memory can get scrambled or amplified in one's mind during duress. As his mother's death became imminent, there would be little time for resolution.

In the room of the morbid death scene stood Louisa with her Aunt Dike, who was Betsey's sister Priscilla. At that moment one of Louisa's most loved family members stood with her, standing near the bed of her dying mother. Just before Mrs. Dike departed the room, Louisa motioned to her brother:

> Louisa pointed to a chair near the bed, but I was moved to kneel down close by my mother, and take her hand. She knew me, but could only murmur a few indistinct words; among which I understood an injunction to take care of my sisters. Mrs. Dike left the chamber, and then I found the tears slowly gathering in my eyes. I tried to keep them down, but it would not be; I kept filling up, till, for a few moments, I shook with sobs. For a long time I knelt there, holding her hand; and surely it is the darkest hour I ever lived.[34]

Mrs. Hawthorne's life came to an end peacefully on August 2, 1849 as she "gradually faded as day fades"[35] without any visible suffering in her last few hours on earth. Sophia believed that she "could not stay through the final hour, but found myself courageous for Louisa's and Elizabeth's sakes; and her disinterested, devoted life exhaled in a sigh, …"[36] Betsey Hawthorne had been a widow for four decades by the time she took her final breath. During those long years she raised her children, suffered an unending longing for her husband, and experienced the ups and downs of her life with gained and lost dreams. As her life neared its end, she enjoyed the love of her children and the blessing of grandchildren.

Nathaniel and his sisters suffered from inconsolable grief at the death of their mother. Sophia wrote that her husband, "came near a brain fever," and "Elizabeth and Louisa are desolate beyond all words."[37] There was suddenly, however, the need to take care of the necessities such as a funeral for Mrs. Hawthorne and the money to cover the expenses. Louisa and her sister Ebe did not sustain the capacity to help as Sophia wrote, "Louisa is not in strong health enough to do anything, and it would be a pain to me to see her making any efforts."[38] Apparently in Sophia's eyes, her sister-in-law Ebe was simply useless: "Elizabeth is not available for every-day purposes."[39] Nathaniel and Sophia made the arrangement for Mrs. Hawthorne's funeral themselves and for her burial in the Manning plot in the Howard Street Cemetery.

After the modest family funeral, Sophia arranged their daily schedule so that Nathaniel could write every day in his study. Louisa at this point was deeply grieving and unable to contribute by helping with the children. Ebe locked herself in her room. Sophia, however, needed to reserve time for her painting, not for recreational purposes but to supplement the family income. Therefore, Nathaniel and Sophia agreed to set aside three hours each day when he would watch the children. During those hours, Sophia had the freedom to address her own creativity and paint.[40]

Once again, as had happened previously, devoted associates came to Hawthorne's financial rescue. They added additional monies to the little of Sophia's savings that remained. George S. Hillard, a Boston orator, writer, and friend of many years, sent the sum of a collection taken. Hillard wrote:

> It is only paying, in a very imperfect measure, the debt we owe you for what you have done for American Literature ... Let no shadow of despondency, my dear friend, steal over you. Your friends do not and will not forget you.[41]

Newspaperman John L. O'Sullivan, Una's godfather, sent Nathaniel one hundred dollars that had been due him for his writings with a promise of an advance if needed. Poet and newspaper editor John G. Whittier followed up on more payments due to Hawthorne for his work.[42]

Thus, Nathaniel under these woeful and challenging circumstances wrote "*immensely*," as Sophia made note that, "I am almost frightened about it."[43] The inspired author worked in his upper floor study, overcome with grief and without the pleasant visits of his mother doting on him. He was writing a story about Puritans, sin, and punishment. After about six months of work, Nathaniel put his pen down to rest on his desk and breathed a long sigh with relief. He had completed one of the most respected American stories ever written, *The Scarlet Letter*, which was published in 1850.

With the publication of this book, Nathaniel, for the first time in his life, had acquired a more positive long-term financial prospect from his writings. In his thoughts, he gave no thanks to Salem. He wrote to Bridge in April of 1850, "As to the Salem people ... I feel an infinite contempt for them ..."[44]

> **THE SCARLET LETTER,**
> A ROMANCE by Nathaniel Hawthorne, just published and for sale by GLADDING & PROUD.

Notice for *The Scarlet Letter*,
Republican Herald, Providence, Rhode Island, March 20, 1850

> **HAWTHORNE'S CELEBRATED ROMANCE,**
> **THE SCARLET LETTER.**
> FIFTH THOUSAND. 1 vol. 16mo.; 75 cents.
> Following immediately a careful perusal of The Scarlet Letter, we have no hesitation in saying that in imagination, power, pathos, beauty, and all the other essential qualifications requisite to the completeness of a first-rate romance, Mr. Hawthorne has equaled if not surpassed any other writer who has appeared in our country during the last half century. The subject is one that needed to be most carefully handled, and no man but Hawthorne could have traced it so delicately and with so much effect. The Scarlet Letter is the work of infamy branded on the bosom of one who has violated the Seventh Commandment; and side by side with the partner of her guilt, the sad heroine walks through a life of retribution crowded with incidents which the novelist has depicted with so much truth and vigor that the interest at every page of his story grapples to the reader with a powerful hold upon his sympathy, and he will not lay down the book till he knows the result at the close. As a great moral lesson, this novel will outweigh in its influence all the sermons that have ever been preached against the sin, the effects of which The Scarlet Letter is written to exhibit.

Review for *The Scarlet Letter*,
New-York Daily Tribune, June 3, 1850

Nathaniel was ready and financially able to fulfill a lifelong desire to leave Salem permanently. Now possessing the means to leave his despised hometown and all those who lived there, Nathaniel looked elsewhere to find a home for his family. The sea and the forest called to him equally. In one of his stories, "Footprints on the Sea-Shore," he had once written, "At intervals, and not unfrequent ones, the forest and the ocean summon me—one with the roar of its waves, the other with the murmer of its boughs ..."[45] He was equally conflicted about which direction he should move with his family.

Nathaniel made the decision to relocate far, far from Salem to the Berkshire Mountains in western Massachusetts. In 1850 he, with his wife and two children, moved into a small rented red-painted dwelling nestled among the rolling and forested hills of Lenox. Hawthorne had disassociated himself from Salem. He was a distance from the familiar Atlantic coastline with its salt air and sea breezes, from the Manning relatives, and his sisters. He had purposely removed himself from all of them. He wanted a change; he chose a drastic one.

For the first time in their lives, Louisa and Ebe, had a choice regarding where they wished to live permanently. They chose to live separately from one another. It is difficult to determine exactly what their relationship was as they grew older. They had lived in the same house, but there is little known about their interactions together. Ebe enjoyed solitude. Louisa was socially oriented. They appeared to make their own visits separately once Louisa was old enough to be on her own. The sisters seemed more interested in their individual relationship with their brother rather than with each other. Their mother and the need for family money for support had kept them together for so many years. Therefore, the sisters decided to pack up their belongings and live in different households.

Louisa, about forty-one years old when her mother died, was welcomed to live in Salem with one of her aunts. Surviving envelopes with letters were directly addressed to Maria Louisa in Salem. However, there are envelopes with letters that were addressed to her at the John Dike residence. Therefore, Louisa possibly moved in with Rebecca Manning, the widow of Robert Manning, or more likely with Priscilla Manning Dike, who was married to and living with her husband John Dike. Louisa continued her life in Salem as she had always done. She was content residing in the loving security of a relative's home and enjoyed the companionship of family and friends. Louisa did not require much to be happy with her life.

Nathaniel's older sister, about forty-seven years old at that time, chose to move out of Salem entirely, first briefly to Manchester. She wasn't entirely satisfied there so she moved again to settle permanently in Montserrat in Beverly, Massachusetts. She lived contentedly renting a room, reading, and lately, "I have been very busy about Cervantes's Tales."[46] She did not articulate if she was studying these tales, editing, or translating them as they were originally written in Spanish. However, there were English versions available. Ebe with this last move, accomplished her long journey into an almost complete seclusion but with certain exceptions as she so dictated. She achieved the life she had always longed for. It was her brother who provided and paid for it.

Although very happy to remain in Salem, Louisa did miss

her brother. He was living farther away from her than he had since his Bowdoin College days a quarter century earlier. Writing to Sophia in August of 1850, Louisa wistfully offered a message for her brother, "Give my love to Nathaniel. If he only did know how I want to see him—but it is not to be told how much!"[47]

The heavy snow accumulated inch by inch to foot by foot as winter nestled in the mountains of western Massachusetts. Ironically, Nathaniel was completing a story about the haunted old Salem he purposely left behind. Although he was "a little worn down with constant work,"[48] he wrote to Louisa. He complained to her, "the pen is so constantly in my fingers that I abominate the sight of it!"[49] He knew that he must take advantage of opportunity while it was afforded to him and while creativity fired up his mind. The book written from September 1850 to about February 1851 in the little red house became a classic in American literature. Published in 1851, *The House of the Seven Gables* depicts a story of curses, death, and retribution. The book would immortalize the house on Turner Street in Salem where Susanna Ingersoll lived and where he and Louisa had spent countless hours playing cards with their friends.

The Hawthornes continued their normal routine in their small abode in the mountains. Nathaniel isolated himself in his study during the morning hours as Sophia tended to their children. At times, Sophia taught them arithmetic, French, geography, and history, drawing from her own reading and educational experiences.[50] At midday, her husband reappeared after hours of concentration in writing to share a pleasant dinner with his family. In the evening after the

My Dear Sister

children were put to bed, Nathaniel and Sophia, as they had done as newlyweds in Concord, spent their, "long, beautiful evening, which we richly enjoy. My husband has read aloud ... I never heard such reading. It is better than any acting or opera. ..."[51]

> CHOICE BOOKS—TICKNOR, REED & FIELDS, Boston, have lately published—
> Grace Greenwood's Poems, with a fine portrait. 75 cents.
> Mr. Hawthorne's True Stories, from History and Biography, with plates. 75 cents.
> Mr. Whittier's Songs of Labor. 50 cents.
> Mr. DeQuincey's Biographical Essays. 75 cents.
> Professor O. W. Holmes's new Poem, Astraea. 25 cents
> In Memoriam, by Alfred Tennyson. 75 cents.
> The Scarlet Letter, 6th Thousand. 75 cents.
> Mr. Giles's Lectures and Essays. $1.50.
> Mr. Giles's Discourses on Life. 75 cents.
> Mr. E. P. Whipple's Lectures on Literature and Life. 62 cents.
> Mr. Longfellow's Evangeline, Illustrated. $5.
> Mr. George Hillard's Address before the Mercantile Library Association. 25 cents.
> Professor O. W. Holmes's Address at the Medical College.
> Mr. Charles Sumner's Orations and Speeches. 2 vols. 16mo. $2.50.
> T. R & F. will shortly issue—
> The Biography of William Wordsworth, by D. Christopher Wordsworth. Edited by Prof. Henry Reed.
> Mr. Hawthorne's The House of the Seven Gables, a new Romance.
> Mr. E. P. Whipple's Essays and Reviews, new and enlarged Edition.
> Grace Greenwood's History of My Pets, with fine engravings.
> Goethe's Faust, translated by Hayward, a new Edition.
> Goethe's Wilhelm Meister, translated by Carlyle.
> DeQuincy's Writings, Third Volume.
> Mr. James Russell Lowell's Nooning, a new Poem.
> Horace and James Smith's Rejected Addresses, new Edition.
> Memory and Hope, a book of Poems on Childhood.
> n27 law4tW

Notice including *The House of the Seven Gables,*
New-York Daily Tribune, November 27, 1851

TRANSITION (1845-1852)

Sophia wrote to her mother in June of 1850:

> We are so beautifully arranged (excepting the guest-chamber), and we seem to have such a large house *inside*, though outside the little reddest thing looks like the smallest of ten-feet houses. Mr Hawthorne says it looks like the Scarlet Letter.[52]

Sophia's love and devotion for her husband seemed to blossom ever more as she wrote, "If I can only be so great, so high, so noble, so sweet, as he in any phase of my being, I shall be glad. I am not deluded nor mistaken, as the angels know now, and as all my friends will know, in open vision!"[53]

Although he purposely removed himself from Salem to a distance far away in the mountains, Nathaniel became annoyed about the lack of correspondence and news received from his sisters. He may have had a valid point as his sisters had spent their lives being supported by other family members, including himself. What do they do each day that would not allow a few moments to write letters? Nathaniel always craved to hear family news, and this desire had not diminished as he aged. He wrote to his sister Ebe in March of 1851, in a tone indicating much exasperation:

> I wish you or Louisa would write to us once in a while, without waiting for regular responses on our part. Sophia is busy from morning till night, and I myself am so much occupied with

235

pen and ink that I hate the thought of writing except from necessity. ... It is my purpose to come to Boston (and of course to Salem) some time in June ... I hope that one of you two will come to see us, after my return. The children would be delighted, and it would afford Sophia great pleasure.[54]

On May 20, 1851, a visitor arrived at the little red house. This visitor was neither Louisa nor Ebe, but one who would stay forever at the Hawthorne home. As Nathaniel had done before, it was to Louisa that he wrote in May, about one year after the move to Lenox, to make an announcement:

You have another niece. She made her appearance this morning at about three o'clock, and is a very promising child—kicking valiantly and crying most obstreperously. Her hair, I understand, is very much the tinge of Una's. Sophia is quite comfortable, and everything is going on well.[55]

The child's name was Rose, whom Nathaniel would take to calling "Rosebud."[56] He seemed to take fancy in the name and had previously incorporated it into his writings. He used the name Rosebud in his story, "Chippings With A Chisel" and again in the story "Edward Fane's Rosebud."[57]

But where were little Rosebud's aunts? Nathaniel, still annoyed at the lack of communication from Louisa, continued writing but with a somewhat scolding tone:

Judging by your long silence, you will not take much interest in the intelligence, nor in anything else which concerns us. I should really like to hear from you once or twice in the course of a twelve-month. Dr. Peabody (who is now here) says that you called in West Street, some time ago; this is our latest news of you. How did you like The House of the Seven Gables? Not so well as The Scarlet Letter, I judge from your saying nothing about it.[58]

Feeling ignored, he may have been most perturbed that Louisa traveled to Boston visiting the Peabody home but not to Lenox to visit him. His attitude improved by the end of the letter as he informed her in a postscript that publisher "Tichnor & Co. want to publish a volume of my tales and sketches not hitherto collected."[59] Nathaniel also needed something. He had two requests for his sister, the reason for his sudden change in tone. He asked Louisa for copies of his stories and, in addition, an 1850's style of necktie, "If you have any, or can obtain them, pray do so. Can you make me a black silk stock, to be ready when I come? ..."[60]

Louisa was confident venturing to Boston, and Ebe too had the opportunity to travel short distances if she ever wanted to. Whether they would visit their brother in Lenox was always in question. Ebe had no desire to travel as far as Lenox. Nathaniel had invited Ebe, but she responded to his invitation in a letter, "I thank you for your invitation, but I do not like to go further from home than I can walk."[61] Those

237

were her self-imposed restrictions on her self-imposed life; she did not wish to travel any distance and not to Lenox.

Ebe commented to her brother that he should have taken a cottage nearby her home and that if he had done so he would have been much happier. She mentioned that Louisa had visited her there a few weeks earlier. It is apparent that Ebe would have been happier with her brother if he lived nearby. She tartly explained to her brother that, "… I would never go out of the sound of its [seashore's] roar if I could help it."[62]

By July of 1851, Nathaniel wrote to Louisa again asking for more pieces of his published works, "If you have any of the magazine articles, mentioned in my last, I wish you would have them sent to B., as he is going to send a package to me within a week or two."[63] Nathaniel was exhausted from writing and explained his reason for not sending Louisa more letters, "I have written a book for children, two or three hundred pages long, since the first of June."[64]

Louisa, not failing her brother's request for articles, sent a package to him. He wrote to her: "Your package and letter were duly rec-d [sic]. I am rather afraid that I shall not be able to collect articles enough for a volume … When I come to Salem, I can ride out with Mr. W.M. and see you. …"[65] Thus, Louisa's work was all in vain for the moment. Nathaniel mentioned in the letter that Sophia had spent some time in West Newton visiting her relatives and taking their daughters along.[66]

This left Nathaniel in Lenox alone with his young son Julian. Together, they embarked into a 19th century version of male bonding between father and son. Day by day, Nathaniel recorded their activities in his journal, creating a sweetly honest yet sometimes quixotic narrative of a father with his five-year old son. The once-in-a-lifetime experience of their adventures would later be published and titled, *Twenty Days with Julian & Little Bunny By Papa*.

Regarding their adventures, Nathaniel wrote, "After dinner ... we walked down to the lake. On our way, we waged war with the thistles, which represented many-headed hydras and dragons ..."[67] It can easily be imagined the father and son swinging fanciful swords to win their hard-fought battle against the enemy before it was time for bed.

Then, there was the pet bunny. Nathaniel may have wished he could have sent Julian's pet bunny away with the dragons because it, "makes me more trouble than he is worth."[68] As luck would have it, due to some unexplainable reason, one day, the bunny took its last breath and died. The dutiful father "dug a hole, and we planted poor Bunny in the garden. Julian said, 'Perhaps to-morrow there will be a tree of Bunnies, and they will hang all over it by their ears.'"[69]

As the three weeks of adventure for father and son neared an end, they both were the better for it. Nathaniel waited for Sophia's return home with their daughters Una and Rose from West Newton. About six o'clock one evening, they did arrive safely as Nathaniel noted, "they have come,—all well! Thank God."[70] He rejoiced in his family being together again.

As he had done throughout his life, Nathaniel wrote to Louisa of his annoyances, and he had several regarding the red house. Although his writing was prolific in that house, he had grown to dislike it; the place had been too small for his liking. He complained to Louisa, "... this is certainly the

239

most inconvenient and wretched little hovel that I ever put my head in."[71]

Ebe may have been correct in her estimation that Nathaniel would have been happier at the seashore. However, his productivity could have suffered if he had chosen that location. The seashore and proximity to family members offered too many distractions. Lenox provided what he needed to write prolifically even though he hated the little red house. He also hated the weather in the Berkshire Mountains. Just how much he noted:

> This is a horrible, horrible, most hor-ri-ble climate; ... I detest it! I detest it!! I de-test it!!! I hate Berkshire with my whole soul, and would joyfully see its mountains laid flat.[72]

However greatly he despised those mountains, this was the place where his prolific writing further solidified his fame and future. It was in the Berkshires and in Lenox, specifically, where Nathaniel lived for a year and a half writing *The House of the Seven Gables*, the diary entries that years later would become *Twenty Days with Julian & Little Bunny by Papa*, the outline for *The Blithedale Romance,* and the children's book, *A Wonder-Book.*

Ebe admired the *Wonder-Book*. However, always opinionated, she wrote to Louisa criticizing Nathaniel's plan to leave Lenox:

> I think it a very poor plan for them to go to Newton when it will be absolutely necessary to

remove again in the spring. I think they might have decided to leave Lenox time enough to find a permanent residence this autumn.[73]

Not one to spare Sophia from any insults, Ebe blamed her for the planned move to West Newton: "I suppose it is Sophia's plan; it is so much like the Peabody's never to be settled. If Nathaniel buys a place, she will have some excuse for leaving it in a year or two."[74]

It is surprising that Ebe would even suggest this as she had been moved about often in her life, not by choice but necessity. Apparently, this fact had slipped her memory. When she was six years old, Ebe was first moved from the Hathorne house to the Manning house on Herbert Street. She was moved to Raymond, Maine, back to Herbert Street, then Dearborn Street, and back again to the Herbert Street house. Nathaniel moved her to the Mall Street house, followed by her stay in Manchester then finally to Beverly. It appears she had little cause to accuse Sophia. However, Ebe took every opportunity to criticize her sister-in-law.

In Lenox, Nathaniel could not lay flat those despised mountains as he had complained, but he could leave them behind. He planned to relocate his family closer to Boston although briefly into borrowed accommodations. The journey away from Lenox provided him with a few moments of unexpected happiness. He recorded in his journal the departure from the insufferable little red domicile:

> We left Lenox Friday morning, November 21, 1851, in a storm of snow and sleet, and took the

cars at Pittsfield, and arrived at West Newton that evening. Happiness in this world, when it comes, comes incidentally. Make it the object of pursuit, and it leads us a wild-goose chase, and is never attained. Follow some other object, and very possibly we may find that we have caught happiness without dreaming of it; but likely enough it is gone the moment we say to ourselves; 'Here it is!' like a chest of gold that treasure-seekers find.[75]

In West Newton, the Hawthornes lived for a few months in a house owned by public education advocate and member of the U.S. House of Representatives Horace Mann. He was Sophia's brother-in-law who, in 1843, had married her sister Mary. While the Manns were in Washington, D.C. for several months, Nathaniel occupied himself writing his next book, *The Blithedale Romance*, with a setting reminiscent of Brook Farm. The book was in the process of being published by springtime of 1852.

Nathaniel, excitedly announced, writing to Louisa, "My book is in Press."[76] In the same letter he expressed his desire for Louisa to visit him stating, "Dear L. You have put off coming to see us so long ..."[77] However, he cautioned his sister that the house was bursting with people because, "The whole family of Manns, great and little, have come home and you may readily conceive that we are anxious to get away."[78] Because of all the commotion at the Mann house, Louisa's visit needed to wait.

With their improved financial outlook from his books,

TRANSITION (1845-1852)

Nathaniel and Sophia had been investigating the possibility of buying their own home. They needed that home quickly. They had three children, and their stay at the Manns must come to a speedy end. The seeds of a home acquisition for the Hawthornes had been planted for some time. Years earlier after Sophia's marriage, Mrs. Peabody wrote a letter to her daughter and included a paragraph about a certain house in Concord owned by the Alcotts, the parents of author Louisa May Alcott:

> Mrs. Alcott has just come in to tell us about her house in Concord. It is at the entrance of a wood, two miles in a direct line to the river. She would enjoy Mr. Hawthorne's having it more than she can express; thinks the house would be forever honored; and, though she might never be so happy as to hear him speak, if she could sometimes see his inexpressibly sweet smile, it would be an enhancement of the value of her property only to be realized by those who know him ...[79]

In 1852, a few weeks before their tenth wedding anniversary, this prospect materialized. Nathaniel bought a house from the Alcotts called Hillside. This would be the only house that the Hawthornes would own and was certainly a dream come true for the author and his wife. The success of his books had given him financial security, and he was reaping the rewards after years of hard work and frustration. Nathaniel and Sophia had come home to Concord, the town where they began their married life ten years earlier in the "Old

My Dear Sister

Manse" and where they had lived glorious years in a paradise of their own making. They quickly renamed their newly purchased home Wayside.

Julian Hawthorne, their son, later reminisced of the move to Concord:

> The family advent was effected in June ... My mother and Una came a day ahead of the others, and with the help of carpenters and upholsterers, and a neighboring Irishman and his wife for cleaning and moving purposes, they soon got human order into the place of savage chaos. The new carpet was down in the study, the walls had been already papered and the wood-work grained, the pictures were hung in their places, and the books placed on their shelves. By the time the father, the boy, the baby, and the nurse drove up in the hot afternoon a home had been created for their reception.[80]

In this home, Nathaniel and Sophia with their three children quickly adjusted to the joys of a new environment. The older children explored the surroundings populated with trees, thick woods, and plenty of land to run around or hide. The parents settled in to make their house a home for their three children. It seemed all the wants and needs in their life were being fulfilled. Except there was one thing missing, Nathaniel's sister, Louisa, and he wished that she come for a visit. So, Nathaniel sat down in his study to write a letter to Louisa.

Chapter 10
Nathaniel's Tears (1852)

> "This was the most painful episode connected with his life ..."
>
> —Julian Hawthorne

Louisa had been contentedly living in Salem, Massachusetts, surrounded by her Manning relatives. Since her early childhood, she had maintained an exceptionally close relationship with her Aunt Priscilla Miriam, a Manning aunt. That closeness extended to Priscilla's husband after her marriage to John Dike. Louisa had been a source of comfort to them when their daughter Mary had died more than thirty years earlier. The Dikes love for Louisa remained warm and steadfast. One June day at their home, a letter arrived addressed to Louisa in care of her uncle John Dike, Esq. The letter dated June 18, 1852, was posted from Concord and signed by her brother, Nathaniel. It contained the latest of his many

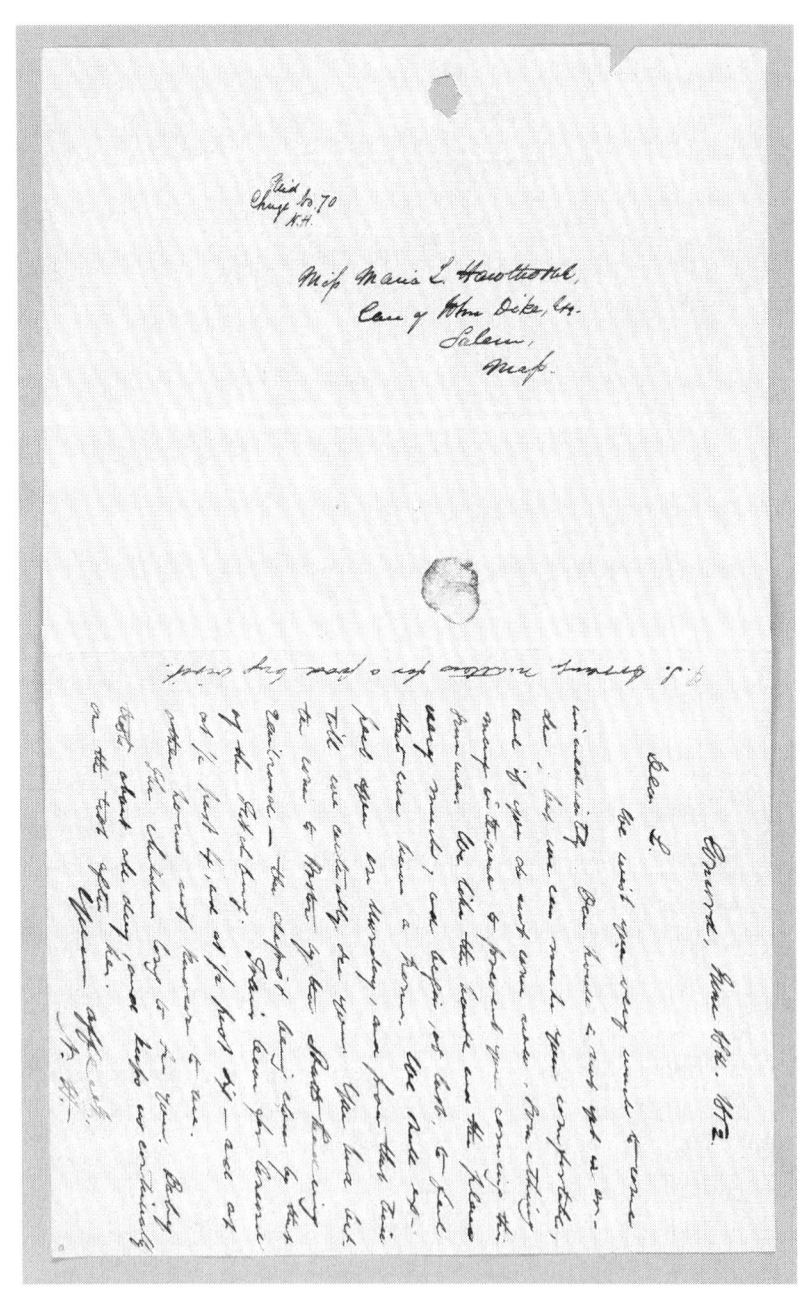

Hawthorne's June 18, 1852 letter inviting his sister Maria Louisa for a visit. Courtesy of the Phillips Library

NATHANIEL'S TEARS (1852)

entreaties encouraging Louisa to visit him. It was a letter that would change the course of her life.

> Dear L—We wish you very much to come immediately. Our house is not yet in order, but we can make you comfortable, and if you do not come now, something may intervene to prevent your coming this summer ...[1]

Neither Louisa nor Nathaniel would know at the time that something terrible would truly intervene with her visit. It was an ominous choice of words on his part, presupposing an act of fate or the dreaded Hathorne curse destined to come between them. As Louisa finished reading the inviting words of his letter, she did not know that she might never see her brother again:

> We like the house and the place very much, and begin, at last, to feel that we have a home. We shall expect you on Monday, and from that time till we actually see you ... The children long to see you. Baby trots about all day, and keeps us continually on the trot after her.—Yours affect.—N.H.[2]

"Baby," as Nathaniel wrote, was his youngest child Rose who had been born in Lenox. His other children Una and Julian had already spent part of their young lives playing with their Aunt Louisa. They were undoubtedly anticipating an upcoming visit. Sophia was equally excited about the

247

prospect of seeing her genial sister-in-law. Using the available space remaining on his letter to Louisa, Nathaniel scribbled a postscript along the left side of the page. His final thoughts to her in the letter urged, "P.S. Arrange matters for a good long visit."[3] Nathaniel wished her to stay not for a short day or two but for perhaps days, weeks, or months.

Two weeks later Nathaniel received a response from Louisa. She explained that her planned visit must be delayed for a few days:

> My dear brother—Mrs. Manning is very ill, and I must put off coming to you till next week. I am glad you like your house, and that you seem at last to be settled.[4]

Wayside, Concord, Massachusetts

NATHANIEL'S TEARS (1852)

Louisa, since early adulthood, had taken on the responsibilities of handling family or household matters. Presently, her aunt needed her caregiving, so Louisa quickly agreed, as it was in her nature to assist her relatives whenever they needed her. Louisa, by this time, was no longer a playful child, but she remained well-loved in the family. They seemed to struggle among themselves as to whom would receive her attention next.

It may be noted that Ebe was quietly content living her solitary life in a neighboring village. It is doubtful her relatives tugged for her attentions because they were aware of her lifestyle choice and understood that she was happy that way. Like her father who chose books to accompany him on his voyages at sea, Ebe chose books as her companions in her rented room. During the last years of her life, Ebe made infrequent trips to Salem, about three miles away, or other close environs when she chose. Her brother had indulged her with invitations for her to visit him in Concord, but she rarely accepted.

Unlike Ebe, Louisa was often out and about visiting family and friends. In her lively letter to her brother, Louisa mentioned to Nathaniel that she had "heard of you in Boston, two or three weeks ago, buying carpets."[5] Nathaniel must have been on a mission for home decorating items, but Louisa was not too impressed, lightheartedly joking about his abilities, "I should have been afraid to trust you."[6]

She proceeded to write in the letter about her own trip to Boston. She had unexpectantly encountered their old friends the "Chancellor" and the "Cardinal" without mentioning their real names in the letter. Nathaniel knew who they were

249

My Dear Sister

without needing to ask. She mentioned that, "The Cardinal ... wished very much to see you, and will meet you in Boston any day you may appoint."[7] Louisa, the ever sociable one, maintained those acquaintances from card games and laughter at the Ingersoll house with David Roberts (the "Chancellor") and Horace Conolly (the "Cardinal").

A week passed, and Rebecca Manning's health improved, allowing Louisa the freedom to travel away from Salem. It may not have been a complete surprise to the Hawthornes when another opportunity kept Louisa from visiting them in Concord. This next sojourn was an indulgence for Louisa, who rarely left the confines of Essex County in Massachusetts. She was invited for a holiday at Saratoga Springs, New York, to take in the spa with her Uncle John Dike.[8] Nathaniel may have been familiar with the upstate New York resort area from his travels with his uncle years earlier. How could he argue for Louisa not to go?

Nathaniel's son, Julian, although a young child at the time, remembered the congenial nature of his Aunt Louisa. He later described her by writing that:

> She was a lady of sociable and gentle disposition, and a great favorite with the children, as well as Mr. and Mrs. Hawthorne. She had never enjoyed robust health, however, and had therefore been prevented from mingling, as much as she would otherwise have done, with the friends who loved her and whom she loved.[9]

A trip to a Saratoga spa may help improve Louisa's lifelong precarious constitution. Saratoga Springs was situated in upstate New York, several miles above Albany and a whisper south of the beautiful Adirondack Mountains. By the mid-19th century, the community had become famous as a destination for the wealthy for restoration of one's health. A summer's day was so much cooler, the air so much fresher, and perhaps the sun shone brighter on lovely Saratoga Springs. Word of mineral springs brought popularity to the Saratoga Springs area. The Columbian Spring, exposed in 1803, offered special therapies as its "water is rich in iron and has a high content of carbon dioxide gas. At one time it was called the 'headache spring,' because some people experience a headache after drinking a quantity of it."[10]

Louisa's train had passed through Concord, without making a stop. Thus, passed an opportunity for the brother and sister to meet, even if only at the depot. They would not know

Columbian Spring, Saratoga,
Saratoga Springs, New York

at the time that it was an opportunity that was lost forever as she and her uncle traveled west to Saratoga Springs. Hidden away amidst the quiet mountains and green pastures of upstate New York, the pair vacationed, relaxed, and enjoyed the spa with its mineral waters, hoping to rejuvenate their delicate conditions. Louisa was forty-four years old, middle-aged. If she was following the same journey as her mother, Louisa's fragile health issues may have become more challenging as she grew older. It was noted later in the newspapers that Maria Louisa, "had been for some time an invalid, and had been greatly benefited by her stay at the Springs."[11]

Interestingly, at the very same time that Louisa and her uncle were guests, a lengthy article appeared in the *New-York Daily Times* regarding Saratoga. The reporter wrote an in-depth description of this resort area at the height of the 1852 summer tourist season:

> Saratoga has seldom been more completely filled with visitors, generally from a distance, than at present ... It is ... in every respect delightful and unexceptionable; composed, as far as we are advised, after every reasonable inquiry, of as fine a class of Summer visitors as could possibly be drawn from the four quarters of this great and happy country. Nearly every state is at present represented, and the cities of New-York, Philadelphia, and New-Orleans largely and highly-respectably so. We have remarked neither pretension nor dissipation. The varied social attractions of the place are made conspicuous

NATHANIEL'S TEARS (1852)

by the free and unrestrained commingling of hundreds of the best citizens and families of North and South, and by a happy and seemingly universal purpose to make the most, in a truly rational sense of "the season ..."[12]

Saratoga Springs was a resort area ready to beckon and entertain the well-connected and wealthy of American society. Louisa was born to the Hathorne family, which had long lost its wealth and prominence. She was raised by the gracious outpourings of the Manning family. Now, she was enjoying an exquisite holiday in Saratoga Springs, where only those who could afford such expensive luxuries frequented. Louisa had avoided a life of destitution that easily could have been hers if not for the generosity of her ardent Salem relatives.

All too quickly, this special resort holiday came to an end as Louisa and her uncle departed from their hotel. Saratoga Springs would continue to entertain the next wave of summertime guests who checked into the local resorts. Meanwhile, Uncle Dike and his niece readied to embark on their journey back to Massachusetts. At second thought, a visit to New York City seemed irresistible, and "They were returning this way that they might view our beautiful Hudson."[13]

Therefore, initial plans for taking the train directly east across the Massachusetts state line to continue to Concord were changed. Louisa and her uncle chose a longer and slower route for their journey, yet it was a most picturesque one, travelling by luxurious passenger steamboat down the Hudson River. The express train from Albany to the great city offered a faster trip. However, the steamboat, taking twice the

253

My Dear Sister

hours, offered an adventure that covered an equal distance but provided wonderful views of charming riverside mansions, imposing mountains, and expanses of luscious landscape throughout the beautiful Hudson Valley. The steamboat offered a casually slow ride, a long glimpse of the Military Academy at West Point, a view of the Hudson Highlands, and a special meal as part of the amenities. Who should miss that when given the opportunity?

Nathaniel was unaware that his sister and uncle had changed their plans to travel by steamboat to the majestic city of New York before returning to Massachusetts. He believed his sister and uncle were traveling cross country east by train to see him. Sophia later wrote, "we expected her here for a long visit."[14] As a result, Nathaniel and Sophia waited patiently at their home anticipating Louisa's arrival.

If Louisa and Uncle Dike had travelled one day earlier or if they had boarded another steamboat at Albany on that morning, fate would have moved in their favor. Nevertheless, early on the sunny morning of Wednesday, July 28, 1852, Louisa, "a tall, fragile, pale, amiable figure"[15] with her elderly uncle John Dike, took the course that would alter her destiny. They boarded the beautiful and practically new, already famous sidewheeler steamboat, *Henry Clay*, at the hectic Albany docks for passage to New York City.[16]

Affixed to her dress, Louisa wore a piece of jewelry, an engraved pin that had belonged to her Aunt Rachel (Hathorne) Forrester.[17] Years earlier, this aunt had provided the perfect gown for Louisa when she attended the autumn ball as a teenager in Salem. Louisa was excited to spend a most splendid day traveling by luxurious steamboat on the scenic

254

NATHANIEL'S TEARS (1852)

and historic Hudson River. What's more, the entire day's 150-mile journey would end with a visit to New York City, "Gotham," as it was demonstrably known. There would be so many memories and stories to tell Nathaniel and Sophia about her adventures in the spectacular city.

On the *Henry Clay*, Louisa and her uncle were in the presence of several prestigious and well-known passengers. Among the hundreds of those on board was Andrew Jackson Downing, a talented landscape architect. Along with his wife, his mother-in-law was also travelling with him, Caroline DeWint. She was the granddaughter of U.S. President John Adams. Stephen Allen, a former mayor of New York City and a director of the Hudson River Railroad, was travelling on the steamboat as well. West Point instructor Jacob Bailey was accompanied by his family and friends. There was an array of attorneys, businessmen, working people, and adventurers onboard that day.[18]

By mid-afternoon, the steamboat would lay as a smoldering hull on the sunbaked beach of Riverdale, which today is a part of the Bronx of New York City. "Mr. D. had left her [Louisa] in the ladies cabin only five minutes before the fire was discovered, to go forward to take the fresh air."[19] Dike, like many other men that afternoon, enjoyed the pastoral sights, viewed beautiful riverside mansions, and anticipated the appearance momentarily of New York City on the horizon.

Many women and husbands had settled in the cabins with their families, an alternative to the steamboat's sunbathed and hot summertime decks. The cabins offered a shaded and quieter place to relax where parents could coax their children to nap or sit in conversation. For travelling women like

255

My Dear Sister

Louisa, there was opportunity to rest in cooler comfort on a hot summer day. For Louisa, reading a favorite book was like spending time with a devoted friend. It offered joy and comfort yet asked for nothing in return. Therefore, she sat contentedly and comfortably while anticipating her upcoming visit to New York City, "reading in the after-cabin, when the accident occurred."[20]

As the steamboat approached Riverdale, interrupting the quiet of children sleeping and adults reading or chatting, the steamboat suddenly burst into fierce flames, which spread quickly across the decks. "Instantly, the fire and smoke rose so densely as to cut off all communication and access between the forward and aft part of the boat."[21] Acting to save lives, the pilot, with skillful maneuvers, turned the flaming steamboat and travelled several minutes before landing onto a sandy beach. The vessel remained intact from the crashing ashore. The forward section of the steamboat was on solid ground, a sandy beach, while the aft protruded into the deep and dark river water.

Within moments, terror reigned upon the passengers of the *Henry Clay*. The blazing inferno engulfed the vessel, trapping hundreds of innocent people in its fiery clutches. Children and adults, the dining staff and ship's crew were all at risk—no one was safe. In the chaos and mayhem of the roaring fire onboard, "… the passengers on the forward part of the boat jumped on the sand bank, while those on the after part were compelled to get ashore the best way they could, by leaping into the water."[22] Did Louisa and Uncle Dike jump ashore at the bow or, like so many others, jump into the menacingly dark depths to possibly drown? Had

NATHANIEL'S TEARS (1852)

they burned to death in the explosion of flames onboard or somehow escaped the burning fires as the steamboat was reduced to smoldering ash?

Uncle Dike, who had always been available to help Louisa, was unable to reach her cabin after fire engulfed the steamboat. The flames blocked passageways, making it impossible for separated family members to reach their loved ones. Many fathers had been on deck while their wives and children were resting in the cabins, "... husbands, wives, parents, and children quickly separated from one another by a dreadful death, when least expecting it. ..."[23] For the first and only time in her life, Louisa, by tragic circumstance, was totally abandoned. There was no family member or friend available to assist her when she truly needed the help, this time to save her life. While Dike helplessly stood on the flaming deck, Louisa helplessly stood terrified inside a cabin as the steamboat burned in flames around them both.

Surrounded by this chaos onboard, Louisa remained alone. She found herself with no safe avenue of escape. If she was able to leave the cabin before it collapsed around her, she then faced an impenetrable wall of flames on deck which could cause her to die in the inferno. Her only other option was to attempt to exit through a door or window and jump overboard, blinded from the smoke, into the deep river water. The waters became crowded with dozens, if not hundreds, of passengers doing the same thing. Louisa most likely did not know how to swim.

If she had jumped, the river water would have immediately soaked into her long dress, adding weight and making it more difficult for her to stay afloat. As she struggled to keep

My Dear Sister

her head above the churning water, gasping for air, other passengers could have jumped from the boat's deck onto her pushing her underwater. Others could have grabbed her, hoping to help themselves stay afloat with each eventually sinking. Could Louisa somehow have gotten herself to shore? Did someone on a rescue boat reach for her to save her? During these horrific moments and in the somber hours to follow, there was no one, whether passenger, rescuer, or witness on shore, who saw Maria Louisa Hawthorne anymore that day.

Two days later, on Friday morning, Nathaniel Hawthorne, unmindful of the tragic events in Riverdale, arose with the thought of passing another joyous day at his home. He had spent the entire month of July wandering his property, reading, composing a story in his mind, and playing with his children. Nathaniel's writings, especially *The Scarlet Letter* and *The House of the Seven Gables*, had given him fame and the outlook for a financial security he had long worked toward. As the Friday morning sun rose in the sky, he looked forward to the good things in his life and a visit from his special sister, Louisa. He expected that she would be arriving at his home at any moment.

To his surprise, it was not Louisa who graced his Wayside that early morning. The unexpected visitor who arrived was William Pike, a long-time friend of Nathaniel's.[24] The news he had to share would shadow darkly over Nathaniel's being. Pike came to inform him of an unexpected and unspeakable tragedy. What is known about Pike's visit that early morning was recorded in a letter that Sophia wrote to her mother that day, July 30th. She described the details of Pike's heartbreaking announcement of the unexpected and horrible news:

NATHANIEL'S TEARS (1852)

> My dearest Mother, —This morning we received the shocking intelligence that Louisa Hawthorne was lost in the destruction of the steamer 'Henry Clay' on the Hudson, on Wednesday afternoon, July 27.[25]

Unfortunately, Sophia confused the date of the steamboat accident as July 27 as indicated in her letter. Due to this correspondence, many books and research materials about Nathaniel Hawthorne had documented the date of July 27th as the day of the disaster. However, that date was an error in her letter possibly due to the extreme stress and sadness she was experiencing. Sophia was correct to write that the *Henry Clay* disaster took place two days earlier on Wednesday, but the actual date for that Wednesday in 1852 was July 28.[26]

Sophia continued to explain in her letter to her mother that Louisa:

> Has been at Saratoga Springs and with Mr. Dike for a fortnight, and was returning by way of New York ... It is difficult to realize such a sudden disaster. The news came in an appalling way ... It struck to my heart that he had come to inform us of some accident ... Mr. Hawthorne opened the door with the strange feeling that he should grasp a hand of air. I was by his side. Mr. Pike, without a smile, deeply flushed, seemed even then not in his former body.[27]

259

Something was terribly wrong but how does one impart heartbreaking news? Pike, not knowing how to inform them otherwise, blurted out the news directly. Sophia, in her delicate voice, questioned him to comprehend what he was telling them:

> "Your sister Louisa is dead!" I thought he meant *his own* sister was dead, for she also is called Louisa. "What! Louisa?" I asked. "Yes." "What was the matter?" "She was drowned." "Where?" "On the Hudson, in the 'Henry Clay'!"[28]

The revelation pierced their hearts. It seemed Wayside had suddenly disappeared, leaving Nathaniel and Sophia to float ungrounded in a foreboding nothingness with only the incomprehensible words "Louisa is dead" in their minds. A moment passed before they were brought back into the present world. There was air to breathe and sunshine to light the day, but it was impossible to discern their existence. As their hearts sank and their throats tightened, they tried to seek out an answer to the question in their minds: Louisa is dead—how could this be true? The shock from the news set itself upon their beings, and Sophia was escorted inside the house. As she later communicated the details of that morning, she continued in her letter to her mother, "He then came in, and my husband shut himself in his study ..."[29]

In her letter, Sophia continued that, "I began to weep."[30] The minutes passed as she tried to compose herself in front of her children. She found it difficult to collect her confused thoughts. Her husband had left the room, but she felt an obligation to stay with her children for their sake. Knowing she must make sense of the tragic news, Sophia wrote to her mother:

> At last, my mind left the terrible contemplation of Louisa's last agony and fright, and imaged her supremely happy with her mother in another world. For she was always inconsolable for her mother, and never could be really happy away from her.[31]

Sophia explained how Una and Julian were understandably distraught over the news. Baby Rose was much too small to understand, but Una was about eight years old and Julian six. They were young, but they could understand that their precious Aunt Louisa, who they had often played with and who had cared for them, was never coming back to them. Sophia confided in her mother that she tried to think of something, anything that would console her children and ease their minds. She frantically looked for the words in her own aching heart but was able only to reiterate what she had said a few moments earlier. Sophia re-affirmed to her children, "Aunt Louisa is with her mother, and is happy to be with her. Let us think of her sprit in another world."[32]

Distraught young Julian tried to be brave as, "A smile shone in his eyes for a moment, but another flood of tears immediately followed. All at once he got up and went to the study,—he had the intention of consoling his father with that idea; but his father had gone on the hill."[33] This hill that Sophia wrote of was a very steep incline that was situated closely behind their house. Nathaniel climbed up the embankment for the purpose of losing himself from the present world to deal with his profound grief. He was alone with the earth and the sky. Although the natural world had always offered comfort to him in his youth, there was no comfort on this day. The news was too much to grasp, too much to rationalize, too much to bear. Louisa was dead.

Ebe was equally struck by the tragedy as Sophia wrote that for her sister-in-law, "It is an unmitigated loss …"[34] Neither she, Nathaniel, nor anyone else in the family was prepared or ever expected that Louisa would be taken from their lives. Sophia mentioned in her letter to her mother that she anticipated Nathaniel would invite Ebe to visit them in Concord "to change the scene."[35]

The day had begun with the expectation of joy and happiness and an expected visit from Louisa. With William Pike's somber news, the entire family was immediately thrown into sadness and grief before the breakfast hour was complete. The questions and scenarios spun in their minds with one agonizing and unanswerable thought whether Louisa, "had leapt into the river, preferring that mode of death to the fire."[36] It was too emotionally painful to even think of the circumstances of Louisa's death.

The images of such events were not foreign to Nathaniel. Nine years earlier, he had witnessed, firsthand, the ravages that drowning placed upon the body when he had volunteered in a search party for a missing nineteen-year-old girl. The events unfolded on the evening of his first wedding anniversary nine years earlier in Concord.[37] A local acquaintance, Ellery Channing, inquired about using Nathaniel's boat to search the river for the missing girl. Her name was Martha whose "bonnet and shoes had already been found."[38]

Nathaniel navigated his small boat in the river for the search. Holding torches illuminating the night darkness, three men, including Channing, searched. They used poles and a rake poking into the dark waters until she was found.[39] Nathaniel was overcome at witnessing the condition of the dead girl's body and later recorded his thoughts in his journal:

> I felt my voice tremble a little ... When close to the bank, some of the men stepped into the water and drew out the body ... I never saw or imagined a spectacle of such perfect horror. The rigidity, above spoken of, was dreadful to behold. Her arms had stiffened in the act of struggling, and were bent before her, with the hands clenched. She was the very image of a death-agony ... But that rigidity!—it is impossible to express the effect of it; it seemed as if she would keep the same position in the grave, and that her skeleton would keep it too ...[40]

Nine years later with such remembrances still in his mind, Hawthorne wrote in similar terms of the drowning death of the fictional character, Zenobia, in his recently completed *Blithedale Romance*:

> Were I to describe the perfect horror of the spectacle, the reader might justly reckon it to me for a sin and shame ... Of all modes of death,

My Dear Sister

methinks it is the ugliest. Her wet garments swathed limbs of terrible inflexibility. She was the marble image of a death-agony … It is impossible to bear the terror of it … as if her body must keep the same position in the coffin, and that her skeleton would keep it in the grave …[41]

Haunted by those images, Nathaniel's mind swirled with terrifying thoughts as he envisioned that his beloved sister had suffered an equally horrible death. His memories of the drowned girl nine years earlier in Concord or his own words in the *Blithedale Romance* may have terrified him enough to caution him from immediately traveling to New York. He found himself living the horror of what he had written. Could he bear to witness Louisa in her final state of death and have that memory etched into his own mind forever? It was all too horrible.

At the disaster site in Riverdale, the air was filled with the residue of burnt wood, smoke, and death. The remnants of the steamboat *Henry Clay* rested on the sand, a dead hulk, serving as a reminder of the tragedy that had occurred. Nearby residents had opened their homes and estates to those who had survived or been injured in the disaster. Other survivors were transported the sixteen miles by train or steamboat to New York City for medical attention or a safe place to sleep. As survivors were sheltered somewhere, family members searched for their missing loved ones, either by walking along the sand of Riverdale's beach or inquiring door-to-door at nearby homes.

The newspapers compiled their own lists of the dead,

missing, and survivors so that relatives and friends unable to travel to the scene could check for mention of their loved ones. Distraught John Dike miraculously survived the disaster. He had been on deck and could jump onto the beach after the boat reached shore. Spending two days searching unsuccessfully for Louisa, the strain had taken its toll. Louisa was nowhere to be found; there was no word of her from anyone; there was no discovery of any of her personal possessions. It was as if she had vanished. Louisa's name appeared on the list of missing in the newspaper as "Miss Hawthorne."[42]

Dike, overcome from exhaustion and worry, no longer sustained the strength to remain at Riverdale. Before departing the scene, he offered a detailed description of Louisa, mentioning also the Rachel Forrester pin that Louisa had adorning her dress.[43] Dike, accepting the reality, telegraphed his wife, Priscilla, of the circumstances making her "almost distracted" that "Maria is lost."[44] Years before, the Dikes had lost a daughter to illness. Now, Louisa, who had been like a daughter to them was gone, too, from disaster. To lose one child in a lifetime is cruel enough. To lose another is beyond words to comprehend and endure.

Robert Manning, Louisa's trusted cousin and the son of her Uncle Robert and Aunt Rebecca Manning, hurried to Yonkers, New York, where the Inquest into the disaster was proceeding. He had stepped in to relieve Nathaniel from traveling to the horrific scene of his sister's death. As a result, Manning would take care of the affairs regarding Louisa's inquest.[45] Louisa's body had been recovered on Saturday from the waters near the disaster site in Riverdale. It was one day after her brother learned of her death and three days following the disaster. Initially, Louisa had been listed #3 on the *New-York Daily Tribune*'s missing roster.[46] Once her body was recovered and identified, her name appeared #54 on the *New-York Daily Times'* list of those who had been lost:

> 54. Miss Maria L. Hawthorne (sister of Nathaniel Hawthorne, the author) of Salem, Mass.[47]

The official identification of her remains was initially made at the inquest in Yonkers by Edward Lefort, who had been appointed an inquest juror for the investigation into the disaster. He testified using the description provided to him by Louisa's uncle John Dike:

> The body he has seen answered the description in every particular, and a pin was found on her bearing an inscription containing the name Forrester; the body was found this afternoon, ... by some boatman, who said they found it in the river in the neighborhood of the wreck; her death was doubtless caused by drowning.[48]

Robert Manning arrived at the Inquest courtroom and was prepared to make his own statement. Louisa had cared

---

54. Miss Maria L. Hawthorne, (sister of Nathaniel Hawthorne, the author,) of Salem, Mass.

Maria Louisa Hawthorne, "List of the Dead,"
New-York Daily Times, August 2, 1852

for him and comforted him many years earlier when he was a young child. Louisa, at the time, had been a young woman herself, then about twenty years of age. More than twenty years had passed since he was that child. Now, the adult Manning stood before the inquest jury in a hot and crowded room filled with witnesses, newspaper reporters, court officials, and bystanders. He needed to find the strength to speak, testify, and identify his dear cousin's remains while holding back the grief that pressed heavy upon his grieving heart.

The identification was not an easy task. For three days, Louisa's body had been floating in the brackish, slightly salty Hudson River water under an unforgiving and scorching summer sun. As a result, Manning was unable to recognize his cousin's disfigured face or features. Instead, he identified her clothing, a monogrammed handkerchief with the initial "H" found in her pocket, and the pin on her dress which bore the name "Rachel Forrester."[49] These simple possessions confirmed that this victim was Maria Louisa Hawthorne and that her life had been taken in the disaster:

> I live in Salem, Mass.; am a nurseryman; Miss Hawthorne was my cousin, and I knew her well; she lived in Salem ... she was a sister of NATHANIEL HAWTHORNE, the author, she was a passenger with Mr. Dyke on the *Henry Clay*, on the 28th inst.; she drowned on that occasion; from the description given by the last witness and from the articles found on her body, which I recognize as having belonged to her, I have no doubt of her identity.[50]

My Dear Sister

The account of the testimony printed in the *New-York Daily Times* on August 2, 1852 added a short commentary:

> The witness recognized a breast-pin, marked with the name of 'Rachel Forrester,' a handkerchief marked 'H,' was also found in the deceased's pocket. Witness was authorized by her family to take the body to Salem for burial, and a certificate was accordingly awarded for the purpose.[51]

After the official identification process had been completed, newspaper reports indicated Louisa's body was transferred into a coffin and shipped via Adams & Co's Express to

> *Robert Manning* sworn and examined—I live in Salem, Mass.; am a nurseryman; Miss HAWTHORNE was my cousin, and I knew her well; she lived in Salem; she was between 35 and 40 years of age, and single; she was a sister of NATHANIEL HAWTHORNE, the author; she was a passenger with Mr. DYK 2 on the *Henry Clay*, on the 28th inst.; she was drowned on that occasion; from the description given by the last witness, and from articles found on her body, which I recognize as having belonged to her, I have no doubt of her identity. The witness recognized a breast-pin, marked with the name of "Rachel Forrester," a handkerchief marked "H," was also found in the deceased's pocket. Witness was authorized by her family to take the body to Salem for burial, and a certificate was accordingly awarded for the purpose.

Robert Manning inquest statement,
New-York Daily Times, August 2, 1852

Salem.[52] In death, she would complete the journey that she had commenced from Saratoga Springs a few days prior. Her coffin was shipped downriver from Yonkers to New York City, where, noted by *The New York Herald*, in its August 4, 1852 edition, it had been placed on a steamer bound for Massachusetts:

> The body of Miss M. Hawthorne passed through this city, *en route* by steamboat to Boston for Salem, Mass; it was enclosed in a metallic coffin and in charge of Uriah Lott, sexton of Williamsburg.[53]

> The body of Miss MARIA L. HAWTHORNE, sister of NATHANIEL HAWTHORNE, Esq., the poet, residing at Salem, Massachusetts, who was in company with Mr. JOHN DYKE, (her uncle,) on board of the *Clay*, and lost her life at the time of the disaster was observed at an early hour on Saturday morning, floating upon the surface of the water, near the wreck. The remains were decomposed, to such an extent as to render recognition impossible yet they were identified by Mr. EDWARD LA FORT, one of the Jurors, with whom a full description was left by Mr. DYKE. A metallic coffin was procured by Mr. LA FORT, in which the body was deposited, and will be forwarded to Salem this forenoon, by ADAMS & Co's Express.

Maria Louisa Hawthorne's death,
The New York Herald, August 4, 1852

269

My Dear Sister

A steamboat had taken Louisa's life. Another carried her lifeless body back to her home. Louisa had lost her life far away from Massachusetts as did her father four decades earlier. Unlike her father, however, Maria's body was going home to Salem for the last time. Plans were that she be buried in the Manning plot in the Howard Street Cemetery. For her surviving brother and sister, words were left unsaid, plans unfulfilled, and dreams crushed.

Memories of Louisa were loving and long lasting. Her nephew, Julian Hawthorne, who was only six years old when she died, remembered details about Louisa and years later wrote of her:

> She was a gentle, rather fragile woman, with a playful humor and a lovable nature ... She was a delightful person to have in the house, and her nephew and niece were ardently in love with her.[54]

Very little was noted about Louisa at the time of her death other than the inquest statements and brief mention in several newspaper articles. There do not appear to be surviving notes in Nathaniel's journals or letters written by him or Ebe to fully understand their thoughts about the untimely and tragic death of their younger sister. It was Sophia, Louisa's sister-in-law, who in her letters, recorded the emotions and grief that consumed the family.

Rebecca Manning remembered Louisa as well:

Louisa Hawthorne was a most delightful, lovable, interesting woman—not at all "commonplace," as has been stated. Her death was a great sorrow to all her friends. Her name was Maria Louisa, and she was often called Maria by her mother and sister and aunts.[55]

Louisa was not remembered as an extraordinary writer like her brother, Nathaniel. Nor was she remembered as someone with a great innate yet untapped talent like that of her older sister Ebe. Louisa was not a woman destined to change the world. Her joy was to brighten the lives of those around her. This included her dear and once very lonely brother, Nathaniel.

There are references in Hawthorne's *The House of Seven Gables* to the character, Phoebe, which reflect on the demeanor of Hawthorne's sister Louisa. These were personal qualities that brought sunshine into dismal circumstances, such as when Louisa lived in the old Manning Herbert Street house:

> Young, blooming, and very cheerful face which presented itself for admittance into the gloomy old mansion. It was a face to which almost any door would have been opened of its own accord … But, even as a ray of sunshine, fall into what dismal place it may, instantaneously creates for itself a prosperity in being there, so did it seem altogether fit that the girl should be standing at the threshold. It was no less evidently proper that the door should swing open to admit her …[56]

My Dear Sister

Throughout the stages of their respective lives, Nathaniel had played games with Louisa, run wild with her, and taught her how to fish in Maine. He danced with her, laughed with her, and had quiet conversations with her at afternoon tea. He instilled in her the pleasures of reading and sought out her kindness whenever he needed someone to listen. Nathaniel appreciated the special clothes she had sewn for him and the manner with which she played with his children. He trusted her as a close confidant throughout her life. He chose her to receive his special letters with important news following his marriage and the birth of his children. He enjoyed the occasion of her infrequent visits. She was supposed to visit Nathaniel in Concord in response to his invitation. Instead, she died on the picturesque but disastrous journey to see him.

> The body of Miss M Hawthorne passed through this city, en route by steamboat to Boston, for Salem, Mass. It was enclosed in a metallic coffin, and in charge of Uriah Lott, sexton of Williamsburg.

Maria Louisa Hawthorne's final journey home,
New-York Daily Times, August 2, 1852

Chapter 11

The Spirits of the Hawthornes

"I should miss your father."

—Elizabeth Manning Hawthorne

The dust of John Hathorne's sin-stained bones remains almost forgotten in the ancient graveyard. However, remembrances of his descendants, the Hathorne and Hawthorne family, remain dispersed around Salem. The house where the children of seaman Nathaniel Hathorne were born still exists. The multiple gabled home once owned by Susanna Ingersoll serves as a tribute to Nathaniel Hawthorne, the author, who wrote *The House of the Seven Gables*. The Manning houses on Herbert and Dearborn Streets remain as well as does the house on Mall Street where Nathaniel Hawthorne wrote *The Scarlet Letter*. All retain memorable pieces of history that contribute to the complexion of the town long ago named for "Peace."

Had the dreaded curse that was pressed upon the Hathorne

Nathaniel Hawthorne as a mature man,
published ca. 1883

family in 1692 crossed the centuries to strike against Louisa exactly 160 years later? How could Louisa, who was loved by everyone she knew, be the target of such a tragic happening? Yet, she was dead from a horrible death in a disaster of epic proportions. Her family, including her brother, were thrust into a drowning by sorrow. Was this the curse the family was to bear?

Nathaniel Hawthorne was completely crushed and heartbroken by the death of his sister. His son Julian would recollect years later his father's reaction when given the news of Louisa's death:

> with its bright sunshine and its gloom and terror; Mr. Hawthorne standing erect at one side of the room, with his hands behind him, in his customary attitude, but with an expression of darkness and suffering on his face such as his children had never seen there before ...[1]

Although his mother's death had brought severe anguish to Hawthorne, Louisa's death precipitated another significant bout of intense grief. Hawthorne was in a state of total loss and confusion. Upon learning the incomprehensible news of his siter's death, he needed to be alone with his thoughts. His son recollected:

> After a while Mr. Hawthorne went out, and was seen no more that day. It was a blow that struck him to the heart; but he could never relieve himself with words.[2]

My Dear Sister

Since his cousin Robert Manning was the family member present at the inquest in New York, Hawthorne was spared the gruesome memory of seeing his beloved sister's defaced body. Louisa's closed coffin was subsequently returned to the town where she was born and had lived most of her life. Once learning of the funeral arrangements, Hawthorne rushed to Salem from his house in Concord to be present one last time for his younger sister. Unfortunately, too late upon arrival, he had missed the funeral. All he could do was look at the recently dug dirt on Louisa's freshly covered grave in the Howard Street Cemetery. She had been buried near her mother on the morning of August 3, 1852. That afternoon, Hawthorne stood there as he had stood for his mother's burial three years earlier almost to the day. Louisa had been standing beside him then. Now, she too was buried beneath Salem soil. Hawthorne would never see her face again, but his memory held the image of the Louisa he had always loved.

Hawthorne filled the dark days after Louisa's death in the same way he had passed the days after his mother's death—with writing. This time, he did not produce another outstanding American novel. He endeavored to write a campaign biography for his dedicated and long-time Bowdoin College friend, Franklin Pierce, who was running for President of the United States. The country had become much larger by that time. Vast lands had been ceded to the United States after the Mexican War ended in 1848. Gold had been discovered in California, beckoning daring prospectors with hopes of instant wealth. The continental United States stretched from the Atlantic Ocean to the Pacific, adding miles of new western coastline. By 1850 the United States consisted of 31 states and several massive territories.

In the throes of grief, Hawthorne picked up his pen and pursued the work of writing in a genre outside his creative realm. The biography was an extremely difficult undertaking for him, but he persevered for Pierce. The work itself, shadowed by the recent death of his sister, proved a strain on Hawthorne's composure. His frustration became evident in his letters to his publisher.

He wrote to William Tichnor on August 22, 1852, only three weeks after Louisa's death that "I'll be d—d if I mean to finish it at all."[3] In another note, he wanted Tichnor to pursue more promotion of the biography, "I think you must blaze away a little harder in your advertisement."[4] In a third letter that month, he informed Tichnor that, "Of course, I shall likewise wish to see the proofs, but I shall probably see you before this is in type. I shall leave for Down East on Wednesday … "[5]

That trip "Down East" was to the Isle of Shoals, an array of small islands located off the coast of New Hampshire. Waiting for Hawthorne's arrival was the fresh salt air of the coastline to clear his head and improve his health. Hawthorne extensively documented his stay in his journal. He set sail for the Isle of Shoals on August 30th, landing at Appledore to check in at Laighton's Hotel. He "delivered a letter of introduction from Pierce."[6] His reservation may have already provided him a room, but this letter assured him of "obtaining the best accommodations that were to be had. I found that we were expected, a man having brought the news of our intention the day before."[7]

Once settled, Hawthorne spent days observing and interacting with various characters on the island. These assorted people provided him an introduction to others who gladly gave him a personal tour of the island's notable features. On Sunday, September 5, as he awaited Pierce's arrival, Hawthorne wrote:

> To-day I have done little or nothing except to roam along the shore of the island, and to sit under the piazza, talking with Mr. Laighton or some of his half-dozen guests.[8]

Then, "Pierce arrived before dinner ..."[9] Hawthorne needed a close friend at his time of grieving for his sister, and Pierce obliged but stayed only briefly. The two could talk and reminisce as if no time had passed since their college days. The encounter served to settle Hawthorne's mind even if only temporarily. Hawthorne, who was a celebrity himself, noted in his journal, "The islanders stared with great curiosity at Pierce."[10]

He sent a letter to Tichnor that, "Pierce arrived here, last night, and returns to the Main land to-day ... I find my health greatly improved."[11] Hawthorne stayed at the hotel for several additional days as he further explored the islands. He visited a lighthouse and the seashore, which quieted the author's nerves and offered him a place of solitude for his thoughts. His visit to The Isle of Shoals may have relieved temporarily some of his despondency over Louisa's death and set Hawthorne's mind on a new course looking forward.

Ebe, leaning on her practical and calculated personality,

fared surprisingly well after Louisa's death. A few weeks later in September while she made a very infrequent visit to Salem, she wrote to her brother, revealing, "In Beverly I can do exactly as I choose, and even appear to be what I am, in a great degree. They are sensible and liberal-minded people, though not much cultivated."[12] She was quite satisfied with her life writing, "I can lose myself in the woods by only crossing the road, and the air is very pure and exilerating, and the sea, but a mile distant."[13]

The following months brought traditional holidays to the Hawthorne home with Thanksgiving, Christmas, and New Year's Day—all without Louisa. There were no longer the letters sent to Louisa for sharing news or invitations for her to visit. However, there were indications that Nathaniel's broken heart was being healed. As in the manner after his mother's death, he needed to address the necessities of his life and support his family into the future.

Franklin Pierce, his Bowdoin friend who had already achieved considerable renown, had been elected President of the United States. With that office came the ability to grant political appointments and with this authority, Pierce offered the Consulship to Liverpool, England, to Hawthorne.[14] Hawthorne needed employment, but he also needed a big change in his life. He and Sophia had mused about the beauty of Italy, which they had only seen in paintings and books. This assignment in Liverpool would bring them to the doorstep of all Europe.

Hawthorne accepted this prestigious and influential job offer a year after Louisa's death. He left his house in Concord in 1853 and along with his family embarked on a new

My Dear Sister

> **The Consul at Liverpool.**
>
> Speaking of NATHANIEL HAWTHORNE, and his snug provision in the Liverpool Consulship, the *Post* says:
>
> "The appointment will emancipate his mind and pen, and hereafter he will be in a condition to do fuller justice to his genius and resources, perhaps, than he has ever yet been able to do. He is just at the age when WALTER SCOTT first created a sensation as a novelist; and there is no reason why the last half of his life should not be as brilliant."

Hawthorne's appointment as Consul,
New-York Daily Times, March 31, 1853

adventure abroad. He crossed the Atlantic Ocean on the steamship *Niagara* to arrive at the country of his forebear, William Hathorne, who had left England for Massachusetts more than two centuries earlier.[15]

Queen Victoria was on the throne, marking the Victorian era. Her husband was Prince Albert. For the Hawthorne's, 19th century metropolitan Liverpool was markedly different from rural Concord. It was a crowded city with significant affluence but contrasted with large numbers of immigrants, working class, and poor trying to make a living. The climate presented its own challenges as well. It took some time for the Hawthorne family to adjust to this new and unfamiliar environment. Hawthorne wrote to his friend William Pike in 1854 that, "My family, however, are beginning to get acclimated, and are much improved in health since I last wrote you."[16]

In December of 1855, Hawthorne, having lived in Liverpool for more than two and a half years, wrote to his sister Ebe. He addressed the letter, "Dear E, ... I am getting tired of Liverpool."[17] He also admonished her for not writing more often, "I don't think it would do you any harm to write oftener."[18] Hawthorne once again had a valid argument since he was monetarily supporting his sister and her chosen life. He asked simply for news from home, something he always longed for throughout his life. The brother and sister were much older now, but the letter writing issue remained the very same problem as in their younger years. They both wanted news but didn't want to write letters. There was an ocean between them, so news took weeks to arrive by letter.

Setting his aggravation aside, Hawthorne shared in his letter that he planned to continue as consul for the term of his assignment. He hoped to save money for an extended stay in Europe, allowing him time to travel with his family and provide an opportunity for him to return to writing. Once again, Hawthorne settled his challenges with focus. He had long ago focused when sequestered in an upstairs chamber to write until he was successfully published. He now focused, along with Sophia, on saving money for a future sojourn in Europe with their children. Sophia's mother had died in 1853 and her father in 1855, so there was no pressing need for Sophia to return home. She and Nathaniel planned for a multiyear long stay in Europe.

By the next year, Hawthorne's own health had suffered during the winter months. He wrote to Tichnor explaining:

My Dear Sister

I feel rather better than when I wrote last, but am not in very good condition. My chief symptoms are the inability to sleep, and disinclination to eat or drink. This heavy and dreary climate affects me dreadfully but I shall do well enough after Spring opens.[19]

The popular newspapers occasionally printed news of Hawthorne's consul work in Liverpool. He may have been more of a celebrity as an American author rather than its consul. Similarly to his days working at the Custom House in Salem, his consulship offered no time for him to seriously sit down and write stories. Four years after arriving in England, he had saved enough money to live comfortably in Europe with his family. Hawthorne, therefore, left his position at the consulate to pursue his own dreams.

The allure of Europe for Hawthorne was one thing, but the additional time spent there was not without trial. Illness often preyed on members of the family. While living in Italy, Una became very ill for several months. She survived with constant attention but suffered from weakened health for the remainder of her shortened life.

Excluding the illnesses that beset the family, Hawthorne's plans had come to fruition. He traveled in Europe and spent much time in Italy. While there, he began work on his novel, *The Marble Faun*, which was published in 1860. It must be noted that a picture of Italy's beautiful Lake of Como had adorned a wall in the "Old Manse" in Concord. Their dream of visiting romantic Italy had become a lived experience.

With clear memories of their wonderful Italian sojourn,

the Hawthorne family traveled back to England and then America in 1860. After a seven-year absence, fifty-six-year-old Hawthorne returned to the one place he had truly felt comfortable—Concord. He returned to his home accompanied by Sophia with their children, Una, now sixteen, Julian at fourteen, and Rose, nine years old.

Hawthorne arrived in an America witnessing the election of Abraham Lincoln to the Presidency in 1860. Shortly thereafter, South Carolina seceded from the Union resulting in the United States coming apart at the seams. The nation was soon at Civil War. Four brutal years of battle, bloodshed, and death would splash across American soil. In Concord, besides the rhetoric from both sides in the war, Hawthorne and his family were safeguarded from any upheaval or danger.

Coming home may have brought painful reminders to Hawthorne that Louisa and his mother were gone. By this time, many of the family members were deceased, both Hathornes and Mannings. Sophia still had her sisters, Mary and Lizzie. The sadness lingering from the loss of loved ones was softened by the years of living overseas, which added new memories to contemplate. In those years, Hawthorne had the chance to write after leaving his consul position. He traveled with his family and with them enjoyed the beauty of another continent.

Hawthorne's sister, Ebe, remained living in Beverly. She missed the children terribly as soon as they left for Europe. She reflected in a letter to Una, "I frequently think of our walks at Concord … Write to me often, and do not wait for me to answer your letters, nor suppose that they make me the less happy because I do not tell you of it by every mail …"[20]

In another letter Ebe wrote, "I wish you and Julian could be here for one day, for a ramble in the woods, which you would enjoy."[21] During those years of their absence, Ebe refused any invitation to travel to Europe to see them. She felt a closeness to her brother's children, but her world centered entirely around the confines of her chosen home.

After returning to Concord, Hawthorne pursued his writing and renewed his long dormant writing partnership with Ebe. She must have been thrilled to restart their collaborations of writing and editing. Her brother sent a letter to her in August of 1860 instructing, "I wish you to correct the proof-sheets, and to be very careful about it. The Essex Institute certainly ought to be grateful to me; for I could get $100 for such an article."[22] Also again, an oversized self-awareness had popped up in Nathaniel's expressions of himself and his self-worth. However, by this time, he had become extremely famous, both nationally and abroad, so it was to be expected.

Ebe eagerly assisted her brother with his endeavors. The activity certainly elicited memories of their collaborations during their youths. As if the intervening years hadn't existed at all, the brother and sister quickly fell back into their effective manner of working together. This time, however, they worked not as children or young adults as in their earlier years. The vibrancy of youth had long passed, with years of maturity between them as they grew older in age.

Ebe visited her brother at his Concord home during the autumn of 1861. This visit was one of the extremely rare visits that she ventured away from her own home. She wrote to her cousin Robert Manning at year end about the trip and complained of the air and the scenery. As she had done her entire life, she took issue with the shortcomings of anywhere she happened to be. She found only Beverly suitable. However, Ebe did enjoy her visit in Concord regardless of the air and scenery, except for one incident. In her letter she mentioned, "Una rowed her father and me across Walden Pond and when we were in the middle of it told me that it was a most dangerous place."[23] Whether Una's escapade was a joke or a serious threat, they all clearly returned safely and dry from the mid-lake adventure.

Hawthorne, still writing and quietly living his life with his family, oversaw several renovations at Wayside. Since he preferred writing on an upper-level floor, he added a second floor to his home complete with a tower to accommodate his study where he worked on writing the last of his stories."[24] When not writing or renovating his house, Hawthorne traveled at times. In early 1862, he journeyed to Washington, D.C. There, he gathered material for his article "Chiefly about War Matters" for the *Atlantic Monthly*.[25]

Almost nine decades had gone by since the Declaration of Independence was signed. Now the fabric of the American experiment was unravelling and divided in battle, North against South. Safety and security anywhere seemed tenuous as soldiers from both sides positioned themselves near the Federal capitol city. While in Washington, D.C., Hawthorne wrote to his daughter Una on March 11, 1862 telling her, "I have arrived safely in Washington, & feel quite well."[26] He assured her that, "I don't think there will be any battle at all--at least, not while I stay here."[27]

Hawthorne's literary fame had served as a curiosity in

My Dear Sister

Washington, D.C., as much as it had in England. Federal doors were graciously opened to him as a result. A few days later, he wrote again to Una, addressing her as "Dear Onion" and writing "I have shaken hands with Uncle Abe, and have seen various notabilities, and am infested by people who want to … [ ] exhibit me as a lion …"[28] Hawthorne had met President Abraham Lincoln. In a letter to his young son Julian, a letter addressed to "Dear Old Boy," his father explained that "I have been employed in the service of my country."[29]

Since returning to Concord from Europe, the author's health had exhibited a slow deterioration which lasted for the remainder of his lifetime. Hawthorne would not live to learn the outcome of the war and that the Union would prevail and survive. He would not know that the famous southern General Lee would surrender to the equally famous northern General Grant at Appomattox in Virginia. Nor would he know that less than a week later, President Lincoln would be dead, a target of assassination at a theater performance he was attending.

Nine months after Hawthorne's trip to Washington, D.C., Sophia wrote to their daughter, Una, "Papa has not a good appetite, and eats no dinners except a little potato. But he is trying to write, and locks himself into the library and pulls down the blinds."[30] As in his youth but now slowed by age and illness, Hawthorne struggled to write. His works were few by this time. One of his last undertakings in 1863 was a book of stories titled, *Our Old Home*, based on his residency in England. Hawthorne's dedication in the book, "To A Friend," was directed to "my dear General," the former U.S. President, Franklin Pierce.[31] Hidden within the paragraphs of this tribute was a message, "farewell, my dear friend …"[32] Within a year, there would be a farewell.

Sophia was extremely concerned about her husband's well-being, writing to Bridge, "I have felt the wildest anxiety about him, because he is a person who has been immaculately well all his life, and this illness has seemed to me an awful dream which could not be true."[33] She had initially been thankful that friend and publisher William Tichnor accompanied her husband on a trip, including to the Astor House in New York City, in order to take "him out of this groove of existence, and intends to keep him away until he is better."[34] The plan came to an abrupt end when Tichnor took ill and died unexpectedly on April 10, 1864.

Tichnor's death hit Hawthorne very hard, and his friends understood how it affected the sick and frail writer. Pierce wrote to Bridge, "Mr. Tichnor's death would have been a great loss and serious shock to H. at any time, but the effect was undoubtedly aggravated by the suddenness of the event and H.'s enfeebled condition."[35] Sophia was consumed with worry.

Historically, this was the time when General Grant and General Lee battled against each other for conquest of the Wilderness in Virginia—North vs. South. As these two war horses clashed, two devoted friends, Hawthorne and Pierce, made plans to travel together to quiet New Hampshire in early May.

A few days later Hawthorne readied for departure from Concord to meet Pierce. Sophia was overcome. She dreaded this planned visit that would take her husband away from her and home, especially following Tichnor's sudden death. Sophia knew that her husband was too sick to travel and didn't want him to leave. She was frightened that this may be the last time she would see him. Possibly, she had a premonition, a nightmare, or at least a foreboding that haunted her heart; Hawthorne may have felt it too. Perhaps, they each knew, but the words were not spoken.

Eight years earlier while living in Liverpool, Hawthorne had written a grateful letter to his friend Bridge:

> It may be superstition, but it seems to me that the bitter is very apt to come with the sweet; and bright sunshine casts a dark shadow ... In this view of the matter I am disposed to thank God for the gloom and chill of my early life, in the hope that my share of adversity came then, when I bore it alone, and that therefore it need not come now, when the cloud would involve those whom I love.[36]

The dying author bore this final journey alone, sparing his family any undue sorrow. Thus, he traveled away from his beloved wife and children as he embarked on this final trip with Franklin Pierce who would later communicate of the author's death.

Horatio Bridge, recovering from an injury, was unable to leave Washington, D.C. He was devastated but had no choice except be absent from the funeral of his dear friend. However, he would later write of the circumstances of Hawthorne's final hours during his fateful journey:

Travelling by easy stages in Pierce's private carriage, they passed through the region so familiar to Pierce until, on the 18th of May 1864, they reached Plymouth, N.H., and stopped at the Pemigewasset House to rest and sleep.

On retiring that last, sad night, they occupied connecting rooms, with the door between them open. Hawthorne slept quietly at first, and Pierce went in two or three times to see to the invalid's comfort. The last time—about four o'clock—he found him lying what seemed to be a quiet sleep; but the heart had ceased to beat. Hawthorne had died—apparently without struggle.[37]

> **Death of Nathaniel Hawthorne.**
> Boston, May 19.—Nathaniel Hawthorne, the author, died to-day.

Death of Nathaniel Hawthorne,
Daily Ohio Statesman, May 20, 1864

As Hawthorne may have wished, Sophia and their children had been spared. They were not with him in New Hampshire to witness his final breaths but home at Wayside. The sorrowful pangs she felt when her husband left Concord a few days earlier had become what she most feared.

Among the necessary announcements that were made, his sister Ebe had been notified of her brother's death. She had

My Dear Sister

declined to attend the funeral writing to Una a self-absorbed explanation:

> The shock was so terrible that I am too ill to make the necessary preparations. I should have been obliged to go to Salem and have a dress made, and to see people. Happy are those who die, and can be at rest. When I look forward I can anticipate nothing but sorrow, few people are so completely left alone as I am—all have gone before me ... But now he will never know

> SUDDEN DEATH. NATHANIEL HAWTHORNE, Esq., the distinguished author, died yesterday morning, at about 3 o'clock, at the hotel in Plymouth. He had been spending some days in Concord with his class-mate and friend of many years, Ex-Pres. Pierce, and both left together on Tuesday morning, in a private carriage, for a journey through a portion of this State and Vermont. Mr. Hawthorne had been ill some time, and, it will be recollected, accompanied the late Mr. Ticknor, of Boston, to Philadelphia, where Mr. T. suddenly died. On this occasion Mr. Hawthorne was traveling for his health. At Plymouth, the room of Mr. H. was adjacent to that of Gen. Pierce, and the latter occasionally went to the bed of Mr. Hawthorne in the night. At 2 yesterday morning he was sleeping quietly, but about an hour afterward, the sufferer was found dead! Mr. Hawthorne was a graduate of Bowdoin College, and was consul at Liverpool during the Presidency of Mr. Pierce. He was about 60 years of age.

Sudden Death. Nathaniel Hawthorne,
New Hampshire Statesman, May 20, 1864

old age and infirmity. I shall always think of him as I saw him in Concord, when he seemed to be in the prime of manhood. It is not desirable to live to be old ...[38]

Pierce wrote to Bridge, "I go to Lowell this afternoon, and shall drive across the county to C. to-morrow evening. I need not tell you how lonely I am, and how full of sorrow."[39] Friends, family, and literary notables gathered in attendance at Hawthorne's funeral as the citizens of Concord grieved for their famous resident writer.

The quiet, fatherless boy and reclusive young man had in adulthood amassed many friends and associates. From college buddies to literary associates, he had earned the respect and admiration of an entire country and from those well beyond its shores. Among Hawthorne's friends who attended the funeral were Franklin Pierce and George Hillard, along with many from the literary community: Henry Wadsworth Longfellow, Ralph Waldo Emerson, James Russell Lowell, and Oliver Wendell Holmes. All came to pay respects to a uniquely gifted author.

Bright sun shone over Concord on the day of the funeral, May 23, 1864, a stark contrast to the mourning hearts of those in attendance. Sophia and her daughters had filled the Unitarian church with fragrant flowers, and Hawthorne's unfinished *Dolliver Romance* had been placed upon the coffin.[40] James Feeman Clarke, who had officiated Nathaniel and Sophia's marriage twenty-two years earlier, performed the funeral service before a stunned and teary-eyed congregation.

Afterward, the funeral procession accompanied

Hawthorne's coffin as it was transported to Sleepy Hollow Cemetery, a fitting place for such an acclaimed author. This burial ground has been known as "America's Westminster Abbey" for all the literary and prestigious notables who would eventually be buried there such as Emerson, Alcott, and Thoreau[41] along with Hawthorne. Another friend, Elizabeth "Lizzie" Peabody, the other Peabody sister to possibly be in love with Hawthorne, would be buried there thirty years into the future.[42]

Hawthorne's gravestone was simple and small with only his last name, "HAWTHORNE" engraved onto its face. A few weeks later Longfellow wrote in tribute, an eloquent poem titled, "Hawthorne" which reflected on the loss for humanity of a gifted author who left stories never to be completed or written.

Years before their marriage while they were secretly engaged, Hawthorne had written to Sophia of their unique bond:

> When we shall be endowed with spiritual bodies, I think they will be so constituted that we may send thoughts and feelings any distance, in no time at all, and transfuse them warm and fresh into the consciousness of those we love. Oh, what happiness it would be, at this moment, if I could be conscious of some purer feeling, some more delicate sentiment, some lovelier fantasy, than could possibly have had its birth in my own nature, and therefore be aware that you were thinking through my mind and feeling

through my heart! Perhaps you possess this power already.[43]

Only the spirit world may attest to such a truth. In the real world, however, after her husband's death, Sophia stayed at Wayside for a few years raising her children and editing her husband's notebooks. She continued her correspondence with Bridge and was grateful for his remembrances of her husband. She wrote to him a year after her husband's death:

> I hope you are well, dear Mr. Bridge. Those friends of my husband's whom he loved so faithfully are very precious to me. There were but few—you and Gen'l Pierce the chief. But I feel vital interest in your and in his health and well-being.[44]

Sophia eventually moved to Germany for her son Julian's education and then relocated again to England. There, she continued editing her husband's personal journals for publication. Sophia died at age sixty-one in England on February 26, 1871, almost seven years after her beloved husband's death. It will never be known if the loving pair shared such a power as described in Hawthorne's letter written long ago. Her place of rest was an ocean apart from her husband as Sophia was buried in England. Their daughter, Una, wrote of her mother's funeral:

> On Saturday we followed her to Kensal Green, and she was laid there on a sunny hillside looking

towards the east. We had a head and foot stone of white marble, with a place for flowers between, and Rose and I planted some ivy there that I had brought from America, and a periwinkle from papa's grave. The inscription is,—*Sophia, wife of Nathaniel Hawthorne;* and on the foot-stone, "I am the Resurrection and the Life."[45]

In a letter of condolence Ebe sent to her now-grown nieces, Una and Rose, she told them, "My heart aches for you."[46] Ebe added that if they were in America she would care for them and sincerely expressed her affection for them. The children had somehow drawn out of her a deep love for them as she expressed, "But remember my dear child, that as much as any one not your mother can, I love you, both of you …"[47] Hawthorne's children were all Ebe had left. Over the years Ebe wrote long and detailed letters to Una reminiscing about her brother's young life. This exercise may have allowed Ebe to relive the incidents in their lives that she remembered and held close to her heart.

Una's life could have been the subject of a tragic figure in one of her father's stories. Long suffering from ill health, she endured the sudden death of the man she was planning to marry, Albert Webster. With her hopes and plans extinguished, Una became a Church of England "district visitor" working with the sick in England and died unexpectedly at the Protestant Convent at Clewer on September 10, 1877.[48] She was thirty-three years of age, coincidentally the same age as her grandfather, Nathaniel Hathorne, when he succumbed to yellow fever. As with her grandfather and mother, Una also

THE SPIRITS OF THE HAWTHORNES

died an ocean away from Massachusetts. She was buried next to her mother in England. Una's death must have been very difficult for Ebe. One by one, she was losing those closest to her.

Hawthorne's two younger children also suffered serious setbacks in their own lives as well. Rose had married but endured a very difficult union with her husband George Parsons Lathrop. She lost her only child, a son, when he was small. Following in her father's footsteps, she, as well as her husband, both engaged in the authorship of books. Following a marital separation from her husband and his subsequent death, Rose trained as a nurse. She became a Catholic nun and devoted herself to caring for the seriously ill in aptly named Hawthorne, New York. At seventy-five years of age, Rose, known as Mother Mary Alphonsa, died July 9, 1926 on what would have been her parents 84th wedding anniversary.

Her brother Julian became a writer, married, and was the father of several children. He wrote authoritative books about his famous father's life and career. In addition, he wrote numerous novels and short stories. He gained negative notoriety, however, when he was convicted of involvement in a mining scandal and sentenced to prison for a year. Julian, the remaining child of Nathaniel and Sophia Hawthorne, died in San Francisco, California on July 21, 1934 at eighty-eight years of age.

It appeared that the romantically handsome Hawthorne and his beloved Sophia would spend their eternities buried on separate continents. It was the same circumstance as Hawthorne's own mother and father. His mother was buried in Salem, his father buried somewhere in South America or at sea. However, in the summer of 2006, the remains of Sophia and Una were disinterred from Kensal Green in England. They were returned to Concord and buried next to Hawthorne's grave in Sleepy Hollow Cemetery in a reverential ceremony.

Hawthorne's surviving sister, Ebe continued to live her chosen solitary life. It was this characteristic that had often been attributed to the entire Hathorne family. For more than thirty years, Ebe contentedly resided in a rented room in Beverly supported by the monies set aside by her brother.[49] Nathaniel Hawthorne had fulfilled his mother's deathbed directive to take care of his sisters. Sophia, dutifully following her husband's death, sent money to Ebe who was curiously grateful. Ebe wrote:

> My Dear Sophia, I am very much obliged by your kind punctuality in sending me the money, which arrived, as it always does when I was much in need of it.[50]

Ebe, like Nathaniel, loved reading books but disliked corresponding. "I dislike letter writing quite as decidedly as you do,"[51] she once wrote to her cousin Robert Manning. Also like her brother, Ebe enjoyed a love of nature. She took long solitary walks, especially by the seashore. She loved intellectual study and writing and had often given her brother assistance with both. Nathaniel recognized Ebe's writing abilities. He once wrote to his sister, Louisa, years earlier:

> I wish Elizabeth will write a book ... She surely knows as much about children as I do ... I do

hope she will think of a subject ... and set to work ... It will be ... profitable to us all.[52]

It is curious that Ebe did not take up this endeavor. Once *The Scarlet Letter* had been published, Nathaniel had strong connections in the publishing world to assist her with her own manuscript. By the mid-1800's, women authors were getting noticed and published like Louisa May Alcott, Harriett Beecher Stowe, George Eliot (Mary Ann Evans), and Charlotte Bronte. Nevertheless, Ebe declined her brother's suggestion for a gainful authorship in her own name.

In addition, Ebe held no inclination to teach children or operate a school like Lizzie and Mary Peabody. She also was uninterested in running a bookshop or publishing which Lizzie Peabody had been involved. With Ebe's level of self-education, she could have accomplished such occupations. Ebe appeared to have little interest in outside productive work, except helping her brother and writing with him. Louisa, on the other hand, was productive with domestic pursuits and family obligations. Ebe seemed to be more attuned to observation, writing long and detailed letters to her relatives and acquaintances about a myriad of topics. Instead of pursuing what would have been an opportunity for a capable and educated woman in the intellectual world, Ebe chose to follow her mother into seclusion.

As a result, Ebe did not write a book. She spent the rest of her life after her brother's death contemplating the memories she had of him. Her extensive correspondence recorded the incidents of her brother's life as well as her own. Her letters and any stories determined to be hers are her bequest to humanity. Rightfully, the letters penned by her sister serve as Louisa's legacy. The surviving letters written by these two sisters, of opposing personalities, remain a significant contribution to the study of Hawthorne and the Hawthorne family. In her elder years, Ebe was thankful for her reminiscences of her brother. She kept him alive for herself with her memories:

> It is a great pleasure to me, now, that my Brother came here, and walked about, and left the memory of his presence in many spots, which will be always associated with him, and him alone, in my mind.[53]

Ebe's sources of consolation after her brother's death were his three children with whom she felt a deep closeness. Her relationship with them was largely maintained through letters, especially while they lived in Europe and through the last years of her life. She often longed to see them, but she rarely left her home. Over the years, Ebe allowed her nearly perfect seclusion to be interrupted by an occasional visitor or a visit to close environs until the day arrived when she wrote, "I am afraid I shall never have energy enough to go to Boston."[54] She was 74 years old.

Regardless of her civility toward Sophia in later years, Ebe maintained her aversion toward her sister-in-law for almost half a century. She blamed Sophia for her brother's and Una's frail health and took the opportunity to mention that to the Mannings:

> But for the troubles of Una's life her Mother is actually responsible, because it was the Roman fever that ruined her constitution, and that she

owed to her abode at Rome, where her Mother kept her family that she might gratify her own love of art; permanently injuring also her husband's health by the same means ...[55]

Ebe lived her life as she desired as much as custom of that era would allow. She never married, most likely by her own design, and organized her time as she wished. She admitted years earlier, in a letter to Sophia, just before her marriage to Nathaniel that:

> I confess I should not have courage to incur any responsibility not forced upon me by circumstances beyond my control. I should not like to feel as if much depended upon me. In this, however, I am aware how much I differ from almost every one else, and how strange it must appear to you, especially just now.[56]

In her childhood, Ebe lived within very fortunate circumstances. The Mannings completely supported her until she was a grown woman. Once her brother became more financially stable, he stepped in to support his sisters and his mother. He also made the necessary arrangements for Ebe to receive money after his own death. If it was not for the privileged situation she had with her relatives, Ebe could have spent her life struggling to make a living for herself. One must ponder if she ever fully realized the gratitude she should have exhibited toward her family and her brother for providing her the best life to do as she pleased.

Hawthorne had been well-aware of his older sister's

peculiarities, especially of her desire for seclusion. He had exhibited the same traits as had his mother. Seclusion and melancholy seemed to impose upon their daily lives, and Hawthorne incorporated such characteristics in some of his stories. He recorded an idea for a story in his journal, "A change from a gay young girl to an old woman; the melancholy events …"[57]

In "The White Old Maid," he wrote "She dwelt alone, and never came into the daylight, except to follow funerals … She is but a shadow!"[58] In another story, "Sylph Etherege," he penned, "and her guardian's secluded habits had shut her out from even so much of the world as is generally open to maidens of her age."[59]

Continuing along the same theme, he may have incorporated a reference to either his mother's or Ebe's particular seclusion in the description of his character, Hepzibah, in his novel *The House of the Seven Gables*:

> So—with many a cold, deep heart-quake at the idea of at last coming into sordid contact with the world, from which she had so long kept aloof, while every added day of seclusion had rolled another stone against the cavern-door of her hermitage …[60]

Despite her age, Ebe maintained her unique sense of humor. She wrote to her cousin Robert Manning, still with her critical and biting edge, yet with a touch of humor that:

> I must not forget to tell you that the name of Montserrat has been changed to Centreville; we

were formerly, to the great disgust of all dwellers of the region, except myself, called Ratters, now we are Villens—Centrevillens; an appellation full good enough for people who are so wanting in taste and ingenuity as to be dissatisfied with a good old name, and yet unable to find a tolerable new one.[61]

Ebe, satisfied with her home, clearly, took issue with the residents who also resided in Beverly. She had not changed. Decades earlier she had also loved Raymond, Maine, but had harbored dissatisfaction toward her neighbors in that village as well.

Elizabeth Hawthorne's name appeared on the 1870 Federal census for Beverly, Massachusetts, as a woman with no occupation or monetary assets.[62] It is curious she should be casting verbal stones at the neighbors considering her position. It was her brother who had provided her with a comfortable life, yet in her mind, she lived a pauper.

She wrote to her cousin, Richard Manning:

> There is Vanderbilt, whose daughter you know is married to a "far away cousin" of mine ... do you think that if I were to write and ask him for an indefinite sum that he would respond liberally. If I were to tell him the precise truth, that I have to live upon about two hundred dollars a year, and <u>that</u> is a slight degree precarious, and that though I know pretty well how to economize, I am utterly destitute of the ability to earn, and that it would be a great pleasure to me to

spend money if I had it ... but if he sent me three or four thousands I should not be in the least ashamed to have every one know it, for it would be pronounced the only sensible thing I ever did.[63]

In lieu of a receipt of such a windfall from the Vanderbilts, Ebe begged her cousin Richard for thirty dollars![64]

Occasionally still venturing a visit to Salem, Ebe, in December of 1882, made plans with the Mannings, "I hope to be able to come to Salem at least before new Year's Day. I want to go to the Shops."[65] If Ebe was able to make that trip, it was her last outside of Beverly. A few days later Ebe's life came to an end in her rented room on New Year's Day, 1883. She was 80 years old.

She had outlived her famous brother by nineteen years and her sister Louisa by thirty-one years. She also outlived her landlords, Mr. and Mrs. Cole, with whom she had boarded for decades. When the Cole's house was sold to the Appletons, Ebe was included with the house in the real estate transaction and remained there in her rented room until her death.[66] Interestingly, her brother had foretold his sister's death in his story, "The Sister Years," as he had written in his story that the old sister was gone at New Year's Day. Elizabeth Hawthorne died as she had willfully lived in her self-imposed, almost completely solitary existence.

Witches and ghosts and supernatural beings intruded insidiously into the lives of Ebe and her brother. She admitted that she "excessively admired Milton's Satan."[67] Hawthorne had been preoccupied since childhood with the prospects of

HAWTHORNE'S SISTER.

Death of Miss Elizabeth Manning Hawthorne, at the Age of Eighty.

Salem Special to Boston Advertiser, Jan. 1.

Miss Elizabeth Manning Hawthorne, the oldest sister of Nathaniel Hawthorne, died yesterday at the residence of Mr. Appleton, at Mont Serrat, Beverly, Mass., at the age of eighty years. She has lived a retired life for the past thirty years in the old homestead where she died. She was the oldest child of Nathaniel and Elizabeth Manning Hawthorne, whose children were Elizabeth Manning, Nathaniel, the poet, and Maria Louise Hawthorne. The youngest sister was lost on the steamer Henry Clay, several years ago. Elizabeth was a lady of pronounced literary tastes and liberal culture. She was a writer, and was given to much study, but so far as is known, has never given any of the fruits of her genius to the world. She was two years older than her gifted brother, who often said of her, that she could attain greater fame than he had done if she would apply herself to literary pursuits. An ardent admirer of nature, she was content to retire among the woods and flowers which she loved. She came to reside with the family of the late Samuel Coles in the house in which she died, outliving the Coles family and descending with the homestead to the present occupants. She was not a lady of large acquaintance, nor a deeply religious person, but she was possessed of excellent qualities of character and sound literary judgment, for which she was held in high esteem by all who were brought in contact with her. Her home was a delightful resort for admirers of Hawthorne and people of culture. Her last illness was very brief. She was ill but a few days before her death.

Hawthorne's Sister,
The Indianapolis Journal, January 5, 1883

witches and curses. These were topics in some of his writings, and he seemed perplexed, if not haunted, by the legends of the Hathorne family history. Oddly, his sister, Ebe, died in a strange seclusion, Louisa's death was untimely, and Hawthorne's after a long undetermined illness. Did the witch's curse come for them too?

It appeared that their sister, Louisa, was not troubled in her lifetime with such other unworldly creatures. For the most part, she lived in the present, savoring life's special moments. It will never be known if the dreaded witch's curse had caused her life to be taken in the fury of a terrible disaster. However, during Louisa's own life, she had lived a grateful and happy existence where her companions were numerous loving relatives and friends.

Hawthorne apparently suffered years of declining health which finally took his life in the springtime of 1864 at age 60. The aspirations of Spring may have freed him from his illnesses and from the curse of the ghosts that had haunted him. He once wrote:

> Thank Providence for Spring! The earth—and man himself, by sympathy with his birth-place—would be far other than we find them, if life toiled wearily onward, without this periodical infusion of primal spirit.[68]

Springtime may have erased the personal ghosts from his memory to bring Nathaniel peace in death. Yet, regardless of those ghosts, possibly in a certain way with their help, Hawthorne became an admired American author. His stories are the stories of early New England, of persecutions and witches, folklore and myth. Many of his stories are based upon his personal experiences or the result of his family history. Others are products of his extraordinary imagination. Nathaniel Hawthorne had written about so many American themes, all quite vividly. Reflecting upon his life, it becomes clear that his was an appropriate occupation for someone born on the Fourth of July.

There is no question that Hawthorne loved both his sisters, Elizabeth and Maria Louisa, despite their personal and personality differences. His sisters, in turn, held a life-long affection toward their brother. They read together, walked together, and played together as children. As they matured, the boundaries in their lives changed and their relationship changed as well. Sometimes, these lifelong adjustments served to cause great emotional stress for each of them. However, no matter their behavior, Hawthorne never abandoned his sisters. Frequently, he needed to practice great patience in dealing with them, and they, in turn, with him.

After the brother and his two sisters had each entered eternity at fate's decided own time, it may be pondered if Nathaniel would walk again with his sisters, as he long ago had written:

> On a pleasant afternoon of June, it was my good fortune to be the companion of two young ladies in a walk …[69]

My Dear Sister

The memories of their lives were documented in handwritten letters, securely sealed in envelopes, and mailed across the distant miles. Written over decades of lifetime, these letters serve as a tribute to the individuality and devotion a brother and two sisters held toward each other. Throughout the years of his life, Nathaniel Hawthorne wrote letters to his sisters including the news of his life, the milestones, his plans, his thoughts. And lovingly addressed them to—

"My Dear Sister …"

Acknowledgements

My husband, Kornel A. Krechoweckyj, for his love, support, and assistance during the many years of my researching, writing, and rewriting this project. For the miles we traveled for researching and site visits. For his expert photography and the hours he spent researching images and using his design and graphic skills for those incorporated into this book. For his computer assistance whenever the computer exacted its revenge for my typing on it.

My editors Andi Cumbo and Caroline Topperman of Mountain Ash Press for their guidance and assistance in making the publication of this book possible.

Tamara Gaydos, Manuscripts Librarian, Phillips Library of the Peabody Essex Museum, Salem, Massachusetts, regarding articles written by Manning Hawthorne for the *Essex Institute Historical Collection* and selected letters from the Nathaniel Hawthorne Papers.

Britta Karlberg, Reference Librarian, Phillips Library of the Peabody Essex Museum, Salem, Massachusetts, for copies of articles written by Manning Hawthorne for the *Essex Institute Historical Collection* and for copies of selected letters from the Nathaniel Hawthorne Papers.

Irene V. Axelrod, Head Research Librarian, Phillips Library of the Peabody Essex Museum, Salem, Massachusetts for copies of selected letters from the Nathaniel Hawthorne Papers.

Kat Stefko, Director, George J. Mitchell Department of Special Collections & Archives, Bowdoin College Library,

Brunswick, Maine, regarding selected letters from the Manning Hawthorne Collection.

Richard Lindemann, George J. Mitchell Department of Special Collections & Archives, Bowdoin College Library, Brunswick, Maine, for copies of selected letters from the Manning Hawthorne Collection.

Olga Tsapina, Norris Foundation Curator of American Historical Manuscripts, The Huntington Library, San Marino, California, regarding selected letters from the Nathaniel Hawthorne Papers.

James D. Parillo, Executive Director, Saratoga Springs History Museum, Saratoga Springs, New York, regarding information related to the Columbian Spring and Columbian Spring Hotel in Saratoga Springs, New York.

Doris Lamont, Archivist, Historical Society of Saratoga Springs, Saratoga Springs, New York, for copies of information regarding the Columbian Spring and Columbian Spring Hotel.

Amy Waywell, formerly of the *The House of the Seven Gables* in Salem, Massachusetts, for her interest in my research and writings about Maria Louisa Hawthorne's death and arranging a speaking engagement at *The House of the Seven Gables.* The enthusiasm received that evening prompted my husband to suggest that I consider writing this book.

The staff of *The House of the Seven Gables* for their interest in my work and for the opportunity to learn more about the history and the features of the house.

The staff of The Old Manse and the Wayside, both in Concord, Massachusetts, and both former residences of Nathaniel Hawthorne, for pointing out certain features in both historic houses.

And, to all my wonderful friends who listened to me and encouraged me during the many years of this endeavor.

Photography and Illustrations

Chapter 1
Birthplace of Nathaniel Hawthorne. Union Street, Salem, Massachusetts. Photography by Kornel A. Krechoweckyj, 2024.

Chapter 2
Richard Manning House. Herbert Street, Salem Massachusetts. Photography by Kornel A. Krechoweckyj, 2024.

Chapter 3
Betsey Hathorne House, Raymond, Maine. Photography by Kornel A. Krechoweckyj, 2024.

A View of Sebago Lake in Maine. Photography by Kornel A. Krechoweckyj, 2024.

Chapter 4
Old Books with Candle, Photography by Kornel A. Krechoweckyj, 2024.

Chapter 5
The Miriam and Ira D. Wallach Division of Art, Prints and Photographs: Print Collection, The New York Public Library. "Bowdoin College Brunswick, Me." New York Public Library Digital Collections. Accessed August 11, 2024. https://digitalcollections.nypl.org/items/510d47d9-7c8b-a3d9-e040-e00a18064a99.

Chapter 6

Betsey Hathorne House on Dearborn Street. Salem, Massachusetts. Photography by Kornel A. Krechoweckyj, 2024.

Susanna Ingersoll House which became famous as the *House of the Seven Gables.* Salem, Massachusetts. Photography by Kornel A. Krechoweckyj, 2024.

Chapter 7

Phillibrown, Thomas, engraver. *Nathaniel Hawthorne,* 1851. [Published] Photograph. https://www.loc.gov/item/93507969.

Gravestones of Hathorne family Members. Old Burying Point Cemetery. Salem, Massachusetts. Photography by Kornel A. Krechoweckyj, 2024.

Marriages. Hill's New Hampshire Patriot, Concord, New Hampshire, July 14, 1842. https://www.loc.gov/item/sn84022903/1842-07-14/ed-1/.

Chapter 8

The Old Manse. Concord, Massachusetts. Photography by Kornel A. Krechoweckyj, 2024.

The Old North Bridge over the Concord River. Concord, Massachusetts. Photography by Kornel A. Krechoweckyj, 2024.

Chapter 9

Salem Custom House. Salem, Massachusetts. Photography by Kornel A. Krechoweckyj, 2024.

Mall Street house, Salem Massachusetts. Photography by Kornel A. Krechoweckyj, 2024.

Notice for *The Scarlet Letter. Republican Herald* [volume] (Providence [R. I.]) 20 March 1850. Chroniciling America: Historic American Newspapers. From the Library of Congress. https://chroniclingamerica.loc.gov/lccn/sn83021460/1850-03-20/ed-1/seq-3/.

Review of *Hawthorne's Celebrated Romance: The Scarlet Letter*. *New-York Daily Tribune*. [volume] (New-York [N.Y.]), 03 June 1850. Chronicling America: Historic American Newspapers. From the Library of Congress. https://chroniclingamerica.loc.gov/lccn/sn83030213/1850-06-03/ed-1/seq-5/.

Notice for *The House of the Seven Gables* in Choice Books—Ticknor, Reed. *New-York Daily Tribune*. [volume] (New-York [N.Y.]), 27 November 1850. Chronicling America: Historic American Newspapers. From the Library of Congress. https://chroniclingamerica.loc.gov/lccn/sn83030213/1850-11-27/ed-1/seq-1/.

Chapter 10

Wayside. Concord, Massachusetts. Photography by Kornel A. Krechoweckyj, 2024.

Hawthorne, Nathaniel, Letter from Nathaniel Hawthorne to Maria Louisa Hawthorne, June 18, 1852, Nathaniel Hawthorne Papers, MSS 68, Box 1, Folder 4. Phillips Library, Peabody Essex Museum.

Bierstadt, Charles. photographer, Columbian Spring, Saratoga. Saratoga Springs, New York, None. [Niagara Falls, N.Y.: C. Bierstadt, Manufacturer of Stereoscopic Views, between 1860-1890] Photograph. https://www.loc.gov/item/2018651558/.

Fourth Day Testimony. *New-York Daily Times*. August 2, 1852.

Incidents-Further Particulars. *New-York Daily Times*. August 2, 1852.

List of the Dead. *New-York Daily Times*. August 2, 1852.

The Henry Clay Calamity. *The New York Herald*. (New York, NY) August 4, 1852. https://www.loc.gov/item/sn83030313/1852-08-04/ed-1/.

Chapter 11

Nathaniel Hawthorne. Ca. 1883. Sept. 17. Photograph. https://www.loc.gov/item/2003654007/.

311

The Consul at Liverpool. New-York Daily Times. March 31, 1853.

Sudden Death. Nathaniel Hawthorne. New Hampshire Statesman. (Concord, NH), May 20, 1864. https://www.loc.gov/item/sn84022932/1864-05-20/ed-1/.

Death of Nathaniel Hawthorne. Daily Ohio Statesman. (Columbus, OH), May 20, 1864. https://www.loc.gov/item/sn84028645/1864-05-20/ed-1/.

Hawthorne's Sister. The Indianapolis Journal. [volume] (Indianapolis [Ind.]), January 5, 1883. Chronicling America: Historic American Newspapers. From the Library of Congress. https://chroniclingameerica.loc.gov/lccn/sn82015679/1883-01-05/ed-1/seq-4/.

Bibliography

Bridge, Horatio. *Personal Recollections of Nathaniel* Hawthorne. London: Forgotten Books. 2012. Originally published 1893.

"Columbian Spring." Collected Papers, Saratoga Springs History Museum, Saratoga Springs, New York.

Final Memorials of Henry Wadsworth Longfellow. Edited by Samuel Longfellow. Boston: Ticknor and Company, 1887.

George J. Mitchell Department of Special Collections & Archives. Bowdoin College Library. Brunswick, Maine. Manning Hawthorne Collection, M223.

Hansen, Kris A. *Death Passage on the Hudson: The Wreck of the Henry Clay.* Fleischmanns, NY: Purple Mountain Press, Ltd., 2004.

Hawthorne, Elizabeth Manning. *Elizabeth Manning Hawthorne: A Life in Letters.* Edited and with Introduction by Cecile Anne De Rocher. Tuscaloosa: The University of Alabama Press, 2006.

Hawthorne, Julian. *Hawthorne and His Circle.* New York and London: Harper & Brothers Publishers, 1903.

Hawthorne, Julian. *Nathaniel Hawthorne and his Wife: A Biography.* Vol. 1. 2nd ed. Boston: James R. Osgood and Company, 1885.

Hawthorne, Julian. *Nathaniel Hawthorne and his Wife: A Biography.* Vol. II. Boston and New York: Houghton Mifflin and Company, The Riverside Press Cambridge, 1884.

Hawthorne, Manning. "A Glimpse of Hawthorne's Boyhood." *Essex Institute Historical Collections* 83, no. 2 (April 1947): 178-184.

Hawthorne, Manning. "Hawthorne's Early Years." *Essex Institute Historical Collections* 74, no.1 (January 1938): 1-21.

Hawthorne, Manning. "Maria Louisa Hawthorne." *Essex Institute Historical Collections* 75, no. 2 (April 1939): 103-134.

Hawthorne, Manning, "Parental and Family Influences on Hawthorne." *Essex Institute Historical Collections* 76, no. 1 (January 1940): 1-13.

Hawthorne, Nathaniel. *Passages from the American Note-Books.* Edited by Sophia Hawthorne. Boston and New York: Houghton Mifflin and Company, The Riverside Press, 1883.

Hawthorne, Nathaniel. *Five Novels: Complete and Unabridged.* New York: Barnes & Noble, 2006.

Hawthorne, Nathaniel. *Tales, Sketches, and Other Papers.* Boston and New York: Houghton Mifflin and Company, The Riverside Press Cambridge, 1883.

Hawthorne, Nathaniel, *Tales and Sketches, A Wonder Book for Girls and Boys, Tanglewood Tales for Girls and Boys.* New York: The Library of America, Literary Classics of the United States, Inc., 1982.

Hawthorne, Nathaniel. *The Gentle Boy: A Thrice Told Tale.* Boston: Weeks, Jordan & Co., New York and London: Wiley & Putnam, 1839.

Hawthorne, Nathaniel. *Twice-Told Tales.* Boston and New York: Houghton Mifflin Company, The Riverside Press Cambridge, 1882.

Higginson, Thomas Wentworth. *Henry Wadsworth Longfellow.* Boston and New York: Houghton Mifflin Company, The Riverside Press Cambridge, 1902.

Indianapolis Journal, The. January 5, 1883. https://chroniclingamerica.loc.gov/lccn/sn82015679/1883-01-05/ed-1/seq-4/.

Latimer, George Dimmick. "Salem." In *Historic Towns of New England.* Edited by Lyman P. Powell. 2d ed. New York & London: G.P. Putnam's Sons, The Knickerbocker Press, 1899.

New-York Daily Times. 27 July 1852 to 2 August 1852.

New-York Daily Tribune. 31 July 1852.

New York Herald, The. 4 August 1852.

Osgood, Charles S. and H.M. Batchelder. *Historical Sketch of Salem 1626-1879.* Salem: Essex Institute, 1879.

Phillips Library, Peabody Essex Museum. Salem, Massachusetts, *Nathaniel Hawthorne Papers* (1804-1864). Letters Sent/Letters Received by Nathaniel Hawthorne. MSS68.

Records and Files of the Quarterly Courts of Essex County. Vol. VIII. Essex Institute. 1921.

Records of Salem Witchcraft Copied from the Original Documents. Vol. I and II. Roxbury, Mass: W. Elliott Woodward, 1864.

Stearns, Frank Preston. *The Life and Genius of Nathaniel Hawthorne.* Reprint. LaVergne, TN: DoDo Press, originally published 1906.

The Huntington Library, San Marino, California, *Nathaniel Hawthorne Papers*, Letters of Nathaniel Hawthorne (1822-1863).

The Story of Concord: Told by Concord Writers. Edited by Josephine Latham Swayne. Boston: The E.F. Worcester Press, 1906.

United States Census Records for Essex County Massachusetts. Village of Beverly. 30 June 1870, 116.

Upham, Charles W. Salem. *Witchcraft with an Account of Salem Village and A History of Opinions on Witchcraft and Kindred Subjects.* Vol. I & II. New York: Fredrick Ungar Publishing Company, 1867.

Notes

Preface
1. Manning Hawthorne, "Maria Louisa Hawthorne," *Essex Institute Historical Collections* 75, no. 2 (April 1939): 104.
2. Julian Hawthorne, *Nathaniel Hawthorne and His Wife: A Biography*, Vol. 1, 2d ed. (Boston: James R. Osgood and Company, 1885), 9.
3. Elizabeth Manning Hawthorne to "My dear Mr. Fields," James T. Fields, December 1870, Elizabeth Manning Hawthorne, *A Life in Letters*, edited and with introduction by Cecile Anne De Rocher (Tuscaloosa: The University of Alabama Press, 2006), 141.

Chapter 1
1. J. Hawthorne, *Hawthorne and Wife*, 36.
2. Manning Hawthorne, "Hawthorne's Early Years," *Essex Institute Historical Collections* 74, no. 1 (January 1938), 2-3.
3. Manning Hawthorne, "Parental and Family Influences," *Essex Institute Historical Collections* 76, no. 1 (January 1940): 8.
4. J. Hawthorne, *Hawthorne and His Wife*, 10.
5. J. Hawthorne, *Hawthorne and His Wife*, 10.
6. Nathaniel Hawthorne, "The Gentle Boy," in *Twice-Told Tales* (Boston and New York: Houghton Mifflin, The Riverside Press, Cambridge, 1882), 85.
7. J. Hawthorne, *Hawthorne and His Wife*, 10-11.
8. J. Hawthorne, *Hawthorne and His Wife*, 10.
9. N. Hawthorne, "The Gentle Boy," 85-86.
10. J. Hawthorne, *Hawthorne and His Wife*, 11.
11. J. Hawthorne, *Hawthorne and His Wife*, 24.
12. Charles S. Osgood and H.M. Batchelder, "Salem Witchcraft," in *Historical Sketch of Salem* 1626-1879 (Salem: Essex Institute, 1879), 24.
13. Osgood and Batchelder, "Witchcraft," 26.
14. *Records of Salem Witchcraft, Copied from the Original Documents*, Vol. I (Roxbury, Mass: W. Elliott Woodward, 1864), 11.
15. *Records of Salem Witchcraft*, Vol I, 17.
16. Osgood and Batchelder, "Witchcraft," 30.

17. Osgood and Batchelder, "Witchcraft," 35.
18. Osgood and Batchelder, "Witchcraft," 37.
19. *Records of Salem Witchcraft, Copied from the Original Documents*, Vol. II (Roxbury, Mass: W. Elliott Woodward, 1864), 220-221.
20. *Records of Salem Witchcraft*, Vol. II, 218.
21. Charles S. Osgood and H.M. Batchelder, "Biographical Sketches," in *Historical Sketch of Salem* 1626-1879 (Salem: Essex Institute, 1879), 239; J. Hawthorne, *Hawthorne and His Wife*, 25.
22. J. Hawthorne, *Hawthorne and His Wife*, 9.
23. Charles W. Upham, *Salem Witchcraft with an account of Salem Village and A History of Opinion on Witchcraft and Kindred Subjects*, Vol I and II, (New York: Frederick Ungar Publishing Company, 1867), 268-269.
24. Nathaniel Hawthorne, "The Custom House: Introductory to *The Scarlet Letter*," in *Five Novels: Complete and Unabridged* (New York: Barnes & Noble, 2006), 101.
25. Nathaniel Hawthorne, "Fancy's Show Box," in *Twice-Told Tales* (Boston and New York: Houghton Mifflin Company, The Riverside Press Cambridge, 1882), 250.
26. N. Hawthorne, "The Gentle Boy," 86.
27. N. Hawthorne, "Custom House: Introductory," 101.
28. Inscription transcribed from the tombstone of John Hathorne located at the Salem Burying Point Cemetery (Charter Street Burial Ground) in Salem, Massachusetts.
29. J. Hawthorne, *Hawthorne and His Wife*, 29.
30. J. Hawthorne, *Hawthorne and His Wife*, 29.
31. J. Hawthorne, *Hawthorne and His Wife*, 31-32, 35-36.
32. J. Hawthorne, *Hawthorne and His Wife*, 29-30, 95.
33. J. Hawthorne, *Hawthorne and His Wife*, 95.
34. J. Hawthorne, *Hawthorne and His Wife*, 36; M. Hawthorne, "Influences," 12.
35. J. Hawthorne, *Hawthorne and His Wife*, 36; Manning Hawthorne, "A Glimpse of Hawthorne's Boyhood," Essex Institute Historic Collections 83, no. 2 (April 1947), 179; M. Hawthorne, "Influences," 12.
36. J. Hawthorne, *Hawthorne and His Wife*, 36-37
37. *Records and Files of the Quarterly Courts of Essex County Massachusetts* Volume III, (Salem: Essex Institute, 1921), 87-88; Nathaniel Hawthorne, *Passages from the American Note-Books*, edited by Sophia Hawthorne (Boston and New York: Houghton, Mifflin and Company, The Riverside Press, Cambridge, 1883), 1837.

38. *Records Files of Courts Essex County*, 88.
39. *Records Files of Courts Essex County*, 88-89.
40. M. Hawthorne, "Early Years," 2-3.

Chapter 2

1. M. Hawthorne, "Early Years," 2-3.
2. J. Hawthorne, *Hawthorne and His Wife*, 98, 99.
3. J. Hawthorne, *Hawthorne and His Wife*, 107.
4. M. Hawthorne, "Hawthorne's Boyhood," 181.
5. George Dimmick Latimer, "Salem," in *Historic Towns of New England*. Edited by Lyman P. Powell, 2d ed. (New York & London: G.P. Putnam's Sons, The Knickerbocker Press, 1899), 156.
6. M. Hawthorne, "Influences, 1-2; "Hawthorne's Boyhood," 180; J. Hawthorne, *Hawthorne and Wife*, 36-38.
7. M. Hawthorne, "Hawthorne's Boyhood" footnote #5, 182
8. M. Hawthorne, "Hawthorne's Boyhood," 179-182; M. Hawthorne, "Influences," 5.
9. J. Hawthorne, *Hawthorne and His Wife*, 99.
10. J. Hawthorne, *Hawthorne and His Wife*, 106; M. Hawthorne, "Early Years," 5; Elizabeth M. Hawthorne to James T. Fields, 26 December 1870, Elizabeth Manning Hawthorne, *A Life in Letters*, ed. C. De Rocher (Tuscaloosa: The University of Alabama Press, 2006), 144.
11. M. Hawthorne, "Hawthorne's Boyhood," 179; J. Hawthorne, *Hawthorne and His Wife*, 104; Maria Louisa Hawthorne to "Dear Natty," Salem, June 11, 1841, Julian Hawthorne, *Nathaniel Hawthorne and His Wife: A Biography*, Vol. 1, 2d ed. (Boston: James R. Osgood and Company, 1885), 231.
12. Elizabeth M. Hawthorne to James T. Fields, 13 December 1870, Elizabeth Manning Hawthorne, *A Life in Letters*, ed. C. De Rocher (Tuscaloosa: The University of Alabama Press, 2006), 141; M. Hawthorne, "Early Years," 4.
13. Elizabeth M. Hawthorne to "My dear Mr. Fields," James T. Fields, December 1870, Elizabeth Manning Hawthorne, *A Life in Letters*, ed. C. De Rocher (Tuscaloosa: The University of Alabama Press, 2006), 140.
14. Elizabeth M. Hawthorne to "My dear Una," Una Hawthorne, Montserrat, 20 December 1865, Elizabeth Manning Hawthorne, *A Life in Letters*, ed. C. De Rocher (Tuscaloosa: The University of Alabama Press, 2006), 101.

15. M. Hawthorne, "Early Years" 5-6; M. Hawthorne, "Influences," 9-10.
16. M. Hawthorne, "Hawthorne's Boyhood," 180; M. Hawthorne, "Early Years" 5-6; M. Hawthorne, "Influences," 9-10.
17. J. Hawthorne, *Hawthorne and His Wife*, 100.
18. J. Hawthorne, *Hawthorne and His Wife*, 96; M. Hawthorne, "Early Years," 9.
19. M. Hawthorne, "Maria Louisa" 105; Elizabeth Hathorne to "Dear Uncle" Richard Manning, Salem, 29 May 1815, Elizabeth M. Hawthorne, *A Life in Letters*, ed. C. De Rocher (Tuscaloosa: The University of Alabama Press, 2006), 47.
20. J. Hawthorne, *Hawthorne and His Wife*, 177.
21. M. Hawthorne, "Early Years," 3, 20; M. Hawthorne, "Influences," 10.
22. Maria Louisa Hathorne to "Dear Uncle" Robert Manning, Salem, 25 August 1816, Box 1 Folder 9, Manning Hawthorne Collection, M223, George J. Mitchell Department of Special Collections & Archives, Bowdoin College Library, Brunswick, Maine.
23. M. L. Hathorne to "Dear Uncle," 25 August 1816.
24. M. L. Hathorne to "Dear Uncle," 25 August 1816.
25. M. L. Hathorne to "Dear Uncle," 25 August 1816.
26. J. Hawthorne, *Hawthorne and His Wife*, 5.
27. J. Hawthorne, *Hawthorne and His Wife*, 5.
28. J. Hawthorne, *Hawthorne and His Wife*, 5.
29. Elizabeth M. Hawthorne to "My dear Una" Una Hawthorne, Beverly, 1 March 1865, Elizabeth Manning Hawthorne, *A Life in Letters*, ed. C. De Rocher (Tuscaloosa: The University of Alabama Press, 2006), 94.

Chapter 3

1. M. Hawthorne, "Early Years," 10.
2. M. Hawthorne, "Early Years," 10.
3. Elizabeth M. Hathorne to "Dear Aunt" Mary Manning, Raymond, August 1816, Elizabeth Manning Hawthorne, *A Life in Letters*, ed. C. De Rocher (Tuscaloosa: The University of Alabama Press, 2006), 48.
4. Elizabeth C. Hathorne to "Dear Brother" Robert Manning, Salem, 11 August 1818, Box 1 Folder 11, Manning Hawthorne Collection, M223, George J. Mitchell Department of Special Collections & Archives, Bowdoin College Library, Brunswick, Maine.

5. Maria Louisa Hathorne to "My Dear Uncle" Robert Manning, Salem, 11 August 1818, Box 1 Folder 11, Manning Hawthorne Collection, M223, George J. Mitchell Department of Special Collections & Archives, Bowdoin College Library, Brunswick, Maine.
6. Elizabeth M. Hathorne to "Dear Uncle" Robert Manning, Salem, 24 August 1818, Elizabeth Manning Hawthorne, *A Life in Letters*, ed. C. De Rocher (Tuscaloosa: The University of Alabama Press, 2006), 51.
7. Elizabeth M. Hathorne to "Dear Uncle" Robert Manning, Salem, 18 August 1818, Elizabeth Manning Hawthorne, *A Life in Letters*, ed. C. De Rocher (Tuscaloosa: The University of Alabama Press, 2006), 50.
8. Maria Louisa Hathorne to "Dear Uncle" Robert Manning, Raymond, 22 September 1819, Box 1 Folder 24, Manning Hawthorne Collection, M223, George J. Mitchell Department of Special Collections & Archives, Bowdoin College Library, Brunswick, Maine.
9. J. Hawthorne, *Hawthorne and His Wife*, 95-96.
10. J. Hawthorne, *Hawthorne and His Wife*, 95-96.
11. M. Hawthorne, "Maria Louisa," 123.
12. Elizabeth M. Hathorne to "Dear Aunt" Priscilla Manning Dike, Raymond, 15 December 1818, Elizabeth Manning Hawthorne, *A Life in Letters*, ed. C. De Rocher (Tuscaloosa: The University of Alabama Press, 2006), 53-54.
13. Elizabeth M. Hawthorne to James T. Fields, N.p. 13 December 1870, Elizabeth Manning Hawthorne, *A Life in Letters*, ed. C. De Rocher (Tuscaloosa: The University of Alabama Press, 2006), 141-142.
14. Nathaniel Hawthorne, *The Scarlet Letter in Five Novels: Complete and Unabridged* (New York: Barnes & Noble, 2006), 158; Maria Louisa Hathorne to "Dear Sister" Elizabeth Manning Hathorne, Raymond, 10 April 1822 Box 1 Folder 55, Manning Hawthorne Collection, M223, George J. Mitchell Department of Special Collections & Archives, Bowdoin College Library, Brunswick, Maine; Maria Louisa Hathorne to "Dear Uncle" Robert Manning, Raymond, 19 May 1819 Box 1 Folder 20, Manning Hawthorne Collection, M223, George J. Mitchell Department of Special Collections & Archives, Bowdoin College Library, Brunswick, Maine.
15. Maria Louisa Hawthorne to "Dear Natty" Nathaniel Hawthorne, Salem, 11 June 1841, Julian, Hawthorne, *Nathaniel Hawthorne and his Wife: A Biography*, Vol. 1, 2d ed. (Boston: James R. Osgood and Company, 1885), 232.

16. Maria Louisa Hathorne to "Dear Uncle" Robert Manning, Raymond, 6 January 1819, Box 1 Folder 17, Manning Hawthorne Collection, M223, George J. Mitchell Department of Special Collections & Archives, Bowdoin College Library, Brunswick, Maine.
17. Mary Manning to "Dear Sister" Elizabeth C. Hathorne, Salem, 4 July 1820, Box 1 Folder 30, Manning Hawthorne Collection, M223, George J. Mitchell Department of Special Collections & Archives, Bowdoin College Library, Brunswick, Maine.
18. M. Manning to "Dear Sister" Elizabeth C. Hathorne, 4 July 1820.
19. Mary Manning to "Dear Sister" Elizabeth C. Hathorne, Salem, 18 July 1820, Box 1 Folder 31, Manning Hawthorne Collection, M223, George J. Mitchell Department of Special Collections & Archives, Bowdoin College Library, Brunswick, Maine.
20. Maria Louisa Hathorne to "Dear Uncle" Robert Manning, Raymond, 6 January 1819, Box 1 Folder 17, Manning Hawthorne Collection, M223, George J. Mitchell Department of Special Collections & Archives, Bowdoin College Library, Brunswick, Maine.
21. M. L. Hathorne to "Dear Uncle" 19 May 1819.
22. Elizabeth C. Hathorne to "Dear Brother" Robert Manning, Salem, 19 May 1819, Box 1 Folder 20, Manning Hawthorne Collection, M223, George J. Mitchell Department of Special Collections & Archives, Bowdoin College Library, Brunswick, Maine.
23. E. C. Hathorne to "Dear Brother," 19 May 1819.
24. M. Hawthorne, "Maria Louisa," 107-108; Elizabeth M. Hawthorne to "My dear Una," Una Hawthorne, Montserrat, Dec. 20th, 1865, Elizabeth Manning Hawthorne, *A Life in Letters,* ed. C. De Rocher (Tuscaloosa: The University of Alabama Press, 2006), 100.
25. M. Hawthorne "Maria Louisa," 108-110; Nathaniel Hathorne to "Dear Sister," Elizabeth Manning Hathorne, Salem, October 31st, 1820, Nathaniel Hawthorne Papers MSS 68, Box 1 Folder 1, Phillips Library, Peabody Essex Museum, Salem, Massachusetts.
26. Nathaniel Hathorne to "Dear Sister," Maria Louisa Hathorne, Salem, 28 September 1819, Julian Hawthorne, *Nathaniel Hawthorne and his Wife: A Biography,* Vol. 1, 2d ed. (Boston: James R. Osgood and Company, 1885), 105.
27. N. Hathorne to "Dear Sister," 28 September 1819, 106.
28. Maria Louisa Hathorne to "Dear Uncle" Robert Manning, Raymond, 3 November 1819, Box 1 Folder 25, Manning Hawthorne Collection, M223, George J. Mitchell Department of Special Collections & Archives, Bowdoin College Library, Brunswick, Maine.
29. M. L. Hathorne to "Dear Uncle," 3 November 1819.

30. M. L. Hathorne to "Dear Uncle," 3 November 1819.
31. Elizabeth M. Hathorne to "Dear Uncle" Robert Manning, Raymond, 13 January 1819, Elizabeth Manning Hawthorne, *A Life in Letters,* ed. C. De Rocher (Tuscaloosa: The University of Alabama Press, 2006), 55.
32. Nathaniel Hawthorne, "Snow-Flakes" in *Tales and Sketches* (New York: The Library of America, Literary Classics of the United States, Inc., 1982), 593.
33. Nathaniel Hathorne to "Dear Louisa" Maria Louisa Hathorne, Salem, 21 March 1820, Nathaniel Hawthorne Papers, MSS 68, Box 1 Folder 1, Phillips Library, Peabody Essex Museum, Salem, Massachusetts.
34. N. Hathorne to "Dear Louisa," 21 March 1820.
35. N. Hathorne to "Dear Louisa," 21 March 1820
36. Mary Manning to "Dear Sister" Elizabeth C. Hathorne, Salem, 6 June 1820, Box 1 Folder 29, Manning Hawthorne Collection, M223, George J. Mitchell Department of Special Collections & Archives, Bowdoin College Library, Brunswick, Maine.

Chapter 4
1. Maria Louisa Hathorne to "Dear Mother" Elizabeth C. Hathorne, Salem, 6 June 1820, Box 1 Folder 29, Manning Hawthorne Collection, M223, George J. Mitchell Department of Special Collections & Archives, Bowdoin College Library, Brunswick, Maine.
2. M. Manning to "Dear Sister" 6 June 1820.
3. M. Manning to "Dear Sister," 6 June 1820.
4. M. Manning to "Dear Sister," 6 June 1820.
5. Maria Louisa Hathorne to "Dear Mother" Elizabeth C. Hathorne, Salem, 4 July 1820, Box 1 Folder 30, Manning Hawthorne Collection, M223, George J. Mitchell Department of Special Collections & Archives, Bowdoin College Library, Brunswick, Maine.
6. M. Hawthorne, "Maria Louisa" 115.
7. Nathaniel Hathorne to "Dear Mother," Elizabeth C. Hathorne, Salem, October 31, 1820, Nathaniel Hawthorne Papers, MSS 68, Box 1, Folder 1, Phillips Library, Peabody Essex Museum, Salem, Massachusetts.
8. M. Hawthorne, "Maria Louisa," 115.
9. M. L. Hathorne to "Dear Mother," 4 July 1820.
10. M. Hawthorne, "Early Years," 17.
11. M. L. Hathorne to "Dear Mother," 4 July 1820.
12. Mary Manning to "Dear Sister" Elizabeth C. Hathorne, Salem, 1

August 1820, Box 1 Folder 32, Manning Hawthorne Collection, M223, George J. Mitchell Department of Special Collections & Archives, Bowdoin College Library, Brunswick, Maine.
13. M. L. Hathorne to "Dear Mother," 4 July 1820.
14. Elizabeth C. Hathorne to "Dear Son" Nathaniel Hathorne, Raymond, 9 August 1820, Box 1 Folder 33, Manning Hawthorne Collection, M223, George J. Mitchell Department of Special Collections & Archives, Bowdoin College Library, Brunswick, Maine.
15. Nathaniel Hathorne to "Dear Mother," Elizabeth C. Hathorne, Salem, 25 July 1820, Nathaniel Hawthorne Papers, MSS 68, Box 1, Folder 11, Phillips Library, Peabody Essex Museum, Salem, Massachusetts.
16. N. Hawthorne to "Dear Mother," 25 July 1820.
17. Mary Manning to "Dear Sister" Elizabeth C. Hathorne, Salem, 18 July 1820, Box 1 Folder 31, Manning Hawthorne Collection, M223, George J. Mitchell Department of Special Collections & Archives, Bowdoin College Library, Brunswick, Maine.
18. M. Manning to "Dear Sister." 18 July 1820.
19. Maria Louisa Hathorne to "Dear Mother" Elizabeth C. Hathorne, Salem, 9 August 1820, Box 1 Folder 34, Manning Hawthorne Collection, M223, George J. Mitchell Department of Special Collections & Archives, Bowdoin College Library, Brunswick, Maine.
20. M. L. Hathorne to "Dear Mother," 9 August 1820.
21. E. C. Hathorne to "Dear Son" Nathaniel Hathorne, Raymond, 9 August 1820.
22. E. M. Hawthorne to "My dear Una," Dec. 20, 1865, *Life in Letters*, 101.
23. M. L. Hathorne to "Dear Mother," 9 August 1820.
24. M. L. Hathorne to "Dear Mother," 9 August 1820.
25. M. L. Hathorne to "Dear Mother," 9 August 1820.
26. Elizabeth C. Hathorne to "Dear Maria" Maria Louisa Hathorne, Raymond, 9 August 1820, Box 1 Folder 33, Manning Hawthorne Collection, M223, George J. Mitchell Department of Special Collections & Archives, Bowdoin College Library, Brunswick, Maine.
27. E. C. Hathorne to "Dear Maria," 9 August 1820.
28. Maria Louisa Hathorne to "Dear Mother" Elizabeth C. Hathorne, Salem, 7 September 1820, Box 1 Folder 36, Manning Hawthorne Collection, M223, George J. Mitchell Department of Special Collections & Archives, Bowdoin College Library, Brunswick, Maine.
29. Maria Louisa Hathorne to "Dear Mother" Elizabeth C. Hathorne, Salem, 7 November 1820, Box 1 Folder 38, Manning Hawthorne

Collection, M223, George J. Mitchell Department of Special Collections & Archives, Bowdoin College Library, Brunswick, Maine.
30. M. L. Hathorne to "Dear Mother," 7 September 1820.
31. M. L. Hathorne to "Dear Mother," 7 September 1820.
32. Maria Louisa Hathorne to "Dear Mother" Elizabeth C. Hathorne, Salem, 19 September 1820, Box 1 Folder 37, Manning Hawthorne Collection, M223, George J. Mitchell Department of Special Collections & Archives, Bowdoin College Library, Brunswick, Maine.
33. M. L. Hathorne to "Dear Mother" Salem, 19 September 1820; Mary Manning to "Dear Sister" Elizabeth C. Hathorne, Salem, 19 September 1820, Box 1 Folder 37, Manning Hawthorne Collection, M223, George J. Mitchell Department of Special Collections & Archives, Bowdoin College Library, Brunswick, Maine.
34. M. L. Hathorne to "Dear Mother," 7 November 1820.
35. M. L. Hathorne to "Dear Mother," 7 November 1820; M. Hawthorne, "Maria Louisa," 117.
36. M. L. Hathorne to "Dear Mother," 7 November 1820.
37. M. L. Hathorne to "Dear Mother," 7 November 1820.
38. M. L. Hathorne to "Dear Mother," 7 November 1820.
39. M. L. Hathorne to "Dear Mother," 7 November 1820.
40. Mary Manning to "Dear Sister" Elizabeth C. Hathorne, Salem, 7 November 1820, Box 1 Folder 38, Manning Hawthorne Collection, M223, George J. Mitchell Department of Special Collections & Archives, Bowdoin College Library, Brunswick, Maine.
41. N. Hathorne to "Dear Mother," October 31, 1820, Phillips Library.
42. M. L. Hathorne to "Dear Mother," 7 November 1820.
43. Mary Manning to "Dear Sister" Elizabeth C. Hathorne, Salem, 27 November [1820], Box 1 Folder 39, Manning Hawthorne Collection, M223, George J. Mitchell Department of Special Collections & Archives, Bowdoin College Library, Brunswick, Maine.
44. M. Manning to "Dear Sister," 27 November [1820].
45. Maria Louisa Hathorne to "Dear Mother" Elizabeth C. Hathorne, Salem, 30 January 1821, Box 1 Folder 41, Manning Hawthorne Collection, M223, George J. Mitchell Department of Special Collections & Archives, Bowdoin College Library, Brunswick, Maine.
46. M. L. Hathorne to "Dear Mother," 30 January 1821.
47. M. L. Hathorne to "Dear Mother," 30 January 1821.
48. M. L. Hathorne to "Dear Mother," 30 January 1821.
49. Maria Louisa Hathorne to "Dear Mother" Elizabeth C. Hathorne,

Salem, 27 February 1821, Box 1 Folder 42, Manning Hawthorne Collection, M223, George J. Mitchell Department of Special Collections & Archives, Bowdoin College Library, Brunswick, Maine.
50. Maria Louisa Hathorne to "Dear Mother" Elizabeth C. Hathorne, Salem, 6 March 1821, Nathaniel Hawthorne Papers, MSS 68, Box 1 Folder 1, Phillips Library, Peabody Essex Museum, Salem, Massachusetts.
51. Nathaniel Hathorne to "Dear Mother" Elizabeth C. Hathorne, Salem, 6 March 1821, Nathaniel Hawthorne Papers, MSS 68, Box 1 Folder 1, Phillips Library, Peabody Essex Museum, Salem, Massachusetts.
52. N. Hathorne to "Dear Mother," 6 March 1821.
53. Maria Louisa Hathorne to "Dear Mother" Elizabeth C. Hathorne, Salem, 30 April 1821, Box 1 Folder 45, Manning Hawthorne Collection, M223, George J. Mitchell Department of Special Collections & Archives, Bowdoin College Library, Brunswick, Maine.
54. Mary Manning to "Dear Sister" Elizabeth C. Hathorne, Salem, 30 April 1821, Box 1 Folder 45, Manning Hawthorne Collection, M223, George J. Mitchell Department of Special Collections & Archives, Bowdoin College Library, Brunswick, Maine.
55. Maria Louisa Hathorne to "Dear Mother" Elizabeth C. Hathorne, Salem, 21 May 1821, Box 1 Folder 46, Manning Hawthorne Collection, M223, George J. Mitchell Department of Special Collections & Archives, Bowdoin College Library, Brunswick, Maine.
56. Nathaniel Hathorne to "Dear Mother" Elizabeth C. Hathorne, Salem, 12 June 1821, Nathaniel Hawthorne Papers, MSS 68, Box 1 Folder 1, Phillips Library, Peabody Essex Museum, Salem, Massachusetts.
57. N. Hathorne to "Dear Mother," 12 June 1821.
58. Nathaniel Hathorne to "Dear Sister," Elizabeth Manning Hathorne, Salem, October 31, 1820, Nathaniel Hawthorne Papers, MSS68, Box 1 Folder 1, Phillips Library, Peabody Essex Museum, Salem. Massachusetts.

Chapter 5
1. N. Hathorne to "Dear Sister" 31 October 1820.
2. N. Hawthorne to "Dear Sister," 31 October 1820.
3. Manning Hawthorne, "Hawthorne's Boyhood," 182.
4. N. Hathorne to "Dear Mother" 6 March 1821, Phillips Library.
5. N. Hathorne to "Dear Mother," 6 March 1821.
6. Nathaniel Hathorne to "Dear Mother," Elizabeth C. Hathorne,

Salem, 13 March 1821, Julian, Hawthorne, *Nathaniel Hawthorne and His Wife: A Biography*, Vol. 1, 2d ed. (Boston: James R. Osgood and Company, 1885), 107.
7. N. Hathorne to "Dear Mother," 13 March 1821, 108.
8. N. Hathorne to "Dear Mother," 13 March 1821, 108.
9. Horatio Bridge, *Personal Recollections of Nathaniel Hawthorne* (London: Forgotten Books, 2012), originally published in 1893, 38.
10. M. Hawthorne, "Early Years," 11-12.
11. H. Bridge, *Recollections of Hawthorne*, 43-44.
12. H. Bridge, *Recollections of Hawthorne*, 44.
13. H. Bridge, *Recollections of Hawthorne*, 32.
14. M. Hawthorne, "Maria Louisa," 122; Maria Louisa Hathorne to "Dear Uncle" Robert Manning, Raymond, 20 February 1822, Box 1 Folder 54, Manning Hawthorne Collection, M223, George J. Mitchell Department of Special Collections & Archives, Bowdoin College Library, Brunswick, Maine.
15. M. L. Hathorne to "Dear Uncle," 20 February 1822.
16. M. L. Hathorne to "Dear Uncle," 20 February 1822.
17. M. L. Hathorne to "Dear Uncle," 20 February 1822.
18. M. L. Hathorne to "Dear Sister," 10 April 1822.
19. M. L. Hathorne to "Dear Sister," 10 April 1822.
20. J. Hawthorne, *Hawthorne and His Wife*, 96.
21. Nathaniel Hathorne to "My Dear Sister," Maria Louisa Hathorne, Brunswick, 14 April 1822, HM 11027-11028, Nathaniel Hawthorne Papers, The Huntington Library, San Marino, California; H. Bridge, *Recollections of Hawthorne*, 40.
22. N. Hathorne to "My Dear Sister," 14 April 1822.
23. H. Bridge, *Recollections of Hawthorne*, 40.
24. H. Bridge, *Recollections of Hawthorne*, 40.
25. H. Bridge, *Recollections of Hawthorne*, 9-10.
26. H. Bridge, *Recollections of Hawthorne*, 11.
27. H. Bridge, *Recollections of Hawthorne*, 11.
28. H. Bridge, *Recollections of Hawthorne*, 35.
29. H. Bridge, *Recollections of Hawthorne*, 35.
30. Elizabeth M. Hathorne to "Dear Mother" Elizabeth Clarke Manning Hathorne, Salem, 14 May 1822, Elizabeth Manning Hawthorne, *A Life in Letters*, ed. C. De Rocher (Tuscaloosa: The University of Alabama Press, 2006), 56-57.
31. J. Hawthorne, *Hawthorne and His Wife*, 101.
32. Nathaniel Hathorne to "My Dear Sister," Maria Louisa Hathorne,

Brunswick, 4 May 1823, HM 11027-11028, Nathaniel Hawthorne Papers, The Huntington Library, San Marino, California.
33. H. Bridge, *Recollections of Hawthorne*, 33.
34. N. Hathorne to "Dear Mother, 25 July 1820, Phillips Library.
35. H. Bridge, *Recollections of Hawthorne*, 32.
36. H. Bridge, *Recollections of Hawthorne*, 14.
37. H. Bridge, *Recollections of Hawthorne*, 14.
38. H. Bridge, *Recollections of Hawthorne*, 18, 19, 23; Nathaniel Hawthorne, "The Life of Franklin Pierce," in *Tales, Sketches, and Other Papers* (Boston and New York: Houghton Mifflin and Company, The Riverside Press Cambridge, 1883), 397- 399, 414.
39. Nathaniel Hawthorne to "My Dear Louisa," Maria Louisa Hathorne, Brunswick, 11 August 1824, Julian Hawthorne, *Nathaniel Hawthorne and His Wife: A Biography*, Vol. 1, 2d ed. (Boston: James R. Osgood and Company, 1885), 113-114.
40. N. Hawthorne to "My Dear Louisa," 11 August 1824, 114-115.
41. N. Hawthorne, to "My Dear Louisa," 11 August 1824, 115.
42. N. Hawthorne, to "My Dear Louisa," 11 August 1824, 115.
43. Nathaniel Hawthorne to "My Dear Sister," Elizabeth Manning Hathorne, Brunswick, 21 April 1825, Julian Hawthorne, *Nathaniel Hawthorne and his Wife: A Biography*, Vol. 1, 2d ed. (Boston: James R. Osgood and Company, 1885), 118.
44. E. M. Hathorne to "Dear Mother," May 14, 1822, *A Life in Letters*, 56-57.
45. E. M. Hathorne to "Dear Mother," May 14, 1822, *A Life in Letters*, 56-57.
46. H. Bridge, *Recollections of Hawthorne*, 5.
47. H. Bridge, *Recollections of Hawthorne*, 41.
48. H. Bridge, *Recollections of Hawthorne*, 41.
49. H. Bridge, *Recollections of Hawthorne*, 4.
50. Nathaniel Hathorne to "My Dear Sister" Elizabeth M. Hathorne, Brunswick, 14 July 1825, Nathaniel Hawthorne Papers, MSS 68, Box 1 Folder 2, Phillips Library, Peabody Essex Museum, Salem, Massachusetts.
51. N. Hathorne to "My Dear Sister" 14 July 1825.
52. H. Bridge, *Recollections of Hawthorne*, 33.
53. H. Bridge, *Recollections of Hawthorne*, 49.
54. Nathaniel Hathorne to "My Dear Aunt," Brunswick, 26 November 1824, Julian Hawthorne, *Nathaniel Hawthorne and his Wife: A Biography*, Vol. 1, 2d ed. (Boston: James R. Osgood and Company, 1885), 116-117.

55. Elizabeth M. Hathorne to "Dear Uncle," Robert Manning, Salem, August 24, 1818, Elizabeth Manning Hawthorne, *A Life in Letters*, ed. C. De Rocher (Tuscaloosa: The University of Alabama Press, 2006), 51.
56. Nathaniel Hawthorne, "Sylph Etherege" in *Tales and Sketches* (New York: The Library of America, Literary Classics of the United States, Inc., 1982), 515.
57. H. Bridge, *Recollections of Hawthorne*, 15.
58. H. Bridge, *Recollections of Hawthorne*, 50.

Chapter 6

1. J. Hawthorne, *Hawthorne and His Wife*, 96-97.
2. J. Hawthorne, *Hawthorne and His Wife*, 125.
3. J. Hawthorne, *Hawthorne and His Wife*, 125.
4. N. Hawthorne, *Passages from the American Note-Books*, June 18, 1835.
5. Elizabeth M. Hawthorne to "Dear Aunt" Mary Manning, Salem, 17 December 1827, Elizabeth Manning Hawthorne, *A Life in Letters*. ed. Cecile Anne De Rocher, (Tuscaloosa: The University of Alabama Press, 2006), 59.
6. H. Bridge, *Recollections of Hawthorne*, 38.
7. H. Bridge, *Recollections of Hawthorne*, 38.
8. J. Hawthorne, *Hawthorne and His Wife*, 124.
9. Nathaniel Hawthorne, *Fanshawe* in *Five Novels: Complete and Unabridged* (New York: Barnes & Noble, 2006), 16.
10. J. Hawthorne, *Hawthorne and his Wife*, 124.
11. Maria Louisa Hathorne to "My Dear Rebecca" Rebecca Manning, Salem, 11 June 1829, Box 1 Folder 61, Manning Hawthorne Collection, M223, George J. Mitchell Department of Special Collections & Archives, Bowdoin College Library, Brunswick, Maine.
12. M. L. Hathorne to "My Dear Rebecca," 11 June 1829.
13. M. L. Hathorne to "My Dear Rebecca," 11 June 1829.
14. M. L. Hathorne to "My Dear Rebecca," 11 June 1829.
15. M. L. Hathorne to "My Dear Rebecca," 11 June 1829.
16. M. Hawthorne, "Early Years," 20; M. Hawthorne, "Maria Louisa," 125.
17. M. Hawthorne, "Maria Louisa," 125.
18. Nathaniel Hawthorne to "Dear Sister," Maria Louisa Hawthorne, Canterbury (N.H.), 17 August 1831, Nathaniel Hawthorne Papers, MSS 68, Box 1 Folder 2, Phillips Library, Peabody Essex Museum, Salem, Massachusetts.
19. N. Hawthorne to "Dear Sister," 17 August 1831.

20. Nathaniel Hawthorne, "The Canal-Boat," from "Sketches from Memory," in *Tales and Sketches*, (New York: The library of America, Literary Classics of the United States, Inc. 1982, 344.
21. M. Hawthorne, "Maria Louisa," 128.
22. M. Hawthorne, "Maria Louisa," 128.
23. N. Hawthorne, *Passages from the American Note-Books*, June 22, 1835.
24. J. Hawthorne, *Hawthorne and His Wife,* 180.
25. M. Hawthorne, "Maria Louisa," 130.
26. M. Hawthorne, "Maria Louisa," 130.
27. M. Hawthorne, "Maria Louisa," 130.
28. Nathaniel Hawthorne to "Dear L" Maria Louisa Hawthorne, Concord, 25 November 1842, Nathaniel Hawthorne Papers, MSS 68, Box 1 Folder 3, Phillips Library, Peabody Essex Museum, Salem, Massachusetts.
29. Nathaniel Hawthorne, "Beneath An Umbrella" in *Night Sketches* in *Twice Told Tales* (Boston and New York: Houghton Mifflin Company, The Riverside Press Cambridge, 1882), 477.
30. J. Hawthorne, *Hawthorne and His Wife*, 128.
31. J. Hawthorne, *Hawthorne and His Wife*, 128-129.
32. J. Hawthorne, *Hawthorne and His Wife,* 128-129; E.M. Hawthorne to James T. Fields, 26 December 1870, *Life in Letters*, 145.
33. Nathaniel Hawthorne, "The Village Uncle" in *Tales and Sketches* (New York: The Library of America, Literary Classics of the United States, Inc., 1982), 222
34. Nathaniel Hawthorne, "Chippings With A Chisel," in *Twice-Told Tales* (Boston and New York: Houghton Mifflin Company, The Riverside Press Cambridge, 1882), 455.
35. Maria Louisa Hawthorne to "My Dear Mother" Elizabeth C. Manning, Newberry Port, 20 July 1835, Box 1 Folder 63, Manning Hawthorne Collection, M223, George J. Mitchell Department of Special Collections & Archives, Bowdoin College Library, Brunswick, Maine.
36. M.L. Hawthorne to "My Dear Mother," 20 July 1835.
37. M.L. Hawthorne to "My Dear Mother," 20 July 1835.
38. M.L. Hawthorne to "My Dear Mother," 20 July 1835.
39. M.L. Hawthorne to "My Dear Mother," 20 July 1835.
40. J. Hawthorne, *Hawthorne and his Wife*, 132, 175-176.
41. N. Hawthorne, *Passages from the American Note-Books*, October 25, 1836.
42. Nathaniel Hawthorne to Maria Louisa Hawthorne, March 3, 1836,

asking for Elizabeth to "concoct" poetry for him, Nathaniel Hawthorne Papers MSS 68, Box 1 Folder 2, Phillips Library, Peabody Essex Museum, Salem, Massachusetts; M. Hawthorne, "Maria Louisa," 129.
43. Nathaniel Hawthorne to "Dear L" Maria Louisa Hawthorne, Boston, 21 January 1836, Nathaniel Hawthorne Papers MSS 68, Box 1 Folder 2, Phillips Library, Peabody Essex Museum, Salem, Massachusetts.
44. Horatio Bridge to "Dear Hath," Nathaniel Hawthorne, Augusta, 16 October 1836, Horatio Bridge, *Personal Recollections of Nathaniel Hawthorne*, (London: Forgotten Books, 2012), originally published in 1893, 70.
45. Horatio Bridge to "Dear Hath," Nathaniel Hawthorne, Augusta, 22 October 1836, Horatio Bridge, *Personal Recollections of Nathaniel Hawthorne* (London: Forgotten Books, 2012), originally published in 1893, 72.
46. Horatio Bridge to "Dear Hawthorne," Nathaniel Hawthorne, Augusta, 25 December 1836, Horatio Bridge, *Personal Recollections of Nathaniel Hawthorne*, (London: Forgotten Books, 2012), orig. published in 1893, 72-73.
47. S.G. Goodrich to "Dear Sir," Horatio Bridge, Boston, 20 October 1836, Horatio Bridge, *Personal Recollections of Nathaniel Hawthorne* (London: Forgotten Books, 2012), originally published in 1893, 79.
48. S.G. Goodrich to "Dear Sir," 20 October 1836, 79.
49. H. Bridge, *Recollections of Hawthorne*, 47-48.
50. Horatio Bridge to "Dear Hawthorne," Nathaniel Hawthorne, Augusta, 25 December 1836, Julian Hawthorne, *Nathaniel Hawthorne and his Wife: A Biography*, Vol. 1, 2d ed. (Boston: James R. Osgood and Company, 1885), 147-148.
51. Nathaniel Hawthorne, "Jonathan Chilley" in *Tales and Sketches* (New York: The Library of America, Library Classics of the United States, Inc., 1982), 614-616
52. Horatio Bridge to "Dear Hawthorne," Nathaniel Hawthorne, Augusta, 1 February 1837, Horatio Bridge, *Personal Recollections of Nathaniel Hawthorne* (London: Forgotten Books, 2012), originally published in 1893, 74
53. H. Bridge, *Recollections of Hawthorne*, 81.
54. Henry W. Longfellow to "My dear Sir" Nathaniel Hawthorne, Cambridge, 9 March 1837, Nathaniel Hawthorne Papers, MSS 68, Box 1 Folder 7, Phillips Library, Peabody Essex Museum, Salem, Massachusetts.

55. Horatio Bridge to "Dear Hawthorne," Augusta, 24 May 1837, Horatio Bridge, *Personal Recollections of Nathaniel Hawthorne*, (London: Forgotten Books, 2012), originally published in 1893, 75.
56. H. Bridge, *Recollections of Hawthorne*, 63.
57. N. Hawthorne, *Passages from the American Note-Books*, 5 July, 1837.
58. J. Hawthorne, *Hawthorne and His Wife*, 97.
59. J. Hawthorne, *Hawthorne and His Wife*, 98.
60. N. Hawthorne, *Passages from the American Note-Books*, 5 July 1837.
61. N. Hawthorne, *Passages from the American Note-Books*, 5 July 1837.
62. Nathaniel Hawthorne, Preface to "The Snow-Image" in *Tales and Sketches* (New York: The Library of America, Literary Classics of the United States, Inc, 1982), 1155.

Chapter 7

1. Recollection of Elizabeth Palmer Peabody, Julian Hawthorne, *Nathaniel Hawthorne and His Wife: A Biography*, Vol. 1, 2d ed. (Boston: James R. Osgood and Company, 1885 177.
2. J. Hawthorne, *Hawthorne and His Wife*, 62-63.
3. J. Hawthorne, *Hawthorne and His Wife*, 198.
4. J. Hawthorne, *Hawthorne and His Wife*, 120-121.
5. J. Hawthorne, *Hawthorne and His Wife*, 179.
6. H. Bridge, *Recollections of Hawthorne*, 6.
7. J. Hawthorne, *Hawthorne and His Wife*, 178.
8. N. Hawthorne, *Passages from the American Note-Books*, 1838.
9. N. Hawthorne, *Passages from the American Note-Books*, 1838.
10. J. Hawthorne, *Hawthorne and His Wife*, 44-45.
11. J. Hawthorne, *Hawthorne and His Wife*, 46, 59-60.
12. Recollection of Elizabeth Palmer Peabody, Julian Hawthorne, *Nathaniel Hawthorne and his Wife: A Biography*, Vol. 1, 2d ed. (Boston: James R. Osgood and Company, 1885), 178-179.
13. E. P. Peabody, J. Hawthorne, *Hawthorne and His Wife*, 178-179.
14. E. P. Peabody, J. Hawthorne, *Hawthorne and His Wife*, 178-179.
15. E. P. Peabody, J. Hawthorne, *Hawthorne and His Wife*, 178.
16. E. P. Peabody, J. Hawthorne, *Hawthorne and His Wife*, 179.
17. E. P. Peabody, J. Hawthorne, *Hawthorne and His Wife*, 179.
18. E. P. Peabody, J. Hawthorne, *Hawthorne and His Wife*, 179.
19. J. Hawthorne, *Hawthorne and His Wife*, 180.
20. E.P. Peabody, J. Hawthorne, *Hawthorne and His Wife*, 179.
21. E. P. Peabody, J. Hawthorne, *Hawthorne and His Wife*, 179.
22. E. P. Peabody, J. Hawthorne, *Hawthorne and His Wife*, 179.

23. E. P. Peabody, J. Hawthorne, *Hawthorne and His Wife*, 179.
24. Elizabeth M. Hawthorne to "Dear Sophia" Sophia Peabody, N.p., April 1839, Elizabeth Manning Hawthorne, *A Life in Letters*, ed. C. De Rocher (Tuscaloosa: The University of Alabama Press, 2006), 61-62.
25. J. Hawthorne, *Hawthorne and His Wife*, 180.
26. J. Hawthorne, *Hawthorne and His Wife*, 189.
27. J. Hawthorne, *Hawthorne and His Wife*, 189.
28. J. Hawthorne, *Hawthorne and His Wife*, 189.
29. Elizabeth M. Hawthorne to "Dear Sophia" Sophia Peabody, N.p., Summer 1838-1840, Elizabeth Manning Hawthorne, *A Life in Letters*, ed. C. De Rocher (Tuscaloosa: The University of Alabama Press, 2006), 60.
30. Elizabeth M. Hawthorne to "My dear Cousins" the Mannings, Montserrat, December 1879, Elizabeth Manning Hawthorne, *A Life in Letters*, ed. C. De Rocher (Tuscaloosa: The University of Alabama Press, 2006), 182.
31. J. Hawthorne, *Hawthorne and His Wife*, 195.
32. Nathaniel Hawthorne, *The Gentle Boy: A Thrice Told Tale*, with an original illustration (Boston: Weeks, Jordan & Co.; New York & London: Wiley & Putnam, 1839).
33. J. Hawthorne, *Hawthorne and His Wife*, 199.
34. Nathaniel Hawthorne to "My Dearest," Sophia Peabody, N.p., 2 June [1840], Julian Hawthorne, *Nathaniel Hawthorne and his Wife: A Biography*, Vol. 1, 2d ed. (Boston: James R. Osgood and Company, 1885), 217.
35. J. Hawthorne, *Hawthorne and His Wife*, 195; Josephine Latham Swayne, ed., *The Story of Concord Told by Concord Writers* (Boston: The E.F. Worcester Press, 1906), 127.
36. N. Hawthorne, *Passages from the American Note-Books*, 9 June 1853.
37. Nathaniel Hawthorne to Sophia Peabody [Boston] 3 January 1840, Julian Hawthorne, *Nathaniel Hawthorne and his Wife: A Biography*, Vol. 1, 2d ed. (Boston: James R. Osgood and Company, 1885), 211.
38. J. Hawthorne, *Hawthorne and His Wife*, 206-213, 218-225.
39. Sophia Peabody to "Best Beloved," Nathaniel Hawthorne [Salem] 31 December 1839, Julian Hawthorne, *Nathaniel Hawthorne and his Wife: A Biography*, Vol. 1, 2d ed. (Boston: James R. Osgood and Company, 1885), 209.
40. Nathaniel Hawthorne "The Sister Years" in *Tales and Sketches* (New

York: The Library of America, Library Classics of the United States, Inc., 1982), 678-679.
41. N. Hawthorne, *Passages from the American Note-Books*, February 11, 1840.
42. N. Hawthorne, *Passages from the American Note-Books*, 15 March 1840.
43. H. Bridge *Recollections of Hawthorne*, 84.
44. Elizabeth M. Hawthorne to "Dear Elizabeth" Elizabeth Peabody, N.p. Spring 1840, Elizabeth Manning Hawthorne, *A Life in Letters*, ed. C. De Rocher (Tuscaloosa: The University of Alabama Press, 2006), 63.
45. Nathaniel Hawthorne to Maria Louisa Hawthorne, Brook Farm, West Roxbury, 3 May 1841, Julian Hawthorne, *Hawthorne and His Wife: A Biography*, Vol. 1, 2d ed. (Boston: James R. Osgood and Company, 1885), 227-228.
46. N. Hawthorne to M. L. Hawthorne, 3 May 1841, 227-228.
47. N. Hawthorne to M. L. Hawthorne, 3 May 1841, 227-228.
48. Maria Louisa Hawthorne to "My Dear Brother," Nathaniel Hawthorne, Salem, 10 May 1841, Julian Hawthorne, *Nathaniel Hawthorne and His Wife: A Biography*, Vol. 1, 2d ed. (Boston: James R. Osgood and Company, 1885), 230.
49. M.L. Hawthorne to "My Dear Brother," 10 May 1841, 229-230.
50. M.L. Hawthorne to "My Dear Brother," 10 May 1841, 229-230.
51. M.L. Hawthorne to "My Dear Brother," 10 May 1841, 229-230.
52. Maria Louisa Hawthorne to "Dear Natty," Nathaniel Hawthorne, Salem, 11 June 1841, Julian Hawthorne, *Nathaniel Hawthorne and His Wife: A Biography*, Vol. 1, 2d ed. (Boston: James R. Osgood and Company, 1885), 231.
53. M. L. Hawthorne to "Dear Natty," 11 June 1841, 232.
54. M. L. Hawthorne to "Dear Natty," 11 June 1841, 232.
55. Maria Louisa Hawthorne to "Dear Natty," Nathaniel Hawthorne, Salem, 3 August 1841, Julian Hawthorne, *Nathaniel Hawthorne and His Wife: A Biography*, Vol. 1, 2d ed. (Boston: James R. Osgood and Company, 1885), 234.
56. Maria Louisa Hawthorne to "Dear Natty," 3 August 1841, 234.
57. Nathaniel Hawthorne to Sophia Peabody, Brook Farm, 22 August 1841, Julian Hawthorne, *Nathaniel Hawthorne and His Wife: A Biography*, Vol. 1, 2d ed. (Boston: James R. Osgood and Company, 1885), 237.
58. N. Hawthorne, *Passages from the American Note-Books*, 22 August 1841.

59. N. Hawthorne, *Passages from the American Note-Books*, 25 September 1841.
60. Nathaniel Hawthorne to "Dearest Heart," Sophia Peabody, Boston, 27 May 1842, Julian Hawthorne, *Nathaniel Hawthorne and His Wife: A Biography*, Vol. 1, 2d ed. (Boston: James R. Osgood and Company, 1885), 238-239.
61. Hawthorne to "Dearest Heart," 27 May 1842, 238-239.
62. Elizabeth M. Hawthorne to "My dear Sophia" Sophia Peabody, Salem, 23 May 1842, Elizabeth Manning Hawthorne, *A Life in Letters*, ed. C. De Rocher (Tuscaloosa: The University of Alabama Press, 2006), 64.
63. E. M. Hawthorne to "My dear Sophia" 23 May 1842, *A Life in Letters*, 64.
64. Elizabeth M. Hawthorne to "My Dear Sophia" Sophia Peabody, Salem, 15 June 1842, Elizabeth Manning Hawthorne, *A Life in Letters*, ed. C. De Rocher (Tuscaloosa: The University of Alabama Press, 2006), 65.
65. Nathaniel Hawthorne to "Dearest," Sophia Peabody, Salem, June 9, 1842, Julian Hawthorne, *Nathaniel Hawthorne and His Wife: A Biography*. Vol. 1, 2nd ed, (Boston: James R. Osgood and Company, 1885), 239-240.
66. Elizabeth Peabody to "My Dearest," Sophia Hawthorne, Boston, no date, Julian Hawthorne, *Nathaniel Hawthorne and His Wife: A Biography*, Vol. 1, 2d ed. (Boston: James R. Osgood and Company, 1885), 264-265.
67. Nathaniel Hawthorne to "Dearest," Sophia Peabody, June 30, 1842, Julian Hawthorne, *Nathaniel Hawthorne and His Wife: A Biography*, Vol. 1, 2d ed., (Boston: James R. Osgood and Company, 1885), 241-242.
68. N. Hawthorne to "Dearest," June 30, 1842, 242.
69. Nathaniel Hawthorne, Preface to *Mosses from an Old Manse* in *Tales and Sketches*, (New York: The Library of America, Literary Classics of the United States, Inc., 1982), 1123.
70. J.L. Swayne, *The Story of Concord*, 156.
71. Nathaniel Hawthorne to "Dear Louisa," Maria Louisa Hawthorne, Concord, July 10, 1842, Nathaniel Hawthorne Papers, MSS 68, Box 1 Folder 3, Phillips Library, Peabody Essex Museum, Salem, Massachusetts.

Chapter 8
1. N. Hawthorne to "Dear Louisa," 10 July 1842.

335

2. N. Hawthorne to "Dear Louisa," 10 July 1842.
3. N. Hawthorne to "Dear Louisa," 10 July 1842.
4. N. Hawthorne to "Dear Louisa," 10 July 1842.
5. Nathaniel Hawthorne wrote extensive descriptions of his first residence in Concord, Nathaniel Hawthorne, "The Old Manse" in Preface to *Mosses from An Old Manse, Tales and Sketches*, (New York: The Library of America, Literary Classics of the United States, Inc. 1982), 1125-1131.
6. N. Hawthorne, Preface to *Mosses from an Old Manse*, 1131.
7. N. Hawthorne, *Passages from the American Note-Books*, August 5, 1842.
8. N. Hawthorne, *Passages from the American Note-Books*, 5 August 1842.
9. N. Hawthorne, *Passages from the American Note-Books*, 5 August 1842; J. Hawthorne, *Hawthorne and His Wife*, 251.
10. Nathaniel Hawthorne to "Dear L" Maria Louisa Hawthorne, Concord, 15 August 1842, Nathaniel Hawthorne Papers, MSS 68, Box 1 Folder 3, Phillips Library, Peabody Essex Museum, Salem, Massachusetts.
11. N. Hawthorne to "Dear L.," August 15, 1842.
12. N. Hawthorne, *Passages from the American Note-Books*, September 1, 1842.
13. N. Hawthorne, *Passages from the American Note-Books*, September 4, 1842.
14. N. Hawthorne, *Passages from the American Note-Books*, October 10, 1842.
15. Nathaniel Hawthorne to "My dear Sister" Maria Louisa Hawthorne, Concord, 12 October 1842, Nathaniel Hawthorne Papers, MSS 68, Box 1 Folder 3, Phillips Library, Peabody Essex Museum, Salem, Massachusetts.
16. N. Hawthorne, to "My dear Sister," 12 October, 1842.
17. N. Hawthorne, to "My dear Sister," 12 October, 1842.
18. N. Hawthorne, to "My dear Sister," 12 October, 1842.
19. Nathaniel Hawthorne to "Dear L" Maria Louisa Hawthorne, Concord, 25 November 1842, Nathaniel Hawthorne Papers, MSS 68, Box 1 Folder 3, Phillips Library, Peabody Essex Museum, Salem, Massachusetts.
20. N. Hawthorne, to "Dear L.," 25 November 1842.
21. N. Hawthorne, to "Dear L.," 25 November 1842.
22. N. Hawthorne, to "Dear L.," 25 November 1842.
23. N. Hawthorne, to "Dear L.," 25 November 1842.

24. N. Hawthorne, to "Dear L.," 25 November 1842.
25. N. Hawthorne, to "Dear L.," 25 November 1842.
26. N. Hawthorne, to "Dear L.," 25 November 1842.
27. N. Hawthorne, to "Dear L.," 25 November 1842.
28. N. Hawthorne, to "Dear L.," 25 November 1842.
29. N. Hawthorne, Preface to *Mosses from an Old Manse*, 1125.
30. N. Hawthorne to "Dear L" 25 November 1842.
31. N. Hawthorne, *Passages from the American Note-Books*, March 31, 1843.
32. J. Hawthorne, *Hawthorne and His Wife*, 274.
33. Nathaniel Hawthorne to "Dear Wife," Sophia Hawthorne, [Salem] 12 March 1843, Julian Hawthorne, *Nathaniel Hawthorne and His Wife: A Biography*, Vol. 1, 2d ed. (Boston: James R. Osgood and Company, 1885), 293.
34. N. Hawthorne to "Dear Wife," 12 March 1843, 293.
35. N. Hawthorne to "Dear Wife," 12 March 1843, 293.
36. Sophia Hawthorne to "Dearest Mother," April 20, 1843, Julian Hawthorne, *Nathaniel Hawthorne and His Wife: A Biography*, Vol. 1, 2d ed. (Boston: James R. Osgood and Company, 1885), 272.
37. N. Hawthorne, Preface to *Mosses from an Old Manse*, 1125.
38. J.L. Swayne, ed., *The Story of Concord*, 130.
39. J.L. Swayne, ed., *The Story of Concord*, 130.
40. J.L. Swayne, ed., *The Story of Concord*, 130.
41. Sophia Hawthorne to "Dearest Mother," Elizabeth Peabody, [Concord] 20 April 1843, Julian Hawthorne, *Nathaniel Hawthorne and His Wife: A Biography*, Vol. 1, 2d ed. (Boston: James R. Osgood and Company, 1885), 273.
42. Nathaniel Hawthorne. to "Dear L.," Maria Louisa Hawthorne, Boston, September 2, 1843, Nathaniel Hawthorne Papers, MSS 68, Box 1 Folder 51, Phillips Library, Peabody Essex Museum, Salem, Massachusetts.
43. J. Hawthorne, *Hawthorne and His Wife*, 273.
44. J. Hawthorne, *Hawthorne and His Wife*, 274.
45. J. Hawthorne, *Hawthorne and His Wife*, 275.
46. J. Hawthorne, *Hawthorne and His Wife*, 275.
47. Nathaniel Hawthorne to "Dear Louisa" Maria Louisa Hawthorne, Concord, 3 March 1844, Nathaniel Hawthorne Papers, MSS 68, Box 1 Folder 3, Phillips Library, Peabody Essex Museum, Salem, Massachusetts.
48. N. Hawthorne to "Dear Louisa," 3 March 1844.
49. N. Hawthorne to "Dear Louisa," 3 March 1844.

50. J.L. Swayne, ed., *The Story of Concord*, 134.
51. J. Hawthorne, *Hawthorne and His Wife*, 276-277, 284.
52. Sophia Hawthorne to "My Dearest Mother," Elizabeth Peabody, April 4, 1844, Julian Hawthorne *Nathaniel Hawthorne and His Wife: A Biography*, Vol. 1, 2d ed. (Boston: James R. Osgood and Company, 1885), 277.
53. Nathaniel Hawthorne to "Dear Bridge," Horatio Bridge, Concord, 1 April 1844, Horatio Bridge, Personal Recollections of Nathaniel Hawthorne, (London: Forgotten Books, 2102), originally published in 1893, 95-96.
54. N. Hawthorne, *Passages from the American Note-Books*, April 14, 1844.
55. Maria Louisa Hawthorne to "My Dear Mother" Elizabeth C. Hawthorne, Concord 27 August 1844, Box 1 Folder 65, Manning Hawthorne Collection, M223, George J. Mitchell Department of Special Collections & Archives, Bowdoin College Library, Brunswick, Maine.
56. M.L. Hawthorne to "My Dear Mother," 27 August 1844.
57. M.L. Hawthorne to "My Dear Mother," 27 August 1844.
58. M.L. Hawthorne to "My Dear Mother," 27 August 1844.
59. M.L. Hawthorne to "My Dear Mother," 27 August 1844.
60. M.L. Hawthorne to "My Dear Mother," 27 August 1844.
61. M.L. Hawthorne to "My Dear Mother," 27 August 1844.
62. M.L. Hawthorne to "My Dear Mother," 27 August 1844.
63. M.L. Hawthorne to "My Dear Mother," 27 August 1844.
64. M.L. Hawthorne to "My Dear Mother," 27 August 1844.
65. M.L. Hawthorne to "My Dear Mother," 27 August 1844.
66. M.L. Hawthorne to "My Dear Mother," 27 August 1844.
67. M.L. Hawthorne to "My Dear Mother," 27 August 1844.
68. M.L. Hawthorne to "My Dear Mother," 27 August 1844.
69. M.L. Hawthorne to "My Dear Mother," 27 August 1844.
70. M.L. Hawthorne to "My Dear Mother," 27 August 1844.
71. M.L. Hawthorne to "My Dear Mother," 27 August 1844.
72. Nathaniel Hawthorne to "Sweetest Phoebe," Sophia Hawthorne, Salem, 20 December 1844, Julian Hawthorne, *Nathaniel Hawthorne and His Wife: A Biography*, Vol. 1, 2d ed. (Boston: James R. Osgood and Company, 1885), 295.
73. N. Hawthorne to "Sweetest Phoebe," 20 December 1844.
74. J. Hawthorne, *Hawthorne and His Wife*, 281.
75. N. Hawthorne, *Passages from the American Note-Books*, 31 March 1843.

76. Sophia Hawthorne to "My Best Mother," Elizabeth Palmer Peabody, [Concord] 7 September 1845, Julian Hawthorne, *Nathaniel Hawthorne and His Wife: A Biography*, Vol. 1, 2d ed. (Boston: James R. Osgood and Company, 1885), 286-287.
77. J. Hawthorne, *Hawthorne and his Wife*, 285.
78. S. Hawthorne to "My Best Mother," 7 September 1845, 286.
79. S. Hawthorne to "My Best Mother," 7 September 1845, 286.
80. Nathaniel Hawthorne to "Dear Bridge," Horatio Bridge, Salem, 7 October 1845, Horatio Bridge, *Personal Recollections of Nathaniel Hawthorne* (London: Forgotten Books, 2012), originally published 1893, 105.

Chapter 9
1. N. Hawthorne, *Passages from the American Note-Books*, October 4, 1840.
2. Julian Hawthorne noted Sophia Hawthorne, had written to Elizabeth Peabody, from Herbert Street in Salem in January 1846, Julian Hawthorne, *Nathaniel Hawthorne and His Wife: A Biography*, Vol. 1, 2d ed. (Boston: James R. Osgood and Company, 1885), 307.
3. J. Hawthorne, *Nathaniel Hawthorne and his Wife*, 307-308.
4. Sophia Hawthorne to "Dearest Mother," Elizabeth Peabody, [Salem] 22 March 1846, Julian Hawthorne, *Nathaniel Hawthorne and His Wife: A Biography*, Vol. 1, 2d ed. (Boston: James R. Osgood and Company, 1885), 308.
5. J. Hawthorne, *Hawthorne and His Wife*, 309.
6. J. Hawthorne, *Hawthorne and His Wife*, 310.
7. J. Hawthorne, *Hawthorne and His Wife*, 419, 422, 424, 425; Nathaniel Hawthorne to "Dear old Boy," Julian Hawthorne, Washington, 27 March 1862, HM 11034, Nathaniel Hawthorne Papers, The Huntington Library, San Marino, California; H. Bridge, *Recollections of Hawthorne*, 187.
8. Nathaniel Hawthorne, "The Intelligence Officer" in *Tales and Sketches* (New York: The Library of America, Literary Classics of the United States, Inc., 1982), 873.
9. Sophia Hawthorne letter dated Salem, 17 November 1846, Julian Hawthorne, *Nathaniel Hawthorne and His Wife: A Biography*, Vol. 1, 2d ed. (Boston: James R. Osgood and Company, 1885), 311.
10. S. Hawthorne, J. Hawthorne, *Nathaniel Hawthorne and His Wife*, 311.
11. Sophia Hawthorne to Elizabeth Peabody, dated Salem, 10 September 1847, Julian Hawthorne, *Nathaniel Hawthorne and his Wife: A*

Biography, Vol. 1, 2d ed. (Boston: James R. Osgood and Company, 1885), 312.
12. S. Hawthorne to E. Peabody, 10 September 1847, 314.
13. S. Hawthorne to E. Peabody, 10 September 1847, 314.
14. S. Hawthorne to E. Peabody, 10 September 1847, 313.
15. S. Hawthorne to E. Peabody, 10 September 1847, 313.
16. S. Hawthorne to E. Peabody, 10 September 1847, 314.
17. S. Hawthorne to E. Peabody, 10 September 1847, 314.
18. J. Hawthorne, *Hawthorne and His* Wife, 328.
19. J. Hawthorne, *Hawthorne and His* Wife, 328.
20. Nathaniel Hawthorne to "Unspeakably Belovedest," Sophia Hawthorne, Salem, 5 July 1848, Julian Hawthorne, *Nathaniel Hawthorne and His Wife: A Biography,* Vol. 1, 2d ed. (Boston: James R. Osgood and Company, 1885), 326.
21. J. Hawthorne, *Hawthorne and his Wife,* 329.
22. Julian Hawthorne, *Hawthorne and His Circle* (New York and London: Harper & Brothers Publishers, 1903), 17.
23. Thomas Wentworth Higginson, *Henry Wadsworth Longfellow,* (Boston and New York: Houghton Mifflin Company, The Riverside Press Cambridge, 1902), 194-195.
24. N. Hawthorne, *Passages from the American Note-Books,* August 22, 1837.
25. T. Higginson, *Henry Wadsworth Longfellow,* 194-195.
26. Henry W. Longfellow to "My dear Hawthorne," Nathaniel Hawthorne, Cambridge, 8 February 1848, Nathaniel Hawthorne Papers, MSS 68, Box 1 Folder 7, Phillips Library, Peabody Essex Museum, Salem, Massachusetts.
27. Nathaniel Hawthorne to Henry Wadsworth Longfellow, "Dear Longfellow," Salem, 21 November 1848, *Final Memorials of Henry Wadsworth Longfellow,* Samuel Longfellow, ed., (Boston: Ticknor and Company, 1887), 29.
28. Nathaniel Hawthorne entry into journal dated Salem, ¼ of 8 o'clock March 1848, Julian Hawthorne, *Nathaniel Hawthorne and His Wife: A Biography,* Vol. 1, 2d ed. (Boston: James R. Osgood and Company, 1885), 324.
29. Nathaniel Hawthorne to "My Dear Little Una," Una Hawthorne, Salem, 7 June 1848, Julian Hawthorne, *Nathaniel Hawthorne and His Wife: A Biography,* Vol. 1, 2d ed. (Boston: James R. Osgood and Company, 1885), 329.
30. J. Hawthorne, *Hawthorne and His Wife,* 340.

31. J. Hawthorne, *Hawthorne and His Wife*, 340.
32. J. Hawthorne, *Hawthorne and His Wife*, 341.
33. J. Hawthorne, *Hawthorne and His Wife*, 347.
34. J. Hawthorne, *Hawthorne and His Wife*, 347-348.
35. Sophia Hawthorne to "My Dearest Mother," Elizabeth Peabody, Wednesday, 1 August 1849, Julian Hawthorne, *Nathaniel Hawthorne and His Wife: A Biography*, Vol. 1, 2d ed. (Boston: James R. Osgood and Company, 1885), 352.
36. S. Hawthorne to "My Dearest Mother," 1 August 1849, 352.
37. S. Hawthorne to "My Dearest Mother," 1 August 1849, 352.
38. Sophia Hawthorne, Salem, 2 September 1849, Julian Hawthorne, *Nathaniel Hawthorne and His Wife: A Biography*, Vol. 1, 2d ed. (Boston: James R. Osgood and Company, 1885), 353.
39. S. Hawthorne, 2 September 1849, 353.
40. S. Hawthorne, 2 September 1849, 353.
41. Geo. S. Hillard to "My Dear Hawthorne," Boston, 17 January 1850, Julian Hawthorne, *Nathaniel Hawthorne and His Wife: A Biography*, Vol. 1, 2d ed. (Boston: James R. Osgood and Company, 1885), 353-355.
42. G. Hillard to "My Dear Hawthorne," 17 January 1850, 353; John G. Whittier to "Dear Friend," Nathaniel Hawthorne, Esq., Amesbury, 22 February 1850, Julian Hawthorne, *Nathaniel Hawthorne and His Wife: A Biography*, Vol. 1, 2d ed. (Boston: James R. Osgood and Company, 1885), 355-356.
43. Sophia Hawthorne, Salem, 2 September 1849, Julian Hawthorne, *Nathaniel Hawthorne and His Wife: A Biography*, Vol. 1, 2d ed. (Boston: James R. Osgood and Company, 1885), 353-354.
44. Nathaniel Hawthorne to "Dear Bridge," Horatio Bridge, Salem 13 April 1850, Horatio Bridge, *Personal Recollections of Nathaniel Hawthorne* (London: Forgotten Books, 2012), originally published 1893, 113-114.
45. Nathaniel Hawthorne, "Footprints on the Sea-Shore," in *Twice-Told Tales* (Boston and New York: Houghton Mifflin Company, The Riverside Press Cambridge, 1882), 504.
46. Elizabeth Manning Hawthorne to "Dear Brother," Nathaniel Hawthorne, Montserrat, May 3, 1851, Elizabeth Manning Hawthorne, *A Life in Letters*, ed. C. De Rocher (Tuscaloosa: The University of Alabama Press, 2006), 68-70
47. Maria Louisa Hawthorne to "Dear Sophia," Sophia Hawthorne, Salem, August 1850, Julian Hawthorne, *Nathaniel Hawthorne and*

His Wife: A Biography, Vol. 1, 2d ed. (Boston: James R. Osgood and Company, 1885), 437.
48. J. Hawthorne, *Hawthorne and His Circle,* 37.
49. J. Hawthorne, *Hawthorne and His Circle,* 37.
50. J. Hawthorne, *Hawthorne and His Wife,* 376.
51. J. Hawthorne, *Hawthorne and His Wife,* 376.
52. Sophia Hawthorne to "My Dearest Mother," Elizabeth Peabody, Lenox, 23 June 1850, Julian Hawthorne, *Nathaniel Hawthorne and His Wife: A Biography,* Vol. 1, 2d ed. (Boston: James R. Osgood and Company, 1885), 366.
53. J. Hawthorne, *Hawthorne and His Wife,* 373.
54. Nathaniel Hawthorne to "Dear E.," Elizabeth Manning Hawthorne, Lenox, 11 March 1851, Julian Hawthorne, *Nathaniel Hawthorne and His Wife: A Biography,* Vol. 1, 2d ed. (Boston: James R. Osgood and Company, 1885), 389-390.
55. Nathaniel Hawthorne to "Dear L," Maria Louisa Hawthorne, Lenox, 20 May 1851, HM 11032, Nathaniel Hawthorne Papers, The Huntington Library, San Marino, California.
56. Nathaniel Hawthorne to "Dear Una," Una Hawthorne, Trinity College, Cambridge, 25 May 1860, HM 2860, Nathaniel Hawthorne Papers, The Huntington Library, San Marino, California.
57. Nathaniel Hawthorne, "Chippings With A Chisel," 462; Nathaniel Hawthorne, "Edward Fane's Rosebud," in *Twice-Told Tales* (Boston and New York: Houghton Mifflin Company, The Riverside Press Cambridge, 1882), 520; J. Hawthorne, *Hawthorne and His Wife,* 410.
58. N. Hawthorne to "Dear L.," 20 May 1851, Huntington Library.
59. N. Hawthorne to "Dear L.," 20 May 1851.
60. N. Hawthorne to "Dear L.," 20 May 1851.
61. E. M. Hawthorne to "Dear Brother," 3 May 1851, *A Life in Letters,* 68.
62. E. M. Hawthorne to "Dear Brother," 3 May 1851, *Life in Letters,* 69.
63. Nathaniel Hawthorne to "Dear L.," Maria Louisa Hawthorne, Lenox 10 July 1851, Julian Hawthorne, *Nathaniel Hawthorne and His Wife: A Biography,* Vol. 1, 2d ed. (Boston: James R. Osgood and Company, 1885), 408.
64. N. Hawthorne to "Dear L, 10 July 1851, 408.
65. Nathaniel Hawthorne to "Dear L.," Lenox, 2 September 1851, HM 2604, Nathaniel Hawthorne Papers, The Huntington Library, San Marino, California.

66. N. Hawthorne to "Dear L.," 2 September 1851.
67. J. Hawthorne, *Hawthorne and His Wife*, 413.
68. J. Hawthorne, *Hawthorne and His Wife*, 411.
69. J. Hawthorne, *Hawthorne and His Wife*, 427.
70. J. Hawthorne, *Hawthorne and His Wife*, 428.
71. Nathaniel Hawthorne to "Dear L.," Maria Louisa Hawthorne, Lenox, July 10, 1851, Julian Hawthorne, *Nathaniel Hawthorne and His Wife: A Biography*, Vol. 1, 2d ed. (Boston: James R. Osgood and Company, 1885), 409.
72. J. Hawthorne, *Hawthorne and his Wife*, 412-413.
73. Elizabeth M. Hawthorne to "Dear Sister" Maria Louisa Hawthorne, N.p. Autumn 1851, Elizabeth Manning Hawthorne, *A Life in Letters*, ed. C. De Rocher (Tuscaloosa: The University of Alabama Press, 2006), 70.
74. E.M. Hawthorne to "Dear Sister," Autumn 1851, *Life in Letters*, 70.
75. N. Hawthorne, *Passages from the American Note-Books*, November 21, 1851.
76. Nathaniel Hawthorne to "Dear L," Maria Louisa Hawthorne, West Newton, 15 May 1852, Nathaniel Hawthorne Papers, MSS 68, Box 1 Folder 4, Phillips Library, Peabody Essex Museum, Salem, Massachusetts.
77. N. Hawthorne, "Dear L.," 15 May 1852.
78. N. Hawthorne, "Dear L.," 15 May 1852.
79. J. Hawthorne, *Hawthorne and his Wife*, 266.
80. J. Hawthorne, *Hawthorne and His Circle*, 61-62.

Chapter 10
1. Nathaniel Hawthorne to "Dear L." Maria Louisa Hawthorne, Concord, 18 June 1852, Nathaniel Hawthorne Papers, MSS 68, Box 1 Folder 4, Phillips Library, Peabody Essex Museum, Salem, Massachusetts.
2. N. Hawthorne to "Dear L.," 18 June 1852.
3. N. Hawthorne to "Dear L.," 18 June 1852.
4. Maria Louisa Hawthorne to "My Dear Brother," Nathaniel Hawthorne, Salem, 1 July 1852, Julian Hawthorne, *Nathaniel Hawthorne and His Wife: A Biography*, Vol. 1, 2d ed. (Boston: James R. Osgood and Company, 1885), 453.
5. M. L. Hawthorne to "My Dear Brother," 1 July 1852, 453.
6. M. L. Hawthorne to "My Dear Brother," 1 July 1852, 453.
7. M. Hawthorne to "My Dear Brother," 1 July 1852, 453.
8. "Statement of Eye-Witnesses," *New-York Daily Times*, 30 July 1852.

9. J. Hawthorne, *Hawthorne and His Wife*, 452-453.
10. Use of quote is Courtesy of the Saratoga Springs History Museum, "Columbian Spring," Collected papers, Saratoga Springs History Museum, Saratoga Springs, New York.
11. "Statement of Eye-Witnesses," *New-York Daily Times*, 30 July 1852.
12. "The Watering Places: Saratoga Springs—The Season—The Waters, &c.," *New York Daily Times*, 27 July 1852.
13. "Statement of Eye-Witnesses, *New-York Daily Times*, 30 July 1852.
14. Sophia Hawthorne to "My Dearest Mother," Elizabeth Peabody, Concord, July 30, 1852, Julian Hawthorne, *Nathaniel Hawthorne and His Wife: A Biography*, Vol. 1, 2d ed. (Boston: James R. Osgood and Company, 1885), 454.
15. J. Hawthorne, *Hawthorne and His Circle*, 16.
16. "Incidents-Further Particulars," *New-York Daily Times*, 2 August 1852.
17. "Fourth Day," testimony of Robert Manning, *New-York Daily Times*, 2 August 1852.
18. "Passengers Missing," "Death of Stephen Allen," "List of the Dead," "Second Day of the Inquest," *New-York Daily Times*, July 30, 1852.
19. "Statement of Eye-Witnesses," *New-York Daily Times*, July 30, 1852.
20. "Rumors and Incidents," *New-York Daily Times*, July 30, 1852.
21. "Statement of Eye-Witnesses," *New-York Daily Times*, July 30, 1852.
22. "Statement of Capt. Tallman of the Henry Clay," *New-York Daily Times*, 30 July 1852
23. "Statement of Eye-Witnesses," "Statement By A Passenger," *New-York Daily Times*, July 30, 1852.
24. S. Hawthorne to "My Dearest Mother," July 30, 1852, *Hawthorne and his Wife*, 455.
25. S. Hawthorne to "My Dearest Mother," July 30, 1852, 454.
26. The newspapers *New-York Daily Times*, *The New York Herald*, and the *New-York Daily Tribune* each had headlines and news stories published in the Thursday July 29, 1852 editions describing the disaster of the *Henry Clay* which had taken place the prior day on July 28, 1852.
27. S. Hawthorne to "My Dearest Mother," July 30,1852, 454-455.
28. S. Hawthorne to "My Dearest Mother," July 30,1852, 454-455.
29. S. Hawthorne to "My Dearest Mother," July 30,1852, 455.
30. S. Hawthorne to "My Dearest Mother," July 30, 1852, 455.
31. S. Hawthorne to "My Dearest Mother," July 30, 1852, 456.
32. S. Hawthorne to "My Dearest Mother," July 30, 1852, 456.
33. S. Hawthorne to "My Dearest Mother," July 30, 1852, 456.

34. S. Hawthorne to "My Dearest Mother," July 30, 1852, 456.
35. S. Hawthorne to "My Dearest Mother," July 30, 1852, 456.
36. J. Hawthorne, *Hawthorne and His Wife*, 457.
37. J. Hawthorne, *Hawthorne and His Wife*, 296.
38. J. Hawthorne, *Hawthorne and His Wife*, 297; J. Swayne, ed., *The Story of Concord*, 139-140.
39. Julian Hawthorne noted an entry that his father made in his journal regarding the search for a missing girl, Julian Hawthorne, *Nathaniel Hawthorne and his Wife: A Biography*, Vol. 1, 2d ed. (Boston: James R. Osgood and Company, 1885), 296-298.
40. J. Hawthorne, *Hawthorne and his Wife*, 298-299.
41. Nathaniel Hawthorne, *The Blithedale Romance* in *Five Novels: Complete and Unabridged* (New York: Barnes & Noble, 2006), 655-656; J. Hawthorne, *Hawthorne and His Circle*, 75.
42. "Missing," *New-York Daily Tribune*, 31 July 1852.
43. "Incidents-Further Particulars," *New-York Daily Times*, 2 August 1852; "The Coroner's Inquests, Fourth Day," Edward Lefert testimony, *New-York Daily Times*, 2 August 1852.
44. Sophia Hawthorne to "My Dearest Mother," 30 July 1852, 456.
45. "Coroner's Inquests, Fourth Day," Robert Manning testimony, *New-York Daily Times*, 2 August 1852.
46. "Missing," *New-York Daily Tribune*, 31 July 1852.
47. "List of the Dead," *New-York Daily Times*, 2 August 1852.
48. "The Coroner's Inquests, Fourth Day," Edward Lefert testimony, *New-York Daily Times*, 2 August 1852.
49. "The Coroner's Inquests, Fourth Day," Robert Manning testimony, *New-York Daily Times*, 2 August 1852.
50. "The Coroner's Inquests, Fourth Day," Robert Manning testimony, *New-York Daily Times*, 2 August 1852.
51. "The Coroner's Inquests, Fourth Day," Robert Manning testimony, *New-York Daily Times*, 2 August 1852.
52. "Incidents-Further Particulars," *New-York Daily Times*, 2 August 1852.
53. "The Henry Clay Calamity," *New York Herald, The*, 4 August 1852.
54. J. Hawthorne, *Hawthorne and His Circle*, 75.
55. Frank Preston Stearns, *The Life and Genius of Nathaniel Hawthorne* (Reprint, LaVergne, TN: DoDo Press, 2009), 152.
56. Nathaniel Hawthorne, *The House of the Seven Gables* in *Five Novels: Complete and Unabridged* (New York: Barnes & Noble, 2006), 322.

Chapter 11
1. J. Hawthorne, *Hawthorne and his Wife*, 456-457.
2. J. Hawthorne, *Hawthorne and his Wife*, 456-457.
3. Nathaniel Hawthorne to "Dear Ticknor" Wm. D. Ticknor, Concord, 22 August 1852, HM10853, Nathaniel Hawthorne Papers, The Huntington Library, San Marino, California.
4. Nathaniel Hawthorne to "Dear Ticknor" Wm. D. Ticknor, Concord, 25 August 1852, HM10857, Nathaniel Hawthorne Papers, The Huntington Library, San Marino, California.
5. Nathaniel Hawthorne to "Dear Ticknor" Wm. D. Ticknor, Concord, 27 August 1852, HM10856, Nathaniel Hawthorne Papers, The Huntington Library, San Marino, California.
6. N. Hawthorne, *Passages from the American Note-Books*, August 30, 1852.
7. N. Hawthorne, *Passages from the American Note-Books*, August 30, 1852.
8. N. Hawthorne, *Passages from the American Note-Books*, September 5, 1852.
9. N. Hawthorne, *Passages from the American Note-Books*, September 5, 1852.
10. N. Hawthorne, *Passages from the American Note-Books*, September 5, 1852.
11. Nathaniel Hawthorne to "Dear Ticknor" Wm. D. Ticknor, Isle of Shoals, 7 September 1852, HM10860, Nathaniel Hawthorne Papers, The Huntington Library, San Marino, California.
12. Elizabeth Manning Hawthorne to "Dear Brother," Nathaniel Hawthorne, Salem, 23 September 1852, Julian Hawthorne, *Nathaniel Hawthorne and His Wife: A Biography*, Vol. 1, 2d ed. (Boston: James R. Osgood and Company, 1885), 465.
13. E. M. Hawthorne to "Dear Brother," May 3, 1851, *Life in Letters*, 68-70.
14. H. Bridge, *Recollections of Hawthorne*, 135.
15. J. Hawthorne, *Hawthorne and His Circle*, 77.
16. Nathaniel Hawthorne to "Dear Pike" William B. Pike, Liverpool, 6 January 1854, HM2856, Nathaniel Hawthorne Papers, The Huntington Library, San Marino, California.
17. Nathaniel Hawthorne to "Dear E" Elizabeth Manning Hawthorne, Liverpool, 6 December 1855, HM11033, Nathaniel Hawthorne Papers, The Huntington Library, San Marino, California.
18. N. Hawthorne to "Dear E.," 6 December 1855, The Huntington Library.

19. Nathaniel Hawthorne to "Dear Ticknor" William Davis Ticknor, Liverpool, 15 February 1856, HM2857, Nathaniel Hawthorne Papers, The Huntington Library, San Marino, California.
20. Elizabeth M. Hawthorne to "My dear Una" Una Hawthorne, Montserrat, 10 November 1853, Elizabeth Manning Hawthorne, *A Life in Letters*, ed. C. Rocher (Tuscaloosa: The University of Alabama Press, 2006), 72.
21. Elizabeth M. Hawthorne to "My dear Una" Una Hawthorne, N.p., 1858, Elizabeth Manning Hawthorne, *A Life in Letters*, ed. C. De Rocher (Tuscaloosa: The University of Alabama Press, 2006), 74.
22. Nathaniel Hawthorne to "Dear Elizabeth" Elizabeth Manning Hawthorne, Concord, 28 August 1860, HM2864, Nathaniel Hawthorne Papers, The Huntington Library, San Marino, California.
23. Elizabeth M. Hawthorne to "My dear Cousin" Robert Manning, Beverly, 31 December 1861, Elizabeth Manning Hawthorne, *A Life in Letters*, ed. C. De Rocher (Tuscaloosa: The University of Alabama Press, 2006), 76-77.
24. J. Swayne, ed. *The Story of Concord*, 141.
25. Nathaniel Hawthorne to "Una Hawthorne," Washington, 11 March 1862, HM2607, Nathaniel Hawthorne Papers, The Huntington Library, San Marino, California.
26. N. Hawthorne to "Una Hawthorne," 11 March 1862.
27. N. Hawthorne to "Una Hawthorne," 11 March 1862.
28. Nathaniel Hawthorne to "Dear Onion" Una Hawthorne, Washington, 16 March 1862, HM11040, Nathaniel Hawthorne Papers, The Huntington Library, San Marino, California.
29. Nathaniel Hawthorne to "Dear old Boy" Julian Hawthorne, Washington, 27 March 1862, HM11034, Nathaniel Hawthorne Papers, The Huntington Library, San Marino, California.
30. Sophia Hawthorne to "My Dearest Una," Concord, 11 December 1862, Julian Hawthorne, *Nathaniel Hawthorne and His Wife: A Biography*, Vol. II (Boston and New York: Houghton Mifflin and Company, The Riverside Press Cambridge, 1884), 326.
31. Nathaniel Hawthorne dedication "To a Friend" Franklin Pierce, The Wayside, 2 July 1863, HM 7173, Nathaniel Hawthorne Papers, The Huntington Library, San Marino, California.
32. N. Hawthorne, "To a Friend," 2 July 1863.
33. Sophia Hawthorne to "My Dear Mr. Bridge," Horatio Bridge, Concord, April 5, 1864, *Personal Recollections of Nathaniel Hawthorne*,

(London: Forgotten Books, 2012), originally published in 1893, 189.
34. S. Hawthorne to "My Dear Mr. Bridge," April 5, 1864, 190.
35. Franklin Pierce to "My Dear Bridge," Andover, May 21, 1864, *Personal Recollections of Nathaniel Hawthorne*, (London: Forgotten Books, 2012), originally published in 1893, 177.
36. Nathaniel Hawthorne to "Dear Bridge," Horatio Bridge, Liverpool, 6 June 1856, *Personal Recollections of Nathaniel Hawthorne* (London: Forgotten Books, 2012), originally published in 1893, 152.
37. H. Bridge, *Recollections of Hawthorne*, 176.
38. Elizabeth M. Hawthorne to "My dear Una" Una Hawthorne, Beverly, 20 May 1864, Elizabeth Manning Hawthorne, *A Life in Letters*, ed. C. De Rocher (Tuscaloosa: The University of Alabama Press, 2006), 87.
39. F. Pierce to "My Dear Bridge," May 21, 1864, *Recollections*, 179.
40. J. Swayne, ed., *The Story of Concord*, 146; J. Hawthorne, *Hawthorne and His Wife*, Vol. II, 347.
41. J. Swayne, ed., *The Story of Concord*, 286-287.
42. J. Swayne, ed., *The Story of Concord*, 227.
43. Nathaniel Hawthorne to Sophia Peabody, Boston, October 1840, Julian Hawthorne, *Nathaniel Hawthorne and his Wife: A Biography*, Vol. 1, 2d ed. (Boston: James R. Osgood and Company, 1885), 223.
44. Sophia A. Hawthorne to "My Dear Mr. Bridge," Concord, November 25, 1865, Horatio Bridge, *Personal Recollections of Nathaniel Hawthorne* (London: Forgotten Books, 2012), originally published in 1893, 196.
45. J. Hawthorne, *Hawthorne and His Wife*, Vol. II, 371.
46. Elizabeth M. Hawthorne to "My poor children" Una and Rose Hawthorne, Montserrat, 2 March 1871, Elizabeth Manning Hawthorne, *A Life in Letters*, ed. C. De Rocher (Tuscaloosa: The University of Alabama Press, 2006), 154.
47. E. M. Hawthorne to "My poor children," 2 March 1871, *Life in Letters*, 154.
48. Julian Hawthorne briefly chronicled Una Hawthorne's remaining life, Julian Hawthorne, *Nathaniel Hawthorne and His Wife: A Biography*, Vol. II (Boston and New York: Houghton Mifflin and Company, The Riverside Press Cambridge, 1884), 372-374; J. Swayne, ed., The Story of Concord, 150.
49. Elizabeth M. Hawthorne to "My dear Sophia," Sophia Hawthorne,

Beverly, 24 November, [1864], Elizabeth Manning Hawthorne, *A Life in Letters,* ed. C. De Rocher (Tuscaloosa: The University of Alabama Press, 2006), 88.
50. E.M. Hawthorne, "My dear Sophia," 24 November, [1864], *Life in Letters,* 88.
51. Elizabeth M. Hawthorne to "My dear Cousin" Robert Manning, Beverly, 31 December, [1861], Elizabeth Manning Hawthorne, *A Life in Letters,* ed. C. De Rocher (Tuscaloosa: The University of Alabama Press, 2006), 76.
52. Nathaniel Hawthorne to "Dear Louisa" Maria Louisa Hawthorne, West Roxbury, 3 August 1841, Nathaniel Hawthorne Papers, MSS 68 Box 1 Folder 3, Phillips Library, Peabody Essex Museum, Salem, Massachusetts.
53. E. M. Hawthorne to "My dear Sophia" 24 November, [1864], *Life in Letters,* 89.
54. Elizabeth M. Hawthorne to "Maria Manning," Montserrat, 9 May [1876], Elizabeth Manning Hawthorne, *A Life in Letters,* ed. C. De Rocher (Tuscaloosa: The University of Alabama Press, 2006), 169.
55. Elizabeth M. Hawthorne to "My dear Cousins" the Mannings, Montserrat, 18 February [1877], Elizabeth Manning Hawthorne, *A Life in Letters,* ed. C. De Rocher (Tuscaloosa: The University of Alabama Press, 2006), 177.
56. Elizabeth M. Hawthorne to "My Dear Sophia" Sophia Peabody, Salem, 15 June 1842, Elizabeth Manning Hawthorne, *A Life in Letters,* ed. C. De Rocher (Tuscaloosa: The University of Alabama Press, 2006), 65.
57. N. Hawthorne, *Passages from the American Note-Books,* 7 September 1835.
58. Nathaniel Hawthorne, "The White Old Maid," in *Tales and Sketches* (New York: The Library of America, Literary Classics of the United States, Inc. 1982), 316, 318.
59. Nathaniel Hawthorne, "Sylph Etherege," in *Tales and Sketches* (New York: The Library of America, Literary Classics of the United States, Inc. 1982), 515.
60. Nathaniel Hawthorne, *The House of the Seven Gables in Five Novels: Complete and Unabridged* (New York: Barnes & Noble, 2006), 302.
61. Elizabeth M. Hawthorne to "My dear Cousin," Robert Manning, Montserrat, 30 June [1871], Elizabeth Manning Hawthorne, *A Life in Letters,* ed. C. De Rocher (Tuscaloosa: The University of Alabama Press, 2006), 158.

62. 1870 United States Census Records for Massachusetts, County of Essex, Village of Beverly, 116.
63. Elizabeth M. Hawthorne to "My Dear Cousin" Richard Manning, Beverly, 6 January 1873, Elizabeth Manning Hawthorne, *A Life in Letters*, ed. C. De Rocher (Tuscaloosa: The University of Alabama Press, 2006), 162.
64. E. M. Hawthorne to "My Dear Cousin" 6 January 1873, *Life in Letters*, 162.
65. Elizabeth M. Hawthorne to "the Mannings" Montserrat, [December 1882], Elizabeth Manning Hawthorne, *A Life in Letters*, ed. C. De Rocher (Tuscaloosa: The University of Alabama Press, 2006), 189.
66. E. M. Hawthorne to "the Mannings," 189; "Hawthorne's Sister," *The Indianapolis Journal*, January 5, 1883.
67. Elizabeth M. Hawthorne to "My dear Una" Una Hawthorne, Beverly, Wednesday, 1 March 1865, Elizabeth Manning Hawthorne, *A Life in Letters*, ed. C. De Rocher (Tuscaloosa: The University of Alabama Press, 2006), 94.
68. Nathaniel Hawthorne, "Buds and Bird-Voices" in *Tales and Sketches* (New York: The Library of America, Literary Classics of the United States, Inc., 1982), 832.
69. Nathaniel Hawthorne, "Alice Doane's Appeal," in *Tales and Sketches* (New York: The Library of America, Literary Classics of the United States, Inc., 1982), 205.

Made in the USA
Middletown, DE
04 February 2025